The Birth Order Book of Love

The Birth Order Book of Love

How the #1 Personality Predictor
Can Help You Find "The One"

WILLIAM CANE

Da Capo

LIFE
LONG

Set in 10 point Sabon by the Perseus Books Group

Cataloging-in-Publication data for this book is available from the Library of Congress.

First Da Capo Press edition 2008
ISBN-10 1-60094-041-2
ISBN-13 978-1-60094-041-5
Published by Da Capo Press
A Member of the Perseus Books Group
www.dacapopress.com

Da Capo Press books are available at special discounts for bulk purchases in the United States by corporations, institutions, and other organizations. For more information, please contact the Special Markets Department at the Perseus Books Group, 2300 Chestnut Street, Suite 200, Philadelphia, PA 19103, or call (800) 255–1514, or e-mail special.markets@ perseusbooks.com.

For Michelle Wolfson

Contents

Introduction ix

An Overview of Our Subject, or What Is
Birth Order? And Why Does It Matter? 1

Part 1 **Firstborns**

1 Older Brother of Brothers 11

2 Older Brother of Sisters 21

3 Older Sister of Sisters 31

4 Older Sister of Brothers 43

Part 2 **Lastborns**

5 Younger Brother of Brothers 55

6 Younger Brother of Sisters 65

7 Younger Sister of Sisters 75

8 Younger Sister of Brothers 85

Part 3 **Only Children, Twins, and Middle Children**

9 The Male Only Child 99

10 The Female Only Child 109

11 Twins 121

12 Middle Children 131

Part 4 **Common Problems and How to Overcome Them**

13	Firstborn Rank Conflict	145
14	Lastborn Rank Conflict	157
15	Sex Conflict	167
16	Communication Problems	177
17	Conflicting Values	191
18	Loss of a Parent or Sibling	203
19	Narcissistic Attraction	211

Conclusion	221
Appendix: Research on Mate Selection and Compatibility	225
Acknowledgments	229
Notes	233
Bibliography	249
Index	257

Introduction

Cupid has been shooting darts into unsuspecting victims for ages, getting people to fall in love, but never having the courtesy to ask, "Will they be *happy* together?" I'm sure you'll admit it's happened to you at one time or another if you stop and think about it. You've seen someone, fallen in love, and before you know it, you're involved in a relationship that's going . . . well, practically nowhere.

It's high time to take a break from Cupid's helter-skelter matchmaking and shed some light on the subject of who's really a *good* match for you.

Until now it has been impossible to do this. Lovers young and old have had to fend for themselves, hoping for happiness with each new relationship. But groundbreaking scientific research has changed all that. Using sophisticated theories of compatibility, compelling clinical data, and revolutionary new birth order research, *it's now possible to predict who your best romantic match is.*

This isn't hyperbole; it's a fact which I intend to prove. And in the following pages I promise to do just that. I'll share this exciting new research with you, and present it in a way that will help you find *your* best romantic match.

Much of this data was compiled by clinical psychologists and social historians of the highest caliber. Before today, the bulk of this research had been largely unavailable to the layman, either because it was published in out-of-the-way journals, couched in arcane language, or written specifically for a professional audience. My long-standing interest in compatibility has led me to access all this information and to meet with the key players in the field of birth order. In addition, my background as a lawyer and college professor has helped me analyze this data and present it in a clear and understandable manner. That's the approach I'm going to take in this book, talking in plain language and ultimately sharing some of the most fascinating new research in a way that will make sense and help *you* find that special someone.

How I Became Interested in Birth Order

I first read about birth order in 1970 in an article by Walter Toman, a German psychologist. He argued that knowing how many siblings you grew up with was the most important thing in predicting personality. Tell him your place in the family (first, middle, last, twin or only child) and how many years separated you from your siblings, and he could tell who your best match was, what career you'd be happiest in, and how well you'd get along with friends and coworkers. After all, almost everyone grows up with a mother and a father, so what makes families *unique* is your sibling constellation, that is, how many brothers and sisters you interacted with during your developmental years.

Intrigued by Toman's ideas, I studied his theory and sought to see if it played out in the real world. While in college I made it a point to discover the birth order of all my friends. Lo and behold, they often fit the pattern, although there were exceptions, too, that I wondered about. In graduate school, I continued to make observations. I practiced law briefly and then began teaching English at Boston College. As a firstborn, I took to teaching like a duck to water. And I always made it a point to find out the birth order of my students. During the course of the semester I would observe their personality, their interactions with others, and their professionalism, creativity, and interpersonal skill—in and out of the classroom.

During the fourteen years I worked as a professor of English, I had an opportunity to observe nearly two thousand students. I noticed how the older sister of sisters often developed a deep rapport with her male teachers. (I'll explain why later.) And how the younger brother of brothers often entertained us with his antics and great sense of humor. (This, too, will be explained later in this book.) I saw how the older brother of brothers was often reserved and conservative but a great help when you needed someone to lead a small group of students in a class project. And I saw how firstborns and lastborns frequently became great buddies and would enjoy enduring friendships. Middle children, twins, and onlies were also well represented, and each had their positives and negatives, which I'll describe in detail in the coming chapters. Each birth order had its own personality, its own strengths and weaknesses.

While teaching, I wrote my first book, *The Art of Kissing*. People always ask me why I chose that topic. The answer is that kissing was the most romantic thing I could think of, and I love romance. The book succeeded beyond all my expectations, and I've been invited to speak about it at hundreds of colleges and universities across North America. I always round up some couples and rehearse them in the different kisses beforehand. Then while I talk, they demonstrate everything from the upside-down kiss to the biting kiss to the French kiss, and more.

I always make it a point to find out the birth order of my student demonstrators. Frequently it's also my responsibility to match up the couples. I quickly saw how two firstborns interacted, as opposed to how two lastborns got along. I saw how complementary relationships (firstborn-lastborn) worked, and also the different dynamics of homogamous relationships (two firstborns, for example, or two lastborns). I saw how lastborn guys loved to get the laughs, how firstborn guys were often a little more diffident onstage, how older sisters of sisters liked to be paired with bad boy types, how lastborn girls loved the chance to be seen in front of an audience. To date I've directed more than three thousand students in these shows, and everything I observed about couples' compatibility is included in this book.

I also lecture about birth order at colleges, talking about celebrity birth order and relating it to the personality of the students in the audience. Afterward I answer questions and counsel individuals and couples with relationship problems. In addition, I've directed more than two thousand actors in plays, television shows, and musicals, invariably finding out everyone's birth order. After thirty-eight years of surveying, I can assure you that birth order is much more than a scientific curiosity. It's a reliable way to find out about personality.

True, there are other factors that go into making us who we are: social class, gender, education, race. I'm also the first to admit that birth order isn't a *perfect* way to predict a person's personality. It *can* fail. But, as Frank Sulloway has pointed out, although birth order is a fallible predictor, it's more accurate and more reliable than any *other* predictor of personality.[1] The fact that it's the most *reliable* predictor should be very exciting news, especially to those interested in romance. Because birth order can help you understand yourself and others in a very real way, it's especially helpful in understanding romantic compatibility.[2]

Why This Book Is Unique

This is the first book on birth order that uses a comprehensive approach to focus exclusively on romantic compatibility. By comprehensive I mean that the advice I give takes into account the work of leading researchers like Walter Toman and Frank Sulloway. Toman's duplication theorem states that opposites attract.[3] Sulloway's research shows that opposites do nothing of the sort; they oppose one another, especially during radical social revolutions.[4] Toman says complementary relationships work best, for example between firstborns and lastborns. Sulloway's research suggests that homogamous relationships might reduce conflict, for example between partners of the *same* birth order.

Although these viewpoints may seem contradictory, in the realm of romantic relationships they really aren't. As I'll explain in the following chapters, opposites do attract, and powerfully so— but so do likes. No picture of romantic relationships can be complete without acknowledging *both* forces. So, in painting the picture of your best match, I'll use the theory that opposites attract, but I'll also take into consideration the fact that many successful relationships are based on like attracting like. Such narcissistic relationships are discussed fully in each of the chapters on the individual birth orders (Chapters 1–12), and also in Chapter 19 on narcissistic attraction.

How This Book Is Organized

I structured this book so that you can use it as a field guide to finding a compatible mate. I suggest you first read the overview chapter for an introduction to the key birth order concepts used throughout the book. Next I recommend you read the chapter about yourself (in Part I, II, or III). When you meet someone new, you can read the chapter on their birth order to find out more about their personality. Eventually I recommend that you read *all* the chapters, because undoubtedly you'll encounter people from all the different birth orders.

In Part IV of the book, we'll look at common problems birth order can produce, such as rank and sex conflict, communication problems, mismatched values, loss and separation issues, and narcissistic attraction. We'll examine how to spot these problems and how to deal with them when they pop up in your own relationships. I've also included an Appendix that reviews some of the relevant clinical research on birth order theory.

Before we go further, I want to emphasize a very important point. *Any* two people can be compatible. I have discussed your best and worst match for theoretical and practical reasons, but if you're already married, keep in mind that human nature is so adaptable and variable that even the match I call "worst" can work wonderfully, provided you understand the dynamics of your relationship. Reading the profiles of yourself and your partner will help you do just that.

I'm not going to use the word *probably* very often in the following pages. There are exceptions to the rules, of course, but for the purposes of outlining the impact of birth order, I'm going to focus on the positive findings—the rules of birth order—rather than on the exceptions.

You'll find yourself profiled in the following chapters, along with your parents, siblings, and friends. Even your employers, co-workers, and romantic partners are here. I'm confident you'll learn something new about yourself and them—even some secrets that may surprise and shock you. I hope you find the discussion enlightening, helpful, perhaps exciting, and most important of all, useful for finding a compatible mate.

An Overview of Our Subject, or What Is Birth Order? And Why Does It Matter?

The beauty of birth order theory is that it's all very easy to understand. Birth order explains how sibling rank (firstborn, middleborn, lastborn, only child) affects personality. If you grew up in a family, you already have a good grasp of all the general principles, and you'll quickly be able to apply the theory to make a good match. Even the research is easy to understand, despite the fact that it sometimes uses complicated-sounding terms. For heaven's sake, one researcher, who published his research in a reputable journal, just stood on a street corner in a big city and asked people who were passing by, "What's your birth order and what's the birth order of your spouse?"[1] You could have done that study yourself with no problem and had time to spare to have a good lunch. That same day, you could have gone home and written up your results.

Let me give you one more example of how easy it is to understand birth order research.

Another researcher used a written questionnaire to ask his questions. One of the things he discovered was that firstborns are slightly more conscientious than laterborns. Conscientious means you do things on time, follow a schedule, and pay attention to details. Do you know how he measured conscientiousness? I'll tell you if you promise not to laugh—he simply measured whether firstborns returned the questionnaires faster than laterborns. You could have done that study too, and then *your* name would appear in the footnotes instead of this researcher's. By the way, he found that firstborns returned questionnaires on average one day sooner than laterborns.[2]

I should mention that the term birth order itself gives some people headaches. Why? Maybe it's that simply hearing the word *birth* brings up in their subconscious the trauma of their own birth, something they don't consciously remember.[3] There's no good way around this. If this problem happens to you, I suggest that every time you hear me say birth order, just think *sibling order*. This entire book is about how brothers and sisters (or lack thereof) impact your personality and your potential for making a good match.

A Brief History of Sibling Study

People have been observing the effects of siblings on personality for a long time, but scientific study on birth order really got started with Alfred Adler, one of Freud's followers. Adler suggested that siblings influence our personality and may even cause feelings of inferiority if they're bigger and more aggressive.[4]

Later theorists have done much to refine Adler's thinking about how siblings impact personality. Walter Toman, a German psychologist, was the first to expand on the personality profiles of all the birth order types. His work has had a profound influence on clinical research as well as on the popular psychology approach to birth order.[5]

Today it's generally agreed upon by social scientists that five traits describe personality fairly completely. These Big Five personality traits, as they're called, include *openness to experience, conscientiousness, extraversion, agreeableness,* and *neuroticism*.[6] But here's something just as big—in 1996 Frank Sulloway convincingly demonstrated that birth order affects these traits and how they shape personality.[7]

That was big news. In fact, it sent shockwaves throughout the scientific community. Sulloway appeared on every major television news show talking about his results. It was such big news that it even upset some people. "Who?" you may ask. "*Who* would get upset at a research finding?"

THE BIG FIVE PERSONALITY TRAITS CORRELATED WITH BIRTH ORDER

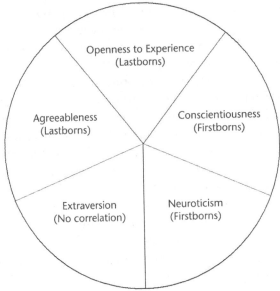

The Big Five personality traits are a way to describe human temperament. Frank Sulloway has made a convincing case that four of these factors are correlated with personality. Firstborns are more conscientious (they tend to plan and to conform to authority) and neurotic (they experience negative emotions like anger, anxiety, and depression), and lastborns are more agreeable and open to experience (they have creative ideas and are interested in art, emotion, and adventure). Extraversion is not correlated with birth order, but two of its components are: lastborns are more sociable, and firstborns are more assertive (Sulloway 1996:74).

Well, I told you birth order produces headaches for some people, didn't I? For researchers who've spent their entire careers arguing that genetics is the biggest influence on human behavior, Frank Sulloway's findings caused a big headache. See, not everyone agrees that birth order has a terrific influence on personality. Judith Rich Harris argues that the effect of birth order on personality has been largely exaggerated[8] and that, to the extent it *is* real, the personality differences occur primarily *within* families, not outside them.[9] She believes that genetic factors are much more important than environmental ones in making us who we are.[10] Certainly genetic factors are crucial in human biology and psychology,[11] but, in the opinion of many eminent scientists,[12] to discount so thoroughly the impact of environment, including birth order, is to miss half the equation.

Dalton Conley also downplays the relation between birth order and personality,[13] comparing birth order to astrology.[14] However, in light of the mass of evidence on the other side of the argument,[15] Harris and Conley sound as convincing as those who initially argued against the Copernican model of the solar system. You remember Copernicus—he discovered that the earth goes around the sun. Not much controversy about that anymore. And although there may still be some controversy about birth order's effects, today most social scientists would readily agree that it plays an important role in shaping personality.[16] In fact, correlations between birth order and personality are so significant, says Sulloway, that the likelihood of these correlations "arising by chance is substantially less than one in a billion."[17]

Birth Order and Romantic Compatibility

Because birth order is so strongly correlated with personality, knowing someone's birth order can help you understand a potential partner better. This, in and of itself, can increase compatibility. For example, knowing that a firstborn wife with a younger brother is going to be maternal and dominant can enable you to deal with those personality traits when they appear.

At this point I'd like to introduce two important theories of personality that seek to explain why people fall in love and marry.

The first is the notion that **opposites attract**. According to this theory, firstborns and lastborns are happily matched because they're opposites. This theory is also called complementarity or the theory of complementary relationships since each partner is said to complement the other, supplying what the other lacks.[18] The notion that opposites attract is the foundation of Walter Toman's *duplication theorem*, and it's the basis of the approach used throughout this book.

The other theory says that **like attracts like**. Social scientists have long observed that people who are similar in age, residence, race, religion, socioeconomic status, and education[19] tend to marry more frequently than people who are vastly different. According to this theory, two firstborns would make the best match, or two last-borns, or two only children, or two twins, or two middleborns.[20] The idea that like attracts like has been popularized by many social scientists, including Edward Hoffman,[21] a New York psychologist, and aspects of this theory are also used throughout this book.[22]

Using the phrases *opposites attract* and *like attracts like* can prove unwieldy, so occasionally I'll substitute the terms *heterogamy* and *homogamy*. Don't let these words frighten you. *Gamy* means marriage, *homo* means same, and *hetero* means different. **Homogamy** is marriage between people who are the same. **Heterogamy** is marriage between people who are different. It's important to point out that these two theories are not mutually exclusive.[23] Homogamy and heterogamy can, and do, operate simultaneously with regard to birth order all the time.[24]

Sulloway's Compatibility Discoveries

Many of Frank Sulloway's groundbreaking discoveries about birth order can be applied to compatibility theory. Let me give you a brief overview of his findings before we jump into the main part of this book.

Sulloway found that, historically, firstborns support the status quo while laterborns rebel against it and support radical social revolutions, such as the Protestant Reformation and the French Revolution. Especially during such revolutions, he suggests, marriages between firstborns and lastborns can be expected to experience conflict based on divergent points of view. Sulloway's findings are essentially a restatement of the notion that like attracts like: first-borns band together during radical social revolutions, and so do laterborns.

But as Toman observes, temperamental differences between firstborns and lastborns more often than not lead to opposites being *attracted*. This is especially true when there are no radical social revolutions occurring. Although those with opposite birth orders might find themselves on opposite sides of political and philosophical issues, in calm times this usually leads to playful and even teasing debates between romantic partners. Put more simply, it need not lead to substantial romantic conflict. However, the possibility *does* exist for such differences in viewpoint to erupt into more serious conflict during times of radical social unrest,[25] and during such periods in history, as Sulloway observes, it would be wise to fully understand where your partner is coming from before getting into heated arguments about deeply held convictions and beliefs.

Key Ideas Used in This Book

I know you're chomping at the bit to get to the profiles of yourself and your potential partners. So I'm going to be very brief in outlining the key concepts you'll need. I'll expand all these ideas later in the book.

• **Rank conflict** is one of Walter Toman's greatest contributions to our understanding of siblings and their effect on personality and explains the two types of conflict that birth order can produce.[26] Rank conflict (see Chapters 13 and 14) occurs when two firstborns enter into a romantic relationship or when two lastborns get together. Firstborns can be expected to fight with each other for dominance and control, whereas lastborns can be expected to squabble with each other over who's got the right to be considered the baby of the relationship. Additionally, as a result of Sulloway's insights, we should be on guard against the possibility of rank conflict flaring up between firstborns and laterborns, especially during radical social revolutions.

• **Sex conflict** (see Chapter 15) occurs when people with no opposite-sex siblings enter into relationships. They can be expected to experience difficulty understanding each other since they didn't grow up with any opposite-sex peers.

• **Narcissistic attraction** (see Chapter 19) entails falling in love with someone who resembles yourself. These are also known as relationships of identification.

- **Interactive relationships** (see Chapter 19) occur between people who are different, such as a firstborn and a lastborn. These are also known as object relationships.

- **Duplication theorem** is Walter Toman's theory that people will be happiest in relationships with those who duplicate their early sibling relationships.[27] For example, an older brother of a sister will be happiest with a younger sister of a brother. More on this later.

Now on to the fun part of the book. The next chapter introduces the expanded birth order profiles. From each profile, you'll pick up another piece of the puzzle. And by the end, you'll have secret insights into just about everyone.

Part 1
Firstborns

1

●○○○○

The Older Brother of Brothers

A firstborn male comes into the world like a king. You're adored and doted on by your parents, and you get plenty of loving attention. Then a few years later, another baby boy comes into the family. By this time you're able to walk and talk, and you're much bigger and stronger than your little brother. As a result you find that you can get your way by dominating him.

Leadership

Your early childhood dynamics explain why you're sometimes perceived as bossy. You're used to getting your way by dominating those under you. In fact, you did it so much as a child that it just seems like the natural way to approach human interactions as an adult. Without even knowing you're doing it, you may adopt an imperious manner. When dealing with others you can appear smug, conceited and overbearing. Obedience is your birthright, and you believe this on both a conscious and an unconscious level. You're genuinely surprised when people don't do your bidding, and you're not afraid of being domineering to get your way. Radio shock jock Don Imus exemplified the hubris of this firstborn. Listening to him, you hear the typical older brother of brothers—condescending, bullying, bossy.

But you have another side: a considerate, guiding side, like a guardian angel. You acquired these kind and helpful qualities because as a child you learned to lead and direct your younger brother. Sometimes you even had to tutor him. As a result, most older brothers of brothers have a magnetic aura about them that attracts men and women and makes people want to follow them.

You have an innate seriousness of purpose. You're a natural leader for great expeditions and undertakings that require a charismatic figure that people, especially men, will follow to the ends of the earth. On some level you're another John Wayne. He played roles that had the aura of masculinity about them, and he embodied the Jungian archetype of the male—active, virile and strong. Wayne had an onscreen presence that radiated strength of purpose, determination and unwavering drive, all characteristics of the older brother of brothers. In real life he was a firstborn with one sibling, a younger brother. Like Wayne's movie characters, you're conscientious, and you strive to do good.

Most firstborn boys who have younger brothers like to lead, but they don't like to take risks, especially risks that threaten their own life. True, you make a good general—sending other men into battle—but you tend to shy away from taking part in the fighting yourself. This reluctance to engage in combat comes from the high regard the firstborn has for his own life and safety. Contrast this aversion with the lastborn of two boys (who usually seeks out danger), and you get a good sense of the way the firstborn approaches the world. The older brother of brothers will gladly let his younger siblings do the bulk of the fighting while he himself orchestrates the contest from the relative safety of army headquarters.

Now, this doesn't mean that you're heartless. On the contrary, you often suffer tremendous guilt and pangs of conscience because of your decisions. Like most firstborns you have a strong conscience and worry that what you're doing may be wrong. Scoring high on conscientiousness, one of the Big Five personality traits, older brothers of brothers want to do the right thing and worry when they don't.[1]

There's another kind of leadership that the older brother of brothers excels at—business leadership. Business may be war, but at least no one is really getting killed when you lead a corporation like

Playboy into battle. Hugh Hefner is three years older than his one sibling, a younger brother. Hefner grew up to be the leader of a worldwide publishing enterprise. When he started the magazine, he felt most comfortable as publisher and editor-in-chief, which meant he was in charge of all major decisions. He also felt comfortable running the day-to-day operations of the company. But compare him to a lastborn (Jay Leno, for example) and you'll notice that, although Hefner appears polite in his interactions with others, he has significantly less charm and agreeableness than a lastborn. This is because firstborns learn early in life that they can get more obedience from their younger siblings by being dominant than by being friendly.

You seek out leadership roles because they reward you with status and recognition, two things firstborns relish above all else. Status and recognition are what make you feel at home. Status in the adult world means the same kind of top-dog position you enjoyed as an older brother during your childhood years, and recognition means the same kind of centrality you enjoyed vis-à-vis your younger brother. For an older brother of brothers, there can be no sweeter success than rising to the top of the hierarchy and enjoying the status and recognition that go along with being king of the hill. You feel that no one deserves the post of top man more than you do. In fact, you're only really happy when you can be number one.

Best Match

You grew up in a family where there's an absence of females your own age. As a result, you sometimes feel at a loss when it comes to understanding women. You may catalog them, classify them, or treat them as if they were unfathomable. One girl described her boyfriend, an older brother of brothers, saying, "He's not romantic at all!" This isn't to say that you can't learn to be charming, certainly you can—only that it'll often be a struggle for you.

Older brothers of brothers often have difficulty choosing a compatible mate. This comes from growing up in an environment where the only female you saw on a day-to-day basis was your mother. Sometimes you yearn for that maternal all-knowing, all-giving love that only a mother can provide, but to expect this from a wife or girlfriend is usually courting disaster since no earthly woman can meet such unreasonable expectations. In fact, the best match for you is a **younger sister of brothers.** She's your opposite, the north to your south, the magnetic feminine that attracts you without your knowing how or why. The younger sister of brothers feels a mutual attraction to the extent that she unconsciously yearns for a boy who can lead like the older brother of brothers. More often than not, however, she feels frustrated when you don't understand her the way she expects, with an intuitive knowledge of her feminine side.[2]

A **middle girl** might also be a good match, provided she had one or more older brothers. You could run into two problems with her, however. First, she might feel you lacked a certain deep understanding of her feminine side. Second, you would tend to fight over leadership, especially if she had a younger brother, since girls with younger brothers like to set the pace and tell guys what to do.

Another potential match is a **younger sister of sisters.** She feels the same attraction toward you, and she needs a natural leader like you to complement her. But here you'll suffer a different problem as a couple: since neither of you grew up with opposite-sex siblings, you'll both feel unsure of your understanding of your partner. Sometimes, however, your mutual handicap in this regard makes things work well in a marriage because neither of you has any advantage over the other.

A **female only child** might be a good match, especially if her mother had one or more older brothers. A **twin** could also be a good match if the girl had a twin brother and if your younger brother is very close to you in age. The twin, however, might feel she needed more closeness and understanding than you could provide, and you, in turn, might feel that your wife is too emotionally needy and demanding of intimacy.

Worst Match

An **older sister of brothers** is a relatively poor match because you'll both want to be the leader. The match between the older brother of brothers and the older sister of brothers is illustrated by the relationship of Bill and Hillary Clinton. Both have forceful, strong personalities, and they like to lead in everything, including marriage. These couples are best together when they live and work side by side, just as Bill and Hillary are often at their happiest when they work together on political campaigns. Otherwise, this isn't a very favorable relationship since it features complete rank conflict.

And yet, even here there *are* factors that can mitigate the problem. For example, if you had major conflict with one or more parents, you would develop characteristics of an honorary laterborn (see page 208). In such a case you might seek out the maternal guiding qualities of the older sister of brothers. You would have to be careful, however, not to fight over who sets the direction in the relationship since you would both want to do this. Another mitigating element in this relationship is the fact that the girl grew up with a younger brother, enabling her to understand you fairly well.

Your worst match would be an **older sister of sisters**. This relationship suffers from a combination of rank *and* sex conflict. You could both have difficulty understanding each other since you both grew up in single-sex families. And you would have the added difficulty that you would both prefer to be leaders in the relationship. To make such a marriage work, you'd need to learn to give up leadership some of the time or to divide leadership into discrete areas—for example, you could lead in matters of career and where you lived, and your wife could lead in matters of domestic design and child rearing. Even so, you would probably find it a rocky road unless other extenuating and mitigating factors, such as narcissistic attraction (see page 211), smoothed over this psychological incompatibility. When narcissistic attraction is operative, this theoretically difficult relationship can actually work surprisingly well.

Advice for Dating the Older Brother of Brothers

The key advice for dating the older brother of brothers is realizing that you're going out with John Wayne. In other words, this is going to be a guy who likes to take charge—of everything. Your date will feel that he's right about everything, that his decisions are correct on all issues, and that he knows what's best for everyone involved, especially you. You've also got to be prepared to be tough. He's going to treat you like a younger brother. He'll expect you to be brave, physically strong, and fearless. He's going to want you to round up the horses, ride like a cowboy, and fight off the bad guys with him. And all through the battle, he'll be giving directions on how to aim, reload, and shoot. This is a man's man, so if you have any manly qualities at all—for example a tomboyish side or a masculine streak—he'll love that aspect of you above all else.

One of the most sophisticated things you can do when dating an older brother of brothers is to use his understanding of men to your *own* advantage. You can do this by flaunting any masculine traits you might possess. One girl called me and complained that her boyfriend, an older brother of brothers and a college football star, never paid any attention to her when a football game was on television.

I suggested that her boyfriend might like it if she wore a football shirt herself.

A few weeks later she told me that the idea had worked—much better than she expected!

"I can't thank you enough," she said. "It was Sunday afternoon and the game was on, and he was glued to the screen as usual. So I put on his football jersey and tied it up nice, and sat down beside him. He went crazy and started flirting with me more than he's ever done before. It was like I had a magic charm. As long as I had that football jersey on, he couldn't get enough of me! Next week I'm planning on wearing the shoulder pads too."

It's these kinds of things that endear a girl to the older brother of brothers. Sure, he knows that girls are different from boys and that they're supposed to be treated with respect and kindness. But he grew up with young brothers, not sisters, so what he's used to doing is horsing around with his peers and treating them like boys. If you can adopt some masculine qualities, even if only in a playful manner like this girl, you'll find the key to his heart.

Advice for Breaking Up

The easiest way to get out of a relationship with the older brother of brothers is to help him save face. This is a very important issue with firstborns. You can't embarrass him in front of his friends or let the story get around town; it'll only annoy him and make him miserable. The most tactful way to break up is to explain your reasons for doing so as logically and calmly as possible. Men like technical explanations, especially older brothers of brothers, so the more detailed you make your reasoning, the better he'll react to it and the more he'll accept it.

An even easier way to make sure that you have a clean break with him is to get one of your friends to show some interest in him. If you can possibly find him a younger sister, that would be ideal. Have this other girl start calling him and flirting with him just before you tell him that you want to break up. That should make the transition easier since he can deflect his interest for you onto her.

As far as your own heart is concerned, you'll find it relatively simple to break up with the older brother of brothers if you continue being friends with him. This will make things easier for both of you. It'll also help if you can get into another relationship—it doesn't have to be romantic, it could just be a friendship—with a boy who has one or more sisters. This boy will be a sounding board for you, listening to your problems. (Sigmund Freud, by the way, had four younger sisters and was a great listener). Talk intimately with your new friend, and before you know it, you'll find your own center and be able to fall in love again.

Friendship and the Older Brother of Brothers

If you're an older brother of brothers, don't be surprised to find that your best friends turn out to be lastborn boys who have older brothers.

Next best will likely be middle boys who have one or more older brothers. These younger and middle brothers will intrigue you with their risky lifestyles, amuse you with funny stories, and inspire you with their creative endeavors. In some cases you'll even want to lead them on expeditions, on trips across the country, or in business ventures. Together you'll have fun, explore the world, and maybe even make some money.

In direct contrast, you'll find older brothers of brothers boring. Not only that, they'll annoy you. They seem stuck up. They're snooty. They're just too into themselves. All the things you dislike most in them are, as Jung pointed out, your own worst faults. To other people, you sometimes appear to be stuck up, snooty, and conceited. But you shouldn't worry about that; in fact, there are some people who will actually find those traits positively charming. They won't think of you as stuck up; they'll see you as confident. They won't think of you as snooty; they'll see you as charismatic. And they won't think of you as conceited; they'll see you as brimming over with leadership skills. These will be the lastborn and middle boys we mentioned, and they're your best bet for great lifelong friends.

Another good friend could be the male only child, who will also admire your leadership and self-determination. An example of how long-lasting this relationship can be is the friendship of firstborn Mick Jagger and only child Keith Richards.

When it comes to women, you'll often find yourself becoming friends with the same types of girls who will be great in relationships—lastborn girls or middle girls who have older brothers. The trickiest friendships will be those with firstborns. You'll often find yourself confused by them, drawn to them with a strange obsession, especially if they're beautiful. Keep in mind that what you like in these girls may simply be what is best in *yourself*—their confidence, their leadership ability, their take-charge attitude. Sometimes these girls will wear you out by driving you to be more of a firstborn yourself, and you'll need to wind down and relax with your lastborn friends, who can help you recharge your batteries.

Of all the male birth orders, you're the closest one to Superman.

You're very hard on yourself, often a perfectionist. So learn to relax with your friends and enjoy their company and companionship.

Career

You do best and find yourself happiest in careers where you're in command.[3] You make a good judge, military officer, or politician. Careers such as captain of a ship, fighter pilot, and astronaut satisfy you on two counts: first, you're at the top of the hierarchy, and second, you're leading others. The one thing you dislike about such work is the risk to your life that's involved; however, once you overcome this fear, you're an inspired leader.

In a corporation, you're dissatisfied unless you can become a midlevel manager or vice president. You make a good hotel manager because this is a safe occupation and you're totally in charge. As a researcher, teacher, or writer you tend to do well when solving puzzles[4] or advocating the status quo. As a religious leader you make a good priest, minister or cult icon. You could be an effective and inspiring captain for a debating society, basketball team, or sports club, especially if the sport isn't too risky. And you make a good taxicab driver because you're taking orders from no one. You like to work for yourself and will do well as a small businessman.

The point is that you feel comfortable in a managing position because you're in charge. You always dream about reaching the top. You work well with other people, provided that they must report to you and do your bidding. But forget about working for a female boss; she would have to defer to you in all matters of importance, or you would fight continually.

You'll find romance on the job if you take the time to relax and associate with female subordinates. Those who respond well to your leadership—the younger sisters—will be your best match. Those who oppose you at every turn—the older sisters and the middle sisters with younger siblings close in age—will make more troublesome life partners. Use your time at work to learn about the temperaments of different women, and you'll soon find that you can make a good match with many of the laterborns.

●○○○○

Celebrity Case Study

BEN AFFLECK

Ben Affleck grew up in Cambridge, Massachusetts, with one younger brother, Casey, who is three years younger. As a firstborn with a brother so close in age, Affleck developed all the traits one associates with older brothers of brothers: dominance, leadership, and masculinity. Unlike John Wayne, however, the roles Affleck usually plays in movies emphasize the guiding qualities of the big brother rather than his dominant take-charge skills. Especially in his early films like *Mallrats* and *Chasing Amy*, Affleck's characters are sympathetic and helpful to others. They even relate well to women, which is the angelic side of the big brother shining through—the side of him that wants to guide and protect those he loves. This quality is one of the nicest features of the older brother of brothers. He genuinely likes to help people, and he can often do this better than anyone else.

Affleck's best friend, Matt Damon, is a lastborn with one older brother about three years older. Their friendship confirms our prediction that firstborns and lastborns often become the best of friends because their personalities are a perfect complement.

Affleck and Jennifer Lopez—the middle sister of three girls—had a very public eighteen-month romance that ended in January 2004. After their breakup, Affleck dated Jennifer Garner, who coincidentally had the same first name and the same birth order as J-Lo. Once you understand birth order, you begin to realize that this might *not* be pure coincidence. It's my hunch that Affleck feels comfortable with middle girls from same-sex sibships. First of all, they have no advantage over him since they have no brothers; in other words, both Affleck and Garner experience *equal* amounts of sex conflict (see page 167). And second, such a partner will alternate between leading and following, a typical middleborn trait. Affleck may like this, too; or at least he may be *used* to it, having just ended a relationship with middleborn J-Lo.

"He's really a gentleman," Garner said about her *Daredevil* costar. "And he's not afraid to laugh at himself or you. And I knew, I just had an instinct that he would take care of me in my first step out there, and he did."[5] Clearly, what she's relating to is Affleck's guiding, helpful side, which is one of the greatest strengths of the older brother of brothers.

Ben Affleck's career demonstrates that the older brother of brothers doesn't have to be John Wayne all the time. He can let his guardian angel side shine through, adopting a helpful and considerate style that will actually leave girls fainting in the aisles with desire.

2

Older Brother of Sisters

You and Cupid, the god of love, have a lot in common. In fact you could say that you're his mortal counterpart. More than other men, you understand women. This is one of your greatest strengths. You're a terrific friend, a good listener, a patient suitor. When you're with a woman, she can feel confident that you'll do your best to understand her feelings and problems. In fact, you may understand her better than she understands herself. This is why women will be drawn to you throughout your life. They sense that you can offer them the kind of understanding that validates their feelings and makes them feel loved.

If you go around telling people that you have these keen insights into the opposite sex, though, they'll think you're conceited. Better keep it to yourself! But read on, it gets even better. . . .

Romantic Charm

Many men have romantic charm, but you have the most complete and consistent ability to focus on your partner in a way that will charm her. The younger brother of sisters has natural charm, and women dote on him too. Some men are so temperamentally pleasant that women fall in love with them simply because they're easy to be with.[1] But in contrast with these kinds of attraction, you have something quite unique. You grew up with a younger sister and learned throughout your childhood that she was special. Your parents taught you to respect her. Girls are different from boys, you learned; they need kindness and consideration. You saw your parents form a romantic duo, and you and your sister formed another kind of duo. This ability to see the relationships of men and women as a natural thing, and to replicate those natural relationships in your adult life, is your special ability.

While the younger brother of sisters charms women by being the lovable baby they want to mother and lavish affection on, you charm women by treating *them* like the object of affection and making them feel special and understood. This proactive approach is in stark contrast to the more laid-back approach of the younger brother of sisters. You remember birthdays, send flowers, and write poems to the women in your life.

Even when you meet someone new, you have the knack of treating her with civility and chivalry.

Jason was only fifteen years old, but having grown up with one sister who was three years younger, he was very comfortable with girls. On the school bus he would joke with them, flirt with them, and talk to them with such ease that other boys seemed like shy dunces in comparison. He almost always had a girlfriend. He went on to date many women, and many women wanted to date him.

You have the ability to strike up a conversation with almost any woman and assure her that you're interested in her as a person, not merely as a sexual object. Of course you can flirt at the drop of a hat, but you know how to start things right by building an acquaintance first. Like Jason, you're comfortable with women.

Best Match

Your best match is a **younger sister of brothers**.[2] You're used to her creativity, rebelliousness, and easygoing nature. She responds well to the kind of attention that you lavish on a woman. And she needs someone who can understand her complex inner nature. True, some older brothers fought with their younger sisters as children,[3] but you usually outgrow such conflicts by the time you're an adult, and you learn to resolve differences with women in a friendly manner.

Your early years with a younger sister prepared you well for a relationship with a woman.[4] And more so than other men, you've been prepared for the role of a father, especially if you had many younger siblings.[5] Women are drawn into your orbit because of your leadership, your kindness, and your attentiveness.

The **younger sister of sisters** is another potential match. You work well with her in non-romantic settings and may find yourself slowly settling into a relationship which the two of you find so comfortable it resembles a long and successful marriage. With her, however, you may miss the deep rapport you're used to with girls who have older brothers.

A **middle girl** can be an exceptionally good match, provided she has at least one older brother. In talking about "the more adjustable personality of the middle born child," one writer made the interesting observation that the "middle born child seems to be like type O blood, suitable to all."[6] While middle girls may be more adaptable and suitable to many different types of boys, the fact that she has one or more older brothers is what makes her match up with you. In this case, you've got one perfectly complementary element in your relationship.

But there are some non-complementary elements too, depending on how many younger siblings she has. The fact that she has one or more younger siblings means that she may be bossy and dominant some of the time, making the relationship a roller-coaster ride for both of you as she goes back and forth from being compliant to being bossy. She's what I refer to as a switch hitter (see page 132). In other words, she has the ability to play both firstborn and lastborn roles. Once you get used to this, however, you may actually enjoy her changeable personality. When she's in lastborn mode, so to speak, you get her docile side, together with all her feisty competitiveness and interactive prowess. When she's in firstborn mode, you get to enjoy all the pleasures of a narcissistic relationship, including having an ally and partner with whom you can identify. In this mode, as one researcher suggests, you might not even fight over leadership but instead align yourselves and actually "escape the re-enactment of juvenile rivalries found in senior-junior pairs."[7]

A **twin** could be a good match, provided she has a twin brother. In that case she would expect even *more* closeness than what the very considerate and caring older brother of sisters typically brings to a relationship. If she also had an older brother, that would make the match even better. If she had only a twin sister and no other siblings, she would demand closeness, but you would miss the subtle and intuitive knowledge of your male nature that you expect in a partner, and at the same time you might feel slightly stifled by the intimacy a twin demands.

A **female only child** is another potential match, although it's a much better match for *her* than it is for you. In fact, you're the *best* match for the female only child. An example of this relationship is the marriage of Humphrey Bogart and Lauren Bacall. With two younger sisters close in age to him, Bogey was the ideal catch for only-child Bacall. His romantic onscreen persona, often ironically combined with a tough guy role, is just what a female only child needs. You'll find that this match works best if the girl's mother had an older brother. In many cases, however, you'll sense that something is missing in this relationship, namely the intuitive connection that you experience with girls who have older brothers.

Worst Match

Your most challenging match is with another **firstborn**. However, it must be said that you're such a ladies' man and have such a keen insight into the opposite sex that you can relate to *any* birth order. As we shall see, your relationship with the older sister of sisters and the older sister of brothers is not entirely negative. The main problem you'll run into, though, is that in both relationships you'll experience total rank conflict.

As a firstborn, you naturally prefer to lead, but the older sister of sisters is not a natural follower. She's a complex person who has a strong tendency to be dominant herself, something she learned vis-à-vis her younger sister. But what makes her particularly interesting is that she also has an underlying, and often unconscious, need to submit herself to the will of an older man, which is a result of her strong relationship to her father. These competing tendencies often war it out in her mind and make her feel a great ambivalence toward men. She sometimes feels that men are no good for her because they don't understand her, they don't treat her right, and they aren't the godlike figure her father was in her life. Of all her potential partners, you have the best chance of understanding her, but she'll feel a conflict when you try to lead, which is your natural tendency.

The older sister of brothers poses a slightly different challenge. She'll be dominant when it comes to men—something she learned by growing up with younger brothers—but the saving grace she brings to the relationship is that she understands you as a man and she respects authority.[8] All older sisters of brothers develop maternal tendencies by virtue of having grown up with younger brothers. What makes this so great is that she'll look out for your best interests. The only problem is that you don't need this kind of big-sisterly help; you're perfectly capable of fending for yourself! In fact, you find this kind of solicitous behavior unnecessary and even a trifle bothersome. If you succumb to her influence, as many husbands do, you may find yourself regressing to an almost babyish state of dependence.[9] This isn't your natural mode of operation, and it's a somewhat limited role for you.[10]

On the other hand, the best way for you to deal with an older sister of brothers is to live side by side with her in a narcissistic relationship, not succumbing to her but instead partnering with her, sharing responsibilities, and relating to her as an equal. She, better than any other girl, will be able to share marital responsibilities and do her fair share of the work to make the relationship click.

Advice for Dating an Older Brother of Sisters

You're in good hands when dating the older brother of sisters. He'll be romantic, attentive, and caring. Conversations with him will be a pleasure because he's a good listener. The best advice for dating him is to relax and be yourself. He'll accept you for who you are.

But if you need to catch this man, here's a tip. More than other boys, he's patient and persistent, especially when the woman he wants is elusive. He likes a challenge. If you can be mysterious and secretive, he'll want to ferret out the mystery and find out the truth. Open up when talking with him and reveal your deepest and craziest thoughts. You won't scare him off. Remember, he's got a little bit of Carl Jung in him, a little bit of the great psychotherapist, so your revelations will intrigue him. Then when you've got him interested, suddenly break off the conversation and tell him you have to go. Leave him wanting more.

Looks are less important to the older brother of sisters than to the older brother of brothers. The older brother of sisters likes beauty, of course, but he can, more easily than other boys, see the inner beauty you possess. Let him see it by revealing yourself to him in all honesty for what you are. He'll accept it all, even things you can't accept yourself.

Another tip for snaring the older brother of sisters—he has a caring big brother side that's a core part of his personality. And he's got a natural affinity for the younger sister of brothers. If you are one, you'll naturally attract him just by being near him, like a magnet. But if you're not, study your friends who *are* younger sisters of brothers. Notice the way they act like little girls around men. Adopt a degree of helplessness. Think of yourself as a damsel in distress who needs to be rescued by your knight in shining armor. He'll be that knight, and he'll come to the rescue. He likes playing the role of Sir Lancelot.

One older brother of sisters told me that both he and his sister are creative. He likes to draw, and so does she. "I like realism," he said. "And all my drawings strive to be realistic. But my sister is the opposite. Her stuff is crazy, like a psychotic dream. You can't understand it." The funny thing is that he himself is drawn to girls who have this craziness in them, this unbounded creativity. If you have such a creative streak, this is what will attract the older brother of sisters to *you.*

Advice for Breaking Up

The best advice I can give you about breaking up with the older brother of sisters is that you can always remain friends with him. In this he's the opposite of many boys who will cut you off and want nothing more to do with you if you're not dating them.

I was visiting a college in North Dakota for a kissing show and, afterward, met many students from the programming council for dinner. While we were talking, one of the guys, a twenty-year-old older brother with a sister three years younger, introduced me to a young woman. He told me that they had dated and that they were now just friends. She happened to be an older sister of a brother. They had broken up after a few dates, as is so often the case with college romances, but they were still good friends. They were both good-looking and had probably been drawn together initially by their physical attractiveness. But their personalities didn't click. Neither felt any resentment. They had decided mutually that it wasn't going to work, and they had moved on to other people.

This is the best way to break up with the older brother of sisters: by maintaining a friendship. You never know when you'll need his help or advice, and there's no one better than an older brother of sisters for helping you with relationship questions and problems later in your life. He's a good person to keep as a friend.

Friendship and the Older Brother of Sisters

The older brother of sisters prefers women friends. This means he can be a very good friend even if things between you aren't romantic, but be careful, because with him things are almost always romantic on some level. He'll be kind and courteous and will probably flirt with you without even thinking about it. Sometimes these friendships develop and become something more than friendship. As a case in point, consider a young law school friend of mine. One day I came into the law review office and found him singing with one of the young women who was part of the staff. The two of them were supposed to be working on an article together, which they did do for a while, but then they began talking about how much they liked singing. Before they knew it, they had launched into a duet. The older brother of sisters is perceptive about women, and he'll quickly find out what you like. If the two of you share an interest or skill, it can lead to singing together or sharing other hobbies and interests.

Men can be friends with him too, although they'll find that he's happiest when they're talking about women, pursuing women together, or girl watching. He's more likely to become interested in your sister than in you. Male friends quickly discover that women are attracted to him, so they befriend him to get access to his large circle of female acquaintances. But it works both ways, and the older brother of sisters will quickly become good friends with his guy friends' girlfriends.

Charlie, a waiter from Tennessee, was going out with Anne, the younger sister of a brother. Doug, one of their mutual friends, was an older brother of a sister. Doug had a great rapport with Anne, but they remained just friends. "I became friends with her over the course of two years while we were in high school and college," he says. "Charlie was always jealous, but he had no reason to be. I kept my distance because Anne was dating him." Doug's ability to maintain a friendship with both Charlie and Anne despite the jealousy of another man, a close competitor, is a hallmark of the older brother of sisters.

Career

You're a natural-born director. Plays, television, films—you name it, you enjoy directing it. Woody Allen, Stephen Spielberg, and Stanley Kubrick are all examples of older brothers of sisters who became accomplished directors.

You also make a great psychotherapist. Like Carl Jung, who had one younger sister, and Sigmund Freud, who had four, you have a wonderful ability to listen. If your interests turn to business, you prefer being a manager. In sales, you do best when you're the head of the sales department. Teaching comes easily to you, and you especially enjoy working with female pupils. As a coach you have a great ability to lead young women to success. As a physician you tend to have a good rapport with female patients, and the specialties of gynecology, pediatrics (where you can meet all the young mothers), and OB/GYN appeal to you more than others. But whatever your career, the key to your motivation and success will always be your relationships with the women around you.

● ○ ○ ○ ○

Celebrity Case Study

PRINCE CHARLES

Prince Charles grew up with one sister, Princess Anne, who is one year and nine months younger.[11] The fact that Princess Anne was so close in age makes Prince Charles a super firstborn, a classic case of the older brother of sisters.

The romance of Prince Charles and Princess Diana is like a fractured fairy tale. During their engagement Diana was dismayed to learn that Charles had sent his old sweetheart, Camilla Parker-Bowles, a gift bracelet. And she was brought to tears after she overheard a telephone conversation in which he told Camilla, "Whatever happens, I will always love you." Charles's actions, however, illustrate how the older brother of sisters is kind to the women in his life, not letting them go, retaining romantic contact despite being married.

Diana grew up with two older sisters and one younger brother, Charles Spencer, who was three years her junior.[12] She and Prince Charles were badly mismatched according to birth order theory. Prince Charles's best match is a lastborn girl. Because he's a firstborn, he'd tend to be bossy in a relationship and expect his partner to be compliant and tractable. Princess Diana was the opposite of what he needed. Since she grew up with a younger brother so close in age, she would naturally dominate men and expect them to obey her. She and Prince Charles must have locked horns on many occasions because they experienced significant rank conflict.[13]

The untimely death of Princess Diana in an automobile accident in 1997 shocked the world. Eight years later, Prince Charles married Camilla Parker-Bowles. As a firstborn with a younger brother and sister, she's another mismatch, and yet their relationship has persisted for many decades. How to account for this love between two firstborns?

My theory is that their relationship is based on narcissistic attraction, a kind of glue holding them together through thick and thin.[14] It's also likely that because he had so much conflict with his father,[15] Prince Charles should be considered an honorary laterborn,[16] which would mean that he would feel a deep connection with any woman who had a younger sibling.

The love life of Prince Charles exemplifies how an older brother of sisters' romantic feelings can persist through many years, waxing and waning but never becoming extinguished. It also illustrates how important it is to consider the firstborn's relationship to his parents (see page 208), for substantial conflict can introduce developmental glitches[17] that predispose him to falling in love with women who have younger siblings.

3

●○○○○

Older Sister of Sisters

Queen of the Amazons—that's the way you appear to others. Strong-willed, determined, possessed of a fierce individualism, you stand out in a crowd because of your dominance and drive. People respect you for your strength and courage, your ability to go against the grain, and your forceful personality. But probably your greatest strength is organizational ability, which comes from an innate sense of what's important and what isn't. More than other girls, you like to have everything in its place. You keep agendas and to-do lists, and you plan ahead better than others. Which isn't to say that you always accomplish everything you set out to do, but you certainly work toward concrete goals, often sacrificing body and mind to achieve them. Ultimately this does bring you more success than others.

If you stop and think about it for a moment, you'll have to admit that you're a perfectionist, pushing yourself to the breaking point in work and play. High standards and performance goals are the way you view the world. If a man doesn't have similar structure in his life, you wonder what's wrong with him. If he does, he reminds you of yourself—or of your father—and you find yourself drawn to him because of this similarity. But at the same time you yearn for a man who's different, someone laid-back and relaxed, easygoing and fun, someone the direct opposite of you (more on this later). Behind your back your friends are saying things like, "She's so driven! Why can't she just relax and let up? Does she have to be so perfect about everything?"

If you have just *one* younger sister, you tend to be a nonconformist, but if you have *two or more* younger sisters, you tend to be much more conforming.[1] No matter how many younger siblings you grew up with, you have strong leadership skills that you developed by virtue of having to take care of younger sisters. You're also extremely conscientious.[2] Teachers like this, and you can use that to your advantage, especially with male teachers.

A good example of how a firstborn girl with one younger sister can be both conscientious and nonconformist is exemplified by an incident that happened while I was teaching a vocabulary class. In this evening college course we used skits to illustrate new words. One night I needed a student to do some ballet dancing in a skit, but I didn't know who to ask. One of the boys suggested that I ask Francine, an older sister of one sister. "She'll do it," he assured me. "She'll have no problems with a skit like this." Sure enough, when Francine entered the room and heard what was needed, she volunteered. She even asked how far she was supposed to dance across the front of the room during the scene. Her ability to jump into such a nonconformist role was due in part to her high level of conscientiousness. "I have no trouble making a fool of myself in your class," she said. "I don't know why, but I'll do anything you need." A director couldn't ask for a better response from an actor, and indeed she did a wonderful job in the skit, which provoked lots of laughter from everyone.

This story illustrates two key traits of the older sister of sisters. First, you're conscientious to a fault. Second, you relate better than other girls to older males and men in authority. On the relationship of the older sister of sisters to older men, Walter Toman says: "She derives her claim to authority and leadership from another person with authority, usually an older man, a man in a high position, or from a law-maker. This frequently includes her own father. She accepts this person's wishes or will unquestioningly and will remain faithful to him for many years."[3] Along the same lines, Frank Sulloway points out that in two-girl families, "Being displaced as the sole object of attention, the elder sister tends to shift her principal identification to her father."[4] This is another reason why the elder of two

Ayn Rand

Novelist and philosopher Ayn Rand grew up in Russia with two younger sisters. A super firstborn, her life and philosophy illustrate all the characteristics of the older sister of sisters. Even as a young girl, Rand was strong-willed, determined, and focused on her career. She struck people as somewhat masculine because of her dominant personality. Arriving in America when she was twenty-one, she pursued her chosen career with singular energy and drive, writing novels, screenplays, and nonfiction that has had a profound influence on American philosophy. Her major contribution was the notion of individualism, which is embodied in all her work, especially *The Fountainhead*, *Atlas Shrugged* and *The Virtue of Selfishness*. The latter encapsulates the mindset of the older sister of sisters— not because she's particularly selfish, but because she knows how to take care of herself, and she realizes her own value and self-worth.

girls in a family with no brothers tends to identify with older men; she transfers her skill in bonding with her father into her romantic life, often developing close ties to men in power, older men, and male authority figures. A good example of this is Sophia Loren, who married Carlo Ponti, a movie producer twenty-five years her senior.

The implications for your romantic life are profound and will be discussed in the next section. People do notice this about you, however, and they talk about you. In fact, if you have a boyfriend he may become jealous of your relationship with older male mentors, employers, or teachers. You may find that you have some confusion about your relationship with older men, and you may even have to force yourself to break off attachments to them in favor of someone closer to your own age.

More than other girls, you have a natural desire to be in control, and you prefer being in control to almost anything, even having fun. When you do have fun, you may feel you're losing control, and it worries you sometimes. You have strong feelings of guilt because your conscience is overly developed. I encourage you to find ways to relax, such as having pets, meditating, or taking walks.

Your greatest weakness is something most firstborns have to watch out for: you're not especially open to new experiences. Put more simply, you often focus on one thing to the exclusion of all else. You have one set of interests, and you don't pursue other things. In some ways this is a strength because it lets you focus, but in other ways it limits you.

Olivia, a seventeen-year-old music prodigy and older sister of two sisters, was traveling by plane to a recital with a male music teacher. Like most older sisters of sisters, she got along famously with her male teacher. When they passed over their music school, her teacher pointed out the window. "There's our school," he said. Olivia, who was sitting by the window, glanced out momentarily. "No, it's not," she said. For the rest of the flight she never looked out the window. She wasn't afraid of flying; she was simply unimpressed by novel experiences to the point that she cut herself off from seeing her school (even though she had looked directly at it!) and the other sights one can view from an airplane window.

To deal with this tunnel vision, encourage yourself to relax, and remind yourself to embrace new experiences, even those that might at first appear trivial or insignificant. It can also help to associate with a lastborn friend, who will naturally notice these things *for* you and point them out to you.

Dominance and Submission

Although one side of you likes to be in control, there's another side that doesn't. Human nature is such that ambivalent feelings, such as love and hate, can coexist simultaneously in the same heart. You have an understandable desire to dominate, originating in your early interactions with your sister, but you have an equally strong, if less conscious and more frightening, desire to be mastered, which comes from your early relationship with your father.

"I like to be dominated," admits one twenty-one-year-old older sister of sisters. Although her personality is direct and forceful, she harbors lingering feelings of wishing to relinquish control and let a man take charge. "I'd like to find a man who'd tell me what to do, and I'd just do it," she says. "But at the same time I fear that desire in myself, and I can't let myself lose control like that. It would be a mistake."

Of all the firstborns, you're the most complex. We usually think of firstborns as being rather simple to understand because they're dominant, conservative, and leadership-prone. The firstborn female, however, is hampered by the fact that, in our society, males are expected to be the leaders, so she experiences her own strength as a masculine trait that she feels ambivalent about, especially when it comes to her relationships with men. Don't be surprised to find yourself fighting with men for dominance part of the time, and fighting with *yourself* the rest of the time as you resist sinking into a state of childish submission to them.

Like the strong female characters in Ayn Rand's novels—Dominique Francon, who enjoyed being ravished by Howard Roark in *The Fountainhead*, and Dagny Taggart from *Atlas Shrugged*, who could only enjoy relationships with men who used physical violence toward her—you have a dangerous desire to let the man in your life take control. Reading Rand may help you vicariously deal with your own tendency to want to let go and be totally controlled by a man.

Best Match

The **younger brother of sisters** is your best match. If you can get him interested it would be worth your while because he's got exactly the kind of personality that will complement you. Whereas you're high-strung, nervous, and pushy, he's relaxed, calm, and agreeable. The two of you are exact opposites, which can often make sparks fly when you're together. However, he may find you too aloof for his tastes, or less of a caregiver than he needs. To improve the match, study your girlfriends who have younger brothers, paying particular attention to how they tease, play with, and baby men. This is what your partner needs.

Another good match is the **younger brother of brothers**. The two of you have total sex conflict (see page 167), but that sometimes isn't an impossible hurdle, especially since in this case neither of you has an advantage over the other. Sometimes two people from a same-sex sibling constellation do very well together. A student of mine, an older sister of one sister, admitted to me on many occasions that she liked another student, a younger brother of brothers. I cast them together in a number of skits. With others she was usually brassy and bossy, but with him she was kind and caring. It was as if being with him magically brought out her best qualities. Relationships between firstborns and lastborns like this often have a great chance for success.

A male **twin** could be a good match, especially if he has a twin sister. He may expect a lot of intimacy and closeness, however, which is something he's used to from his sister. If he has a twin brother, he may expect you to be more masculine than you're comfortable with, but since firstborn girls often have a lot of masculine traits,[5] this may actually work.

Very often the male only child is your best match. He has two big advantages over other guys as far as you're concerned. First, he has a lot of lastborn traits—he's relaxed, affable, and easygoing—which is just your cup of tea. And second, because he's also a firstborn he'll appeal to you on a narcissistic level. The only thing you're going to have to watch out for is that the male only child comes with a huge ego—consider William Shatner or Jean-Paul Sartre, for instance—so he's going to want to be center stage all the time. In your opinion that's where *you* belong, but if you can work together like two superstars, you'll satisfy both egos and be happy. Just beware that his mother will be jealous of you all your life, no matter what she says to the contrary.

If you'd like to experience the ultimate in narcissistic relationships, date an **older brother of sisters**. He's very romantic, genuinely lovable, and will take care of you like no other man. The *younger* brother of sisters, your theoretical best match, would let you fend for yourself while he acts like a baby, but the older brother of sisters will do just the opposite; he'll tend to your every wish and desire and care for you sometimes more than you feel necessary. Many older sisters of sisters have told me that they feel a great deal of satisfaction in relationships with an older brother of sisters. As in any relationship with a firstborn, however, you'll experience rank conflict. He'll want to tell you what to do and how to do it, but if you can get over your annoyance at his bossiness, you'll see that in most cases he's got your best interests at heart.

Worst Match

The **older brother of brothers** is theoretically your worst match if we follow a pure duplication theorem point of view, because you suffer from rank *and* sex conflict. You're both natural-born leaders and will argue over who's going to be in charge, and neither of you has opposite sex siblings so you may find it difficult to understand each other at times.

And yet . . . and yet . . .

Despite these theoretical difficulties, which are very real, I've heard from many older sisters of sisters who swear that they have terrific relationships with older brothers of brothers. The reason lies in the fact that two firstborns will feel narcissistic attraction. You'll see the best qualities of yourself reflected in your partner. This mirrorlike reflection can lull you into a sense of security. It's like falling in love with yourself, which is sometimes a very easy thing to do. In such a relationship you'll want to watch out for the potential of your partner to get bossy and dictatorial, a fault that older brothers of brothers fall into more than other men. If you can share the reins, though, this can be a very powerful experience.

At one college I visited, the director of the student programming board, Rachel, an older sister of two sisters, was dating an older brother of a brother. I expected her to tell me that they fought over leadership issues, but I was surprised. "We never fight," she said. "If I get annoyed he says, 'I'll talk to you when you're not upset.' Then he waits for me to calm down. Justin's very quiet. He doesn't talk much, and neither did my dad."

Rachel's mother and father had divorced when she was only thirteen. Missing her divorced father, she had apparently stumbled upon a relationship that would provide someone just like her father—a quiet, noncommunicative firstborn.

The next day they drove me to the airport, and during the ninety-minute ride Justin almost never spoke. Clearly he and Rachel were in a narcissistic relationship that was working well for both of them, but I also sensed that Rachel wasn't completely happy. "I'm hesitant to commit to marriage," she admitted, "because my parents divorced, and I don't want that to happen to me."

Narcissistic relationships like the one between Rachel and Justin can work even better if you have a lastborn friend who brings some interactive fun into the picture, something firstborns need to calm them down and keep them amused. Ideally this lastborn would be friends with both you *and* your boyfriend.

Advice for Dating an Older Sister of Sisters

An older sister of sisters can be rather harsh with the men in her life. Because she grew up without brothers, who often dominate sisters, she has learned that she has a strength that can be projected into the world almost without limitation. Known as instrumental traits, these forceful personality characteristics may strike others as harsh and masculine.

Olivia grew up with one younger sister and is a classic case of the dominant firstborn. She has a good relationship with Larry, her music teacher, who's twenty-five years older. Occasionally she drives Larry to concerts, and while working as his driver, she unselfconsciously raises her voice and barks instructions at him, telling him to fill up the gas tank or get food from a drive-in. After awhile Larry began to get the impression that Olivia didn't like him, but as they pulled out onto the road one evening, she said, "Please don't take it personally; I do that to everyone. I honestly don't know how to stop. It's just my personality." Indeed you've got to get used to her being bossy, opinionated, tough-minded, and, frankly, somewhat harsh in temperament. Some men actually thrive on this kind of personality and find it challenging and refreshing to be with a woman who's so similar to themselves. If you keep in mind that she's forceful by nature and that she isn't being overly aggressive just toward *you*—she's acting this way with everyone—you'll get along better with her, and you'll learn to enjoy the company of a strong woman, someone you can truly rely on in times of crisis.

Advice for Breaking Up

The older sister of sisters is a good friend and a loyal one, but she can be rather neurotic.[6] She may have quirky hang-ups about diet, clothes, or the way she spends her time. She may be inflexible and rigid about how she does things. One older sister of two girls that I know regularly has to go to the gym for a workout every day at 4:00 p.m. Even when she's on an afternoon date with a guy, she breaks it off when it's time to go to the gym. Her boyfriend was perplexed by this inflexibility, and they broke up over it. His approach was to talk with her, but she was so inflexible that she couldn't listen to his complaints.

When breaking up with an older sister of sisters, you sometimes have to be careful. One former student of mine, who was only twenty years old and who had three younger sisters, told me that she broke up with her boyfriend in a novel way. "He was dating another girl and I found out," she says. "We were in my car when he admitted it to me. I stopped the car, slapped him in the face, and punched him. He was bawling his eyes out, and begging me to calm down. I opened his door, told him I never wanted to see him again, and then I kicked him out onto the road. I drove off, leaving him six miles from home." This kind of violent reaction can occur because the firstborn can be very moralistic and take a hard position on matters of infidelity. When breaking up with an older sister of sisters, be mindful that she may have a mindset that can't be changed. Your best bet is to wait for her to calm down.

Friendship and the Older Sister of Sisters

An older sister of sisters often has more male friends than female ones. Though she gets along well with girls her own age, she has a superior ability to bond with men. It's not uncommon for her to have male friends at school, work, and in her clubs and church. When it comes to girlfriends, she often enjoys the company of younger sisters of brothers because she can learn how to deal with men from them. Abigail, the eldest of two girls, told me that she liked talking with Janet, who has two older brothers. "Janet has a lot of insights into relationships," says Abigail. "I learn things from her. When I have questions sometimes, I call her up to get her opinion. She hasn't been wrong yet!"

One of the most noticeable characteristics of the older sister of sisters is that, when she's with her girlfriends, she's the one who usually sets the agenda.

"Carrie's always telling us what to do," says one friend of an older sister of sisters. "She plans things out weeks in advance. It's nice and all, but sometimes it can get kind of funny, like when she told us where we'd be going for spring break, how much it would cost, and what hotel we'd be staying in—four months before we went!"

Her propensity to plan ahead is a way for the older sister of sisters to minimize her own free-floating anxiety about the future. By planning all the details, she can feel that she has every contingency under control. The way to deal with a friend like this is to encourage her to become a travel agent. In all seriousness, you should feel free to rely on her and be thankful she's so organized. Offer to help her plan and organize things occasionally, and she'll be grateful to have you share the burden she usually takes upon her own shoulders.

Career

If you're an older sister of sisters, you make a good coach, athletic trainer, teacher, or editor. Although you grew up without brothers, you relate well to men, which will have an important influence on your career. You expect men to be good at what they do, and in many cases you want them to let *you* help them reach their goals. In fact you often develop strong relationships with artists, writers, and athletes precisely because of your good judgment about their work.

For this reason you make a superior talent or literary agent, music director, or team coach. Teaching is also something you do well, but you have trouble sometimes with male students who fight with you for authority, especially the firstborns. No matter what you do, you prefer to be in charge, and managing is something you enjoy and are comfortable with. You work especially well under a man in authority, such as a dean, senator, or senior executive.

A student of mine, who was an older sister of one sister, went on to work with a leading talk show host when he was in his sixties and she was only twenty-two. "People say he's more relaxed now and feels more confident about his ability to get the show rolling," she says. "We have a great working relationship."

Such relationships sometimes lead to marriage. Brigitte Bardot married film director Roger Vadim, clearly a male authority figure, when she was only eighteen.

●○○○○

Celebrity Case Study
JACQUELINE KENNEDY ONASSIS

With an age gap of only three and a half years between her and younger sister Caroline, her only sibling, Jacqueline Kennedy Onassis was a super firstborn. She was highly organized, had a forceful personality, was a nonconformist, and was comfortable in the company of powerful older men.

After graduating from Vassar, Jackie worked in Washington as a photographer, which is how she met Senator John F. Kennedy. They married in Newport, Rhode Island, in 1953. Seven years later Kennedy was elected president. As First Lady, Jackie brought a nonconformist sensibility to the White House and insisted that it be completely redesigned to match her taste. After JFK's assassination in 1963, she moved to New York City and, in 1968, once again demonstrated nonconformist taste by marrying Aristotle Onassis, a Greek billionaire twenty-three years her senior—quite the controversial match, as many Americans wanted her to remain faithful to the memory of JFK.

After Aristotle Onassis's death in 1975, Jackie worked as an editor at Doubleday in New York City. She also began associating with a new boyfriend, Maurice Tempelsman.

Jackie's life and romances should sound familiar if you're an older sister of sisters. She sought out the company of older men, and men in power, and related so well to them that they fell in love with her. A true nonconformist, she married Onassis despite public disapproval, then went around with Tempelsman despite the fact that he was a married man. In many ways her life demonstrates that the older sister of sisters does things her own way—and makes a name for herself in the process.

CHAPTER
4
●○○○○

Older Sister of Brothers

You are the Earth Goddess incarnate—maternal, articulate, and confident. You're bold where other women are docile, solicitous where others are inattentive, and above all a defender of the low, a protector of the vulnerable, and a champion of those in need. Beware to those who cross you! Like most firstborns, you're dominant, conservative, and religious. Your dominance often causes you to seek leadership roles.[1] Dominance is usually thought of as a masculine trait, but you can be very feminine. Just consider Paris Hilton, for example, an older sister of two brothers, who has plenty of femininity and yet is more of a controller and a leader than the average gal.

As Frank Sulloway points out, firstborns are "more dominant, tough-minded, competitive, inflexible, lacking in empathy, conservative, conventional, and quick to anger"[2] than laterborns. Your conservative nature is often exemplified by political affiliations, such as joining the Republican Party, advocating conservative religious and political values, and supporting the status quo. This is understandable in light of the often excellent relationship you had with your parents. Girls who have good parental relations typically adopt more conservative values than their younger siblings.

Religiosity and birth order are also related,[3] and you tend to be more religious than other girls.[4] You adopt your parents' traditional religious values and have high levels of spiritual feelings, often seeking out friends and soulmates who share your views. If you had significant conflict with one or both parents, however, your spiritual feelings may be more nontraditional.

Very often you meet men at a church club, school, or political meeting and become romantically involved very quickly. That's how strong your tendency to become infatuated is, and the closer in age your brother is, the more you tend to fall in love at first sight. In just a moment I'm going to tell you how to use your great romantic bonding capacity to find the right match. . . .

Maternal Instinct

But what's your chief characteristic? Here's the good news. While it may seem disadvantageous to be dominant and conservative—especially if you're a college student trying to be popular!—the great thing about your birth order is that it brings together two strong personality traits (dominance and conservatism) in a way that men love. Yes, men love this about you.

Aren't you dying to know what this trait is?

Of course you are! And it can be summarized in just two words. . . .

Above all other girls, you have the strongest maternal instinct. This doesn't mean you want to have the most babies! It means you want to baby your men, take care of them, and help them be the best that *they* can be. Now do you see why they flock to you?

Did you ever notice how you often take a protective role in a relationship, looking out for a guy's well-being, as if you were trying to prevent him from slipping off a curb and falling flat on his face? It's a maternal kind of thing, and I'm telling you that some guys really enjoy it.

Liz was like that. She was a sixteen-year-old student in an English class I taught. She had a perpetual tan, and she wore her hair pulled back tightly behind her head so that it looked like she had on a swimming cap. She would hover around me while I worked. One day when she was standing at my side during a break in class, she reached out and gently adjusted the position of the handkerchief in the breast pocket of my jacket, pulling it out a bit further from the pocket so that it would look better.

The Psychological Mirror

What if you could gaze into a psychological mirror? Would you do it?

What's *that*, you ask?

Well, it's like a glass mirror, only it doesn't show you your *physical* reflection—instead it shows your *inner self.* How would you like to see *that!*

It may sound scary, but there's nothing to be afraid of because the inner you has some very wonderful qualities that you might not even know you possess. You've heard of Julie Andrews, right? The beautiful actress who played Mary Poppins, the magical nanny who wins the hearts of children—and men. In *The Sound of Music* she was a governess, taking care of kids in the Alps, and once again she won the heart of the leading man. Whatever you do, watch those movies! Maybe you've seen them as a child, but rent them and watch them again now that you're an adult. Here's why—

Julie Andrews is an older sister of a brother. Not only is her personality like yours, but in those films she plays a character that is very much like yours. She's helpful, organized, dominant—when the situation requires her to be strict with the children—and loving. She has a wonderful way with children, and her maternal skill wins the heart of the little ones . . . as well as the men in her life.

Guess what? By examining Julie Andrews and her characters, you've just looked into your very own psychological mirror. By studying a famous older sister of brothers, you've seen yourself, your *inner* self, in action.

These older sisters are very insidious about the way they help you. They sneak up on you and help you when you least expect it. In fact, if you're like me, you *don't* expect it at all. It comes out of the blue, and suddenly there you are, assisted, aided, and abetted before you know what hit you.

Helpfulness: this is the hallmark of the older sister of brothers. It's a quality that will win you high marks with men no matter where you go or what job you pursue. And it's a trait that will win you the heart of the man who's perfect for you. More about *him* in a moment. . . .

We have to talk about you a bit more. You don't mind that, do you?

I didn't think so! As a firstborn, you like recognition. But you also feel that your younger brother got a bit more of the spotlight than he deserved. In fact, you secretly harbor some jealousy regarding the little upstart getting all that undeserved coddling from your parents. It's not fair! Just because he's a boy he got more attention. In a way you were slighted. But this unconscious feeling of being slighted by your brother makes you especially considerate around men. You seem to want to help them in everything they do. And they love you for it!

Best Match

The **younger brother of sisters** and you make a heavenly match.[5] He's used to a gal who can rein him in, appreciate his kooky ideas, and enjoy his irrepressible humor. You're used to a guy who's laid-back, adventurous, easygoing, and sweet. The two of you were meant for each other, and the best advice I can give you is to actively seek out this kind of guy. Sometimes he can be so relaxed and laid-back that you won't find him initiating contact with you. He may be so immersed in some pet project of his—he has so many!—that you might literally have to drag him out of the darkroom, away from his racing horse, or into a cozy corner where the two of you can talk. He'll amaze you with his inventiveness and his boyish charm. Don't let this one get away!

Another very good match for you is the **younger brother of brothers**. He's just as creative and easygoing as the younger brother of sisters, and he may win your heart simply because he's so much fun to be with. He'll be getting slightly more out of the relationship since you'll understand him better than he understands you, but he's your next best match.

Almost equally good is the **older brother of sisters**. You and he

Cleopatra

Maybe you don't think of yourself as a *femme fatale*, but you are! In fact, you and the *sexiest woman in history* have a lot in common. . . .

Of course I'm talking about Cleopatra. She beguiled men throughout her life. Plutarch describes her this way: "For her actual beauty, it is said, was not in itself so remarkable that none could be compared with her, or that no one could see her without being struck by it, but the contact of her presence, if you lived with her, was irresistible; the attraction of her person, joining with the charm of her conversation, and the character that attended all she said or did, was something bewitching."[6]

Like you, Cleopatra was a firstborn. She had two younger brothers, making her a super firstborn. And like her, you have a way with men, a way of charming and beguiling them so that they can't resist.

Isn't it nice to know that you've got that Cleopatra touch? Set your sights on the man of your choice, and it's going to be impossible for him to resist.

will have what's called a narcissistic relationship (see page 211), meaning you'll love *in* him what's best in *yourself*: that take-charge, can-do attitude. You two, though, may find yourselves coming apart at the seams because of all your arguments over who's in control in the relationship. Let him lead most of the time, and find those areas where he allows you to take control. By sharing power like that, you'll make it work all the better.

An **only child** or a **twin** could be a good match, especially if the singleton's father had an older sister or the twin has a twin sister. In the former case, the guy will adopt some his father's lastborn characteristics, which will make your life easier and more comfortable. In the latter case, your partner will understand your feminine side and expect a lot of intimate closeness, maybe even more than you're comfy with. There could be worse things! Lucky the girl who gets a guy who wants intimacy and closeness.

Worst Match

You and the **older brother of brothers** don't usually work out too well, and it's easy to see why. As a couple you suffer from both rank *and* sex conflict.

Rank conflict means he's going to want to be the boss all the time, and so are you! Sex conflict (in this instance it's only partial) means that *he* has some difficulty understanding you since he grew up without sisters. Coming on top of rank conflict, that's two strikes against you.

In such a relationship, you both may have terrific egos at the end of the day since you'll be relating to someone so similar to yourself. Avoid getting into arguments about who's in control. Instead, try to discuss leadership and power issues, realizing that this is an area where your partner is going to feel most vulnerable. As a firstborn, you don't want to let anyone else tell you what to do. Neither does he. Once you come to terms with that dilemma, you may find things getting easier.

Advice for Dating an Older Sister of Brothers

The older sister of brothers will be very romantic and will be happy to go to places that are quiet and cozy where you can be alone together. She'll also be very considerate of your needs. You can count on her, but don't abuse her trust. She'll take offense if you trick her or tell her lies. Always try to be as honest and up-front as you can. Tell her your dreams, your ideas, your fantasies of success—anything that comes into your mind. You'll never astonish her. She'll listen to you better than other girls, and more than that, she'll dig deep inside you to find your hidden strengths. In fact, she can listen so well you might feel you're talking with a therapist. So don't overdo it— let her talk too.

She's going to have ideas of her own about how you should do things. Let her speak up and voice her opinion. Listen to her ideas, and in most cases you'll find that she's very thoughtful and helpful.

When it comes to talking about your career, the older sister of brothers will be able to help you with guidance, and at times she may sound like a business associate. Yes, you can even talk about business with her while on a date. She doesn't mind. She loves hearing your plans, and she can even help you realize your dreams.

Advice for Breaking Up

The best way to break up with her is to tell her flat out that you're not compatible because she's too much of a take-charge gal. She'll claim she's comfortable with you taking the lead, but this is just talk. Don't be fooled by her sweet ways. Like any woman, she can act like a little girl at times, but more often than not she's going to play the maternal role. If this isn't your cup of tea, get out while the getting is good. In other words, don't waste her time—or yours! Be up-front and honest with her. She can deal with it. In fact she'll remain a lifelong friend and won't hold a grudge against you if you're honest. She might even have a crush on you for the rest of her life— that's how sweet these older sisters of brothers are. They really do like you and want you to succeed. O lucky man!

Friendship and the Older Sister of Brothers

She likes to be friends with guys, and she has lots of male friends. Often older men become infatuated with her and try to form a relationship by starting out as platonic friends. Her best friend is usually a guy who has older sisters. Because this is also her best romantic match, she may find herself torn between feelings of friendship and feelings of romance. Sometimes these friendships turn into love affairs.

Another thing to keep in mind is that she's very comfortable with men, so much so that girlfriends mean less to her as a general rule. She does have close female friends, but they must usually defer to her in matters of planning and deciding what to do. When with her girlfriends, she prefers to talk about her boyfriends—and *their* boyfriends! Be careful that she doesn't steal your man from you. (Actually she has a strong conscience and is very honorable, so you can bet she'll *try* to be good.) But sometimes she just can't help herself, and if your boyfriend happens to show up, you may find she's focusing her attention on him to the exclusion of you. Don't be jealous; it's her nature to focus on men. You might want to ask her to help your boyfriend in his career—she's very good at that!

When together with her, you'll find that she likes going to religious events, she enjoys organizing parties and directing people at these get-togethers, and she likes things to be planned in advance. You may find her calling you weeks prior to some event to plan it. When you go to a party with her, don't be surprised if she begins to talk in a loud voice and tell people what to do, what games to play, and where to sit. It's her bossy firstborn self coming to the forefront, so don't hold it against her.

Career

Let's start with something you probably never even considered. Are you sitting down? Because I don't want to shock you when you hear this . . .

Okay, here it is: You're a great publicist! In fact, you make the *best* publicist of all the birth orders. Why is that? It's because you're able to see things of value in your clients that even *they* can't see. And you can talk up a storm. People listen to you. You're tactful too, which is important when dealing with the media. You know how to suggest things subtly to make important people—or people who *think* they're important—believe that your suggestions were their *own* ideas. Brilliant strategy! And most importantly, when you have a male client, you're able to peer into his soul and find all the good and creative things there that the world will admire.

But that's not all—not by a long shot!

You're a great teacher. You especially like working with children. Remember Mary Poppins and Julie Andrews? Well, that's you, and that's a skill you have in spades.

You do better than average in school,[7] and on top of that you also have a great bedside manner with children, so being a pediatrician is another good career choice.

You're also a very accomplished manager or administrator. I guess you could say you like being in charge. Sound familiar? (You know what people are saying behind your back, don't you? "She's strict. She's bossy. She's always telling me what to do!") Well, for heaven's sake, it's second nature for you to tell people what to do! Besides, somebody's got to be in charge here, right?

Just remember to take it easy with people. These aren't your siblings in the real world on the job, they're coworkers! They might not take too well to your bossing them around. But you *can* be tactful. That's another skill you developed when dealing with your younger brothers. You learned to almost trick them into doing what you want. In the employment world, you don't have to trick people, you simply have to guide and suggest.

One of your strongest abilities is your vision when it comes to artistic men. Perhaps helping their careers and seeing them succeed gives you vicarious pleasure. You'd do well as the manager of a talent or literary agency, a director of student activities at a college or university, or a corporate officer to whom other people must report. The work of a supervisor or coach suits you perfectly. You also like the idea of being the principal of a school, especially an elementary school. And those kids will love you.

●○○○○

Celebrity Case Study

HILLARY CLINTON

Hillary Clinton grew up with two younger brothers very close in age. That makes her a super firstborn, a very dominant, take-charge individual. In fact, she should be even more of a leader than Bill Clinton! Comparing their personalities, it's clear that Hillary has a more tough-minded tone. Bill Clinton, in contrast, seems almost boyish and sweet compared to his no-nonsense wife. Indeed, Bill Clinton is more of an only child than a firstborn because of the large age gap with his younger brother.[8]

Politics isn't the only area in which you can learn from Hillary Clinton. Notice that she selected a husband who was functionally an only child. While a better match would have been a boy with an older sister, an only child has both firstborn and lastborn traits, so in some sense this was a favorable relationship. She would respond best to the lastborn nature of Bill Clinton, but one can imagine them arguing when he acted like a firstborn since they would then be two leaders fighting for control.

When Bill Clinton had affairs with Gennifer Flowers and Monica Lewinsky, Hillary stood by her man. This, too, is typical of the older sister of brothers. Some may think she did it for political reasons, but the fact is that the Clintons remained together despite mistakes they may have made along the way. This ability to keep a relationship alive is one of the strengths you possess. Not surprisingly, you also have a great romantic nature, and you can find yourself infatuated with a man quite quickly. Rumors that Hillary might have had affairs may be unfounded,[9] but one could easily imagine *you* falling in love with a man and acting on those feelings. So watch that wayward heart of yours. Flirting is okay, and you certainly know how to do that!

Part 2
Lastborns

Younger Brother of Brothers

There are so many good things to say about you it's hard to know where to begin. As a lastborn, you have all the creativity, openness to experience, and social skills that are the special birthright of the baby of the family. People find you easy to approach and friendly. They like your company. They often wish they had your terrific sense of humor.[1] You're also rather unpredictable. You have an impulsive streak and can surprise everyone with your words and actions. Sometimes you like becoming a magician because you truly enjoy entertaining people. This is a trait you developed in response to having an older brother who was often a tyrant. You had to keep him laughing to prevent him from bullying you as a child, and you're still entertaining people and making them smile.

Another great thing about you is your sense of wonder about the world. Things never cease to amaze you. Your active curiosity leads you to pursue interests that would bore your older brother—things like anarchy, oddball philosophies, UFOs, mythology, radical political movements, protest marches, and travel.[2] In fact, of all the birth orders, you become the best at world traveling.

George, a postal worker from New York City, grew up with two older brothers. When Mount St. Helen's exploded in the summer of 1980, he was intrigued by the news and all the excitement surrounding the event. People were warned that they should stay as far away from the volcano as possible. This just fired George's imagination. Friends and family were startled two days after the eruption when George announced that he was going to make a trip to Washington to visit the site of the volcano. Despite the threat of a second eruption, dense smoke pollution, and locally chaotic conditions, he made the trip and came back with photos to prove he was there. This is the kind of challenge that the younger brother of brothers relishes.

Risk-Taking Behavior

If there's a war going on, you're one of the first to want to join the military. The whole prospect of fighting for something seems exciting. Younger brothers like adventure. Be careful of this tendency because it can draw you into life-threatening situations. More than other men, you choose to participate in dangerous sports like boxing, hockey, football, or skateboarding. The danger and fast pace excite you. You're also drawn to things like running with the bulls in Pamplona.

White-water rafting seems like just the kind of thing to do, doesn't it? You probably wouldn't think twice about the fact that you could fall into the rapids or get crushed by a boulder. The adventure is what calls to you. Bungee jumping sounds like fun. So does scuba diving—at night! Big game hunting, parachuting, motorcycle racing—all things your wife will be gnashing her teeth about, hoping you come home in one piece. Give your friends a break! Take time to think before jumping at the opportunity to do some of these risky activities. But then again, you would agree with Nietzsche that the secret to really enjoying life is to live dangerously.[3] That's your credo, whether stated explicitly or not—of all the birth orders, *you* were born to be wild.

Laterborns travel more frequently than those who come before them in the family, and the younger brother of brothers travels furthest of all. But it's not on planned cruises or tours that you have your fun. You want to set out on your own and conquer new territory. Many of the men who sailed with Ernest Shackleton on his Imperial Trans-Antarctic Expedition in 1914 were younger brothers of brothers, including Frank Worsley and Tom Crean.[4] When

Famous Younger Brothers of Brothers

Casey Affleck
Ray Bradbury
Samuel Beckett
Edgar Rice Burroughs
Kevin Costner
Ian Fleming
Dustin Hoffman
Jared Leto
Groucho Marx
Arnold Schwarzenegger

their ship, *Endurance*, became stuck in the ice and sank, Worsley and Crean accompanied Shackleton in the *James Caird*, a twenty-three-foot whaler, on the most dangerous open-boat journey ever attempted, traveling 800 miles across the most perilous seas in the world from Elephant Island to South Georgia during the Antarctic winter of 1916.[5] These are the kinds of adventures that quicken the hearts of younger brothers of brothers!

Best Match

Girls find you so adorable that you're going to have lots of potential partners. What they like most is your easygoing personality. Many will want to mother you, and actually this is precisely what you need in a woman. Your best match is the **older sister of brothers**. She's got exactly the kind of maternal qualities that you'll enjoy.[6] She'll also help you in your career. If you're an artist, which many younger brothers become, she'll be your dedicated publicist. Even if you don't wind up with the older sister of brothers, keep her as a friend and confidant. She can give you sage business advice, so heed her words. This girl, however, may feel that you don't pay enough attention to her. You haven't got any sisters, so she may experience some lack of romantic connection, but your winning ways and genuinely pleasant personality can often more than make up for the fact that you grew up without female peers. Use your charm to win her over, and this could be a match made in heaven. For similar reasons, you're also great with a middle girl who has one or more younger brothers.

Another excellent match is the **older sister of sisters**. You two have no rank conflict, which is very good for a relationship. She'll be organized and like to take charge of things, while you'll be relaxed and will let her do a lot of the planning. She'll love your easy-going, friendly personality, which is in contrast to her rather driven and goal-oriented demeanor. You'll love her take-charge attitude and aggressive personality. While you'll suffer total sex conflict, since neither of you has opposite-sex siblings, this may work to your advantage because she won't have any special ability to read your mind the way an older sister of brothers would. The older sister of sisters won't presume to understand you, so you'll have to explain yourself and make her see what's important to you. Once you do that, you'll both find the relationship very comfortable.

A **twin** is another good match, especially if she has a twin brother. She'll expect closeness from you and an intuitive understanding of her feminine psychology. This relationship is easier for you if your brother is close in age. You may find that this girl expects too much closeness, but if you're comfortable with her need for intimacy, she can be a wonderful match, especially if she also has a younger brother or sister.

An **only child** is a potential match, especially if her mother has younger siblings. In that case, the girl will have learned to take a leadership role in a relationship, and as a result she'll be able to provide some of the big-sister personality that you enjoy. If her mother was an only child, the girl will tend to seem aloof and cool to you, and you'll find the relationship more challenging.

Worst Match

Watch out for **younger sisters of brothers**! They'll mesmerize you, as they do most men, but remember that you're both lastborns and rank conflict is *not* what you want in a romantic relationship. The two of you could paint the town red being kids together, but who's going to set the agenda, see that important details are taken care of, and make plans for the future? The prognosis isn't good, unless you happen to have plenty of friends and family members who can pitch in and help you get organized. Such a relationship might also work during times of political unrest, when you might band together to work toward some common radical political or philosophical goal.[7]

If, however, the girl's brother is six or more years older, she'll be a functional firstborn.[8] In that case, your compatibility could be high. For example, Ulysses has a brother four years older, and when he was a student, he was dating Jessica, who's also a lastborn. I called him recently to ask about their relationship, expecting him to tell me they had problems because they were both babies of the family. "I married her," he said. "I'd rate the relationship ten out of ten! We get along great. Jessica is like a firstborn, she's organized and keeps me on track." At first I was puzzled, but then he reminded me that the age difference between Jessica and her older brother is five and a half years, which would make her a functional firstborn and explain her high degree of compatibility with Ulysses. The fact that she had some lastborn traits would also work on a narcissistic level, giving them the best of both worlds.

Your worst match is with a **younger sister of sisters**. You suffer both rank *and* sex conflict with her, which means you'll have trouble making decisions and you won't understand one another. True, you're both creative and easygoing, which is a good thing, but too much creativity and relaxation can often take its toll on a relationship. Being two lastborns, neither of you is going to want to step up to the plate and lead. This match can be helped if the girl's mother had younger brothers, because younger sisters can learn how to deal with men by observing their mother. Otherwise, this relationship will tax you to the limits. With your easygoing personality, you usually get along with everyone, so if you find yourself in this situation, don't despair. She'll love you, like most women do, although your life will probably be one big party.

Advice for Dating the Younger Brother of Brothers

You'll have a lot of fun dating the younger brother of brothers, especially if you yourself have one or more younger brothers. He'll keep you entertained, he'll amuse you with his great sense of humor, and he'll surprise you with his offbeat observations about the world. On the other hand, if you're a younger sister, you may find that you have little to talk about. This is because you're both romantic counterpunchers. This is a term taken from the world of boxing, meaning a fighter who waits for a punch from his opponent before replying with an attack of his own. In the world of dating, a lastborn is often a counterpuncher in the sense that he waits for input from you before making any remarks himself.

He'll observe you carefully, noticing things that pass others by. His keen ability to perceive the environment is one of the greatest pleasures of this birth order. To enjoy his company to the maximum, you've got to be willing to be playful. Tease him, challenge him, and you'll find that he responds with wit, a ready smile, and good humor.

Adventurous dates are the name of the game when going out with the younger brother of brothers. He'll be up for virtually anything—the wilder the better! Stretch your creative imagination to the limits, and you'll be sure to find him ready to follow you into the wilds of a jungle, to an amusement park, or to an action movie. Some things are safer for you! Boys like this love to take on a challenge. Water skiing, race car driving, and target practice are all fun activities. Just don't expect to do anything boring with him. He'll make every get-together a mini adventure.

If you can come up with something exciting, he'll enjoy being with you all the more. Don't be afraid to suggest ideas. Remember that this guy loves to respond to suggestions made to him more than to initiate ideas for dates himself. Be bold, be creative, and open your horizons. He'll be the perfect companion on these fun dates.

Don't expect too much in the way of romantic outpourings from him. He's not averse to saying nice things, but he tends to wait for nice things to be said to him. He's got a sweet disposition, so you'll find yourself wanting to baby him. The big sister approach is best, but this boy can play hard, too! Once you get the idea that he's a fun guy, you'll understand the best way to approach him—with a lighthearted spirit, a sense of adventure, and a commitment to doing something new and fun.

Advice for Breaking Up

This boy is one of the easiest to break up with because he's so easygoing and nice that he won't make a fuss or cry about your leaving. If you decide that you need to end the relationship, simply explain your reasons. He may have a hard time understanding you, but just explain it as best you can. The younger brother of brothers doesn't always prioritize the romantic relationships in his life, tending to place more emphasis on creative pursuits, male buddies, or having exciting adventures. He does have a heart, however, and it may depress him to see a good relationship end. You may find that he wallows in this sense of failure as a result of your breakup. Don't let that make you feel guilty. He'll get over you rather quickly, so keep yourself grounded by looking for a new boyfriend as soon as possible. You can often remain friends with the younger brother of brothers, and he's so much fun to be with that you may very well *want* to remain friends with him. You may find yourself drawn back to him for another try at that romantic relationship too! This is what happened to Elizabeth Taylor when she divorced Richard Burton.[9] He was so friendly to everyone that she actually married him a second time!

Friendship and the Younger Brother of Brothers

Younger brothers of brothers make great friends. They're outgoing, sociable, and fun to be with. Scoring high on the agreeableness aspect of the Big Five personality traits, they're easy to get along with in a relationship, mingle well at parties, and are generally entertaining and friendly.

The best male friend for the younger brother of brothers is the older brother of brothers. A good example of how well this friendship can work is the relationship of Matt Damon and Ben Affleck.

Together the two in this duo inspire one another to achieve great things and accomplish more than each one would alone. The synergy of their friendship taps into the leadership and organizational qualities of the firstborn and pairs those skills with the creativity and competitive qualities of the lastborn. They complement each other and enjoy one another's company and personality.

Another good friend for a younger brother of brothers would be a middle boy who has one or more younger brothers. This middle child has an older brother himself, which means that their relationship will have a narcissistic element that may be a source of some satisfaction to both.

The older brother of sisters is another good potential friend. This boy can teach the younger brother of brothers something about relating to women, and the younger brother of brothers may seek out this boy's counsel in matters of romance. The older brother of sisters may admire the manliness of the younger brother of brothers and his fearlessness in the face of adversity. Since this friendship is of a lastborn and a firstborn, there is no rank conflict or leadership disputes to speak of.

Other younger brothers of brothers may be chosen for friends, but there will be an underlying issue of competition with them that may annoy them both at times.

Female friends could include any of the birth orders, but especially the older sister of brothers or middle girls who have one or more younger brothers. With these friends, the younger brother of brothers will feel like he's in good company. He'll enjoy sharing his creative ideas, and she will often give him useful suggestions on how to organize his career and romances. In many cases these friendships may have an element of romance to them that both find fun.

Career

You do well in careers where you can work under the guidance of a male mentor, such as being vice president, assistant director, or secretary to an executive. Creative endeavors are also a perfect career. Famous writers who share your birth order include Ray Bradbury,

Edgar Rice Burroughs, Samuel Beckett, and Ian Fleming. Because of your love of travel and your competitive nature, you might be tempted to join the military or work overseas. Languages come easily to you, so work as a translator or foreign correspondent is a good choice. Not infrequently, you'll take a routine job just to support yourself while you pursue a creative career, such as acting, music, or comedy.

Finding love on the job is easy because women are drawn to your warm nature and easygoing personality. You like women who are voluptuous and maternal, even though you rebel against being told what to do. If they have tact and respect, they'll be good for you. Always remember to choose a woman who's willing to help with your career. More often than not, this will be a firstborn or middle child who has younger brothers, and together you'll be perfect.

○○○○●

Celebrity Case Study
ARNOLD SCHWARZENEGGER

Raised in a home with a strict father and a brother who was about one year older, Arnold Schwarzenegger is a super lastborn with enhanced traits of the younger brother of brothers. His personality exemplifies many of the hallmarks of this birth order, including a competitive nature, artistic inclinations, and affability—even his political enemies admit he's a likeable guy.

As a boy Arnold had a competitive drive that was fueled by the discipline enforced at home by his father, an Austrian police officer, who insisted that his sons shine his shoes and write reports about museums they had visited.[10] Arnold's father enforced a strict curfew and ruled the home with the kind of discipline that makes a child need to rebel.

Schwarzenegger moved to the United States in 1968 and began training at Gold's Gym in Santa Monica, California.[11] He went on to win Mr. Olympia five times and Mr. Universe seven times. The documentary *Pumping Iron* (1977) shows a young man dedicated to making a name for himself in the bodybuilding world.

Lastborns like attention, and they usually do an excellent job as actors. This is because when they were growing up they had to do something to get attention from their parents and older siblings, and acting, being funny, and getting laughs is a good strategy. Lastborns are also very good at learning new languages, and Arnold quickly learned English and steadily worked on ridding himself of his accent. You can hear his improvement from movie to movie.[12]

Schwarzenegger parlayed the name recognition he had garnered as an actor to enter politics at a high level, and in 2003 he was elected governor of California. His wife, Maria Shriver, has four brothers, three of whom are younger. Her older brother is one year older, but having three younger brothers makes her a super older sister, which is just what Schwarzenegger needs for compatibility.[13] This couple has won the hearts of Americans for the way they work harmoniously.

Like Schwarzenegger, you have the ability to entertain people. You're possessed of a competitive nature that will drive you to succeed. Women will flock to you, and if you take your time and choose wisely, you'll find the right one, especially if she has a younger brother. Finally, like Arnold, you're the master of many fields, so diversify and try your hand at various careers—that's the way to a fulfilling life.

6

○○○○●

Younger Brother of Sisters

You're the darling of the gods—the female gods, that is! They think of you, no matter where you are or what you do; they dream of you, and they want to be yours. And you, with your carefree ways and your nonchalance, doing nothing to draw them in but being your own sweet self, you're blessed above all men when it comes to attracting the fair sex. Something about you sets their hearts afire, and though you may *think* you have troubles in this department, compared to other men you lead a charmed life.

Why should this be so? Maybe it's because . . .

- You have an older sister who treated you with loving affection, almost as if you were her baby, at least until you could walk and talk.

- Even now your older sister lavishes attention on you.

- As the focus of all this attention, you've become comfortable in groups of people.

- Your older sister was bigger, smarter, and more physically powerful for the first few years of your life, so you learned that the best way to get attention from your parents was by being funny and telling jokes, singing, acting, or doing something creative.

Since your older sister was usually the serious one, you may have a streak of comic genius born of a need to impress your parents, to make them notice you, and to get your sister to stop teasing you. As a result of this early environment, you certainly developed into a friendly, agreeable, and socially conscious young man. You care about the underdog and under-reported issues, whether it's American Indians, the environment, or whales.[1] You have more intuitive insight into how people feel than other boys. You've got a knack for getting along with girls and making them like you. These are skills you developed without even having to think about it, and they'll serve you well in your adolescent and adult years, where you'll find you have an almost uncanny ability to make women dote on you.

Take Howard Stern, for example. Whether or not you enjoy his style of scandalous humor, you have to admit he's got a terrific rapport with women. No matter who his guest is, Stern always manages to talk with her in an intimate way and often convinces her to do outrageous things on the air. He also has a great working relationship with sidekick Robin Quivers. In many ways Howard Stern represents some of the best qualities of the younger brother of sisters—he's great with women, they all seem to love him, and he has a creative side that fascinates both men and women. He's also a rebel at heart and doesn't care what the establishment thinks. In fact, he gets a thrill from doing things differently and thumbing his nose at the status quo.

Rebelliousness

Yes, you love challenging the status quo, don't you? But did you realize that doing that can make you even more attractive to the opposite sex? Here's a story to prove the point.

I was teaching a class that involved acting, and I had one student in the class, Marvin, who was a lastborn with four older sisters. Because of my knowledge of birth order, I felt he might make an excellent actor. The only problem was that Marvin had trouble speaking and was very self-conscious. In fact, he had what amounted to a slight stutter. He also had problems with his other classes—he had difficulty accepting teacher authority and wasn't doing well relating to his professors. This didn't particularly bother me because I also knew that the younger brother of sisters has a rebellious streak, and I thought Marvin might be acting out his conflicts with his older sisters by rebelling against his teachers. When I offered to make him one of the lead actors in our class skits, he seemed surprised that I would consider him for such a role, especially in light of the difficulty he had speaking. Most of the other students were also surprised at my casting choice. But from the first moment he stepped in front of the cameras, he had us all mesmerized. Marvin had an uncanny ability to get into any role he played, and through physical gestures, pauses, and eventually even through his nearly inarticulate speech, he had us all fascinated by his performance. He sounded like Marlon Brando, who also was known to speak in an indistinct voice that was close to unintelligible at times. After many of our class skits, I would see Marvin surrounded by two or three girls who were smiling and talking with him about his performance. All of a sudden the school bad boy had become the class star.

Best Match

Your best match is the **older sister of brothers**. She has a maternal side that's very good for you.[2] In fact, she'll also help you in your career. What could be nicer than that? You tend to be so creative and lackadaisical about things that you actually need someone with her superior planning skill to keep you on track and take care of the little details of day-to-day living. The only downside in this blissful relationship is that your roles are the opposite of what we're socialized to expect from men and women. In other words, she's taking the dominant role, and you're taking the passive role, which may annoy you. The best way to cope with this reversal is to think of her dominance as protective and nurturing, as if she were your guardian angel. When she suggests that you do something, imagine that she's working for you as your personal assistant, as if you gave her the authority to tell you what to do in order to remind you of what's best for yourself.

Here's an example of how this relationship can work, despite its role-reversal problems.

Tom has a sister two years older. He's the sweetheart of his family and everybody loves him. His wife, Rachelle, is a firstborn with three younger brothers. Although she can be kind, maternal, and caring, she also has a strict, domineering side that showed in her relations with her husband. She would tell him what to wear, what to do around the house, and what to eat for dinner. In effect, she was treating him like one of her younger brothers. Tom was such a sweet guy he took most of this without complaint, but after five years of living with her, he reached a breaking point, and they separated.

I told them that they were meant for one another but that Rachelle needed to lighten up on Tom and realize that he's an adult who needs to figure a few things out for himself. "Let him make some decisions, even if you don't agree with them," I said. "It won't kill you, will it? After all, what does it matter if he wears a blue or a green shirt?" She resisted even this suggestion. "But I know best," she said.

"I *would* like to decide for myself," said her mild-mannered husband. At this, Rachelle looked surprised, her eyes opened wide, and she turned to him. "You would?" she said. "Yes," he replied. For a moment Rachelle hesitated. Then she said, "I never realized it." They got back together, and things were better between them.

And for older sisters, the lesson of this story is simple: If you let your partner decide some things for himself, he'll be happier and more content. Above all, be tactful in how you make your suggestions. If you can get him to think they're his ideas, he'll be more likely to get along with you.

Another good match for the younger brother of sisters is an **older sister of sisters**, but in this case your partner may be dominant and bossy without having much intuitive insight into what makes you tick. This relationship is better for *her* than it is for you. She gets a guy who's friendly, laid-back, and easy to get along with— just what she needs. You get a leader who can organize things, which is what you need, but you'll miss the maternal qualities that an older sister of brothers could bring to a relationship.

A **twin** might be a good match, especially if she has a twin brother and if you're very close in age to your older sister. Even in this case, though, the twin will expect more intimacy from the relationship than you think is necessary.[3]

A **younger sister of brothers** is a potentially good match. Two of my students fit this pattern. The boy was one of the friendliest people in class, the girl, slightly more subdued. These two lastborns often partied all weekend and came into class a little bedraggled on Monday. Two lastborns typically have a lot of fun together, but they have more difficulty getting the fine details of a relationship in order—things like planning for the future, making sure insurance payments are submitted on time, and organizing the bookkeeping chores of a household. They're often drawn together by narcissistic attraction. Another thing they have going for them, which might make such a relationship easier, is the fact that they're both the most agreeable of all the birth orders. Lastborns are rated as more friendly and approachable than any other birth order. They'll enjoy each other's company and have terrific conversations as well as marvelous sex (lastborns being more adventurous in this department than firstborns).[4]

WORST MATCH

An **only child** is your worst match, especially if her mother was also an only child, in which case the quality of being a singleton is multiplied. It might work better if her mother had a younger brother, in which case she would have learned from her same-sex parent the kind of big sisterly skills that you prefer in a partner.

A **younger sister of sisters** is not your best match for two reasons. The first is that you have total rank conflict with her. The second is that you have partial sex conflict. Although this girl is very feminine, you may think of her as too much of a baby for your tastes. You want that particular role, for you've enjoyed the attention the baby of the family gets in your own family. She'll want the same thing. The younger sister of brothers has the same problem, but in her case she makes up for it by the fact that there's no sex conflict. The one factor that could make a younger sister of sisters a good choice is the possibility that the narcissistic attraction between you may rule the day. If this is the operative element in a relationship—that is, if you see yourself in her and she sees herself in you, or if you share a lot in common as far as careers and hobbies—then this relationship may have a better chance of fulfilling your interpersonal needs.

Advice for Dating a Younger Brother of Sisters

Everything you know about the younger brother of sisters may prepare you for a guy who's lovable, offbeat, fun to be with, and spon-

J. D. Salinger

Having grown up with one older sister, J. D. Salinger has all the classic traits of the lastborn. Creative from an early age, he began publishing stories in magazines when he was in his twenties. Drafted to fight in World War II, he participated in the invasion of Normandy. Returning home, he wrote *The Catcher in the Rye* and then decided to retreat from public view.[5] He moved to a small town in New Hampshire in 1953, where he developed a keen interest in many occult and unorthodox philosophies and practices, including Zen, acupuncture, homeopathy, Scientology, talking in tongues,[6] and others that are quite outré.[7] Married in 1955 to a woman sixteen years younger, who was also a lastborn, he had two children but refused to let them be seen by a doctor, instead taking them to a swami. His eccentricities contributed to his divorce in 1967. He subsequently had an eight-month affair with eighteen-year-old novelist Joyce Maynard.[8] At the age of sixty he married a young nurse—which is exactly the kind of wife a younger brother needs—and he's reportedly happily living with her to this day. As is the case with many younger brothers, women have been attracted to him all his life. He's so open-minded that he quickly becomes enamored of strange theories, many of dubious scientific value. If you see something of yourself in this portrait, congratulate yourself on possessing the traits of the charmingly creative younger brother of sisters.

taneous. But nothing can really prepare you for his personality. Descriptions can only give you a hint of the wild and wonderful world he lives in, which he'll give *you* access to when you're dating him. So the best advice is to be prepared for the unexpected. Try to remain calm when he introduces you to some strange and outlandish philosophy. Do your best to remain receptive to his sometimes kooky beliefs. Take it all in stride, as if you were his big sister, and let him go on about his bizarre ideas. This is par for the course with the younger brother of sisters, and part of the fun!

The way to deal with a younger brother of sisters when he tells you bizarre things is to listen patiently and try to understand what it all means to him emotionally.[9] You don't have to believe what he believes, but at least try to listen with an open mind. He's so quick to adopt new ideas and offbeat philosophies that he can bewilder you, but if you show real sympathy and listen, you'll win him to your side.

Finally, don't be insulted or overly jealous if you find other women doting on him—even while you're on a date. A younger brother of sisters naturally has many women admirers. They'll materialize throughout his life, and you've got to learn to accept the fact that you're with a kind of romantic superstar. If you can deal with this, then he's the man for you!

Advice for Breaking Up

There's no easy way to weather a breakup with a younger brother of sisters. He's so friendly and lovable that breaking up may be traumatic. When Salinger broke up with Joyce Maynard, he simply told her "It's over" and ordered her to leave his house on short notice. She was devastated and cried her eyes out and spent the next two years trying to get over him.[10] So be prepared for the hold he'll have on your emotions, and do your best to forget him and get on with your life. Many younger brothers of sisters won't even want to remain friends with you after a breakup, so you'll just have to find other people to associate with to help you deal with the blow to your pride and ego. My best advice is that, even when dating a younger brother of sisters, it's important to have other male friends who you associate with on occasion and who are confidants so that you can fall back on their help if and when you need to.

If you're the one who wants to end the relationship, it's much easier. He won't stand in your way, cry, or make a fuss. He'll let you go. It may hurt his feelings, but he won't make you feel guilty. Just tell him your reasons and end it. To be kind, you may wish to remain friends with him, if he'll allow it. But be prepared for his resentment and the fact that he might cut you off if you break up with him.

Friendship and the Younger Brother of Sisters

The younger brother of sisters is a great friend. He's relaxed, creative, and easy to get along with. He makes an especially good friend for women. They like his company, find him funny and lovable, and they often wish to take care of him and mother him. He's also intriguing because his mind is often working at a furious pace to come up with new ideas and interests. The younger child usually has more diverse interests as a rule than older children and firstborns, so be prepared for him to be interested in a multitude of things such as music, art, philosophy, books, ideas, radical political causes, and ecology. Anything different and novel will intrigue him. If you have an open mind and are interested in new ways of looking at the world, be friends with a younger brother of sisters. You won't be disappointed.

Career

The best career for the younger brother of sisters is one where you're working with people on a daily basis. You make a great salesman because you're so affable and personable, and you get enthusiastic about things you love. You're so creative you do well as a writer, singer, or actor. In fact, some of the most gifted actors of our time are younger brothers of sisters, including Robert Downey Jr., Johnny Depp, and Marlon Brando. But remember that acting is such an iffy profession, you'll need something as a backup.

In the sciences, you do well devoting yourself to a specialty in research and development. You work brilliantly as a craftsman such as carpenter, plumber, master electrician, or director of photography, where you can combine technical competence with creative insights.

Whatever career you choose, you'll find women waiting for you. But don't rush into things; instead, pay particular attention to those gals who are nurturing, helpful, and guiding. Some women will act like mentors toward you, especially those with younger brothers. They'll support you in your work, and they'll also make the best romantic partners.

○○○○●

Celebrity Case Study

ROBERT DOWNEY JR.

Robert Downey Jr. has one older sister, Allyson, three years his senior. This close age gap makes him a super lastborn with very strong traits of the younger brother of sisters. As a young man he lived for a time with middleborn Sarah Jessica Parker. His creative energy was obvious to the many directors who sought him out, but he also had a serious substance abuse problem that often interfered with his work. The fact that he checked into rehab in 2001 was a sign that he wanted to focus on getting his life right. He's made numerous movies that won critical acclaim, including *Chaplin* (1992), *Two Girls and a Guy* (1997), and *A Scanner Darkly* (2006).

If you're a younger brother of sisters, you'll find many examples of your strengths played out in Downey's life. He's creative, he's a magnet to women, and he's spontaneous and funny. Like Downey, you have a kooky side, you come up with new ideas, and you have the ability to make people believe you, which is the essence of acting. Women flock to you, and they always will. Even if you don't notice this in your life, if you look for it, you'll see it's true. Sometimes these women are near you just as friends, but believe it or not, many of them have developed deeper feelings for you than you may realize. And you certainly have a knack for being charming and funny. All these skills and abilities are your special birthright, and you can make the most of them by being aware of how they make you lovable.

○○○○●

7

Younger Sister of Sisters

I hesitate to call you a little princess for fear of injuring your pride; you'd probably rather be compared to a queen or even to Venus, goddess of love. Comparisons, I know, are somewhat of a sore spot with you since you've been comparing yourself with a bigger, stronger older sister from as far back as you can remember. But if ever a girl could be called a little princess, it's you! Born into a loving home in which there's already a big sister, during your first year of life you were treated like a doll by everyone, including your sister. This warm welcome has lifelong effects that ripple out and impact your social ability, career, and romantic potential, as we shall see.

Your parents began by focusing their love and attention on you, but before long most of that attention came from Mom. By the time you were two or three years old, Dad and your older sister were likely to interact together more frequently, while your mother looked after you. So you became used to the loving attention of both an older sister and a mother, and you're comfortable when surrounded by women and girls. Dad, of course, still found you charming, and you had a good relationship with everyone in your family.

The one cloud hanging over this happy home was that your older sister sometimes acted bossy. She was taller, stronger, and more intelligent by virtue of being a few years older, and she used these advantages to lord it over you. At first you didn't think there was anything unusual in this, because it was the world you were born into, and you knew no other. To keep your big sister in a happy frame of mind, you learned to be charming and friendly. You found that this personality worked wonders with your mother and father too. Before you knew it you had become the most sociable person in the family. You told jokes at the drop of a hat. You learned to sing and dance. Your smile lit up the lives of those around you, and kept them loving you. By the time you became an adult, your charm and grace had made you one of the friendliest people in your social circle, and your ability to flirt leaves other girls jealous.

Charm and Creativity

You have lots of charm—and men know it! In fact, you tend to charm both men *and* women. In a group, you're the easiest one to talk to, and you love meeting new people at parties and hearing their life stories. Men find it easy to approach you, and you're comfortable with them, especially older brothers or middle boys who have younger sisters. The same way you entertained your big sister and parents, you now have the ability and the tendency to entertain people at work and in social settings.

Your other strong point is your creativity. More than other children, you grew up with an active imagination. In fact, you have such a good imagination that sometimes it gets away with you and seems to lead you astray. You get so many creative ideas—some of them good, some of them just kooky—that you don't know how to deal with them all. Sometimes you feel bewildered because so many ideas come swarming into your brain, and you'd like to pursue them all. For instance, when you look up a word in the dictionary, you come across so many other interesting words along the way that you often wind up studying *them* and forget the original word you were trying to find! Your imagination often leads you to become a writer, and there's no question that you do have a way with words. It's not that you want to be precise like a lawyer writing a contract, or argumentative like a politician in a debate; what you like is expressing yourself and having an audience.

One of your greatest strengths is your ability to focus on different things on the spur of the moment. Another way of saying this is that you're easily distracted. You could be working on something very important, but if someone calls or you get an email or read something in the paper, it'll catch your attention. This is known as openness to experience, and of all the birth orders you have it the strongest. You're quite hypnotizable too. I wouldn't say you're disorganized, but you *are* relaxed about your workplace. Hey, not everyone can be as obsessive-compulsive about neatness like your older sister, and thank goodness! You don't care as much about social recognition as you do about beauty and finding beauty in the world—in literature, in art, in people. You're fascinated by everything mystical and magical, and if someone comes up with a new theory, you're the first one to embrace it. In fact, the whole idea of birth order is fascinating to you.

Even more than other girls, you love people who listen to your ideas. That's why, for you, going to therapy is bliss. Like Anna Freud, the great psychologist's youngest daughter who had numerous older sisters, you love being in analysis. If you can find a therapist, a minister, or a doctor to listen to you, that would be heaven on earth. You pour your heart out and feel that someone understands you at last.

Best Match

Your best match is an **older brother of sisters**. You find him romantic and attentive. You like the way he listens to all your rambling thoughts. And you enjoy the fact that there's no rank conflict in the relationship; he takes the lead, and you're willing to follow because his plans encompass the two of you and seem to be so well thought out.

There's also a good potential for you with the **older brother of brothers**. In some ways, this is an even better match because neither has an advantage in that neither grew up with opposite-sex siblings. In this relationship, however, you'll each have some difficulty understanding one another. This sex conflict, however, isn't an insurmountable obstacle (see box on next page).

How to Overcome Sex Conflict

- Explain yourself to him more than you would to a girlfriend so that he can understand you.
- Ask him to tell you what's going through his mind so that you get a chance to understand him better.
- Realize that he's a perfectionist, and be patient when he tries to do everything perfectly.
- Get away with your girlfriends regularly.
- Let him go out with his male friends alone.
- Remember that you're not a mind reader, and you need to hear him verbalize his thoughts.

Another good match is a **middle boy** who has one or more younger sisters. Having older siblings himself, he'll have a creative bent, like you, and he'll understand your vivid imagination. You'll also enjoy how he takes the lead in matters of romance and sex, as men with younger sisters do.

A **twin with a twin sister** could be a good match too, although he might feel that you can't give him the kind of understanding that he was used to from his twin sister and that he seeks in any romantic relationship. To make this relationship rock, get as snugly close to him physically as you do psychologically.

Another potential good match is a **younger brother of sisters**. This is a narcissistic relationship since you're so similar, having both grown up with older sisters. In this relationship, however, you would suffer from total rank conflict and might have lots of fun together but then be at a loss when it comes time to plan for the future or organize your mutual responsibilities vis-à-vis the kids, property, or your life together. When dating a younger brother of sisters, be sure to have plenty of organized friends and acquaintances who can help you plan and prioritize, something lastborns need help with in most cases.

Worst Match

A relatively poor match for you is a **younger brother of brothers**. Because you're both lastborns, you'll suffer total rank conflict in such a relationship. You'll also have to deal with sex conflict since neither of you grew up with opposite-sex siblings.

Your worst match is a male **only child**. Since you're both lastborns, you'll have all that rank conflict to deal with, which is sure to make decisions tricky, to say the least. Also, neither of you has opposite-sex siblings, so you'll run into problems understanding one another. With decision-making *and* communication problems, this relationship is challenging. You, however, have a knack for relating well to people, so you could probably even make a go of this matchup. The point is, why fight an uphill battle? If the boy's father had younger sisters, it might make things easier because a male only child learns to imitate his father's birth order. But it would still be a rocky road that could challenge even the most accommodating younger sister of sisters.

Cameron Diaz–Jared Leto Mismatch

After dating for four years, lastborns Cameron Diaz (who has one older sister) and Jared Leto (who has one older brother) split up in 2005. Diaz's sister is only two years older, making the superstar a super lastborn with very strong younger sister traits, including sociability, a good sense of humor, and an undercurrent of ambition. Sources close to the couple say that Leto didn't do many things with her, leading one to conclude that although they were undoubtedly physically attracted—which is easy to understand—they didn't really enjoy each other's company that much. This, too, is understandable since they suffer from both rank *and* sex conflict. A much better match for Diaz would be someone like Brad Pitt, who has a younger sister. A much better match for Leto would be someone like Paris Hilton, who has a couple of younger brothers and who could become the maternal angel this bad boy needs.

Advice for Dating a Younger Sister of Sisters

More than other women, the younger sister actively seeks a man who will let her pursue her financial interests or who will provide for her financially and make her secure. She has her feet planted firmly on the ground when it comes to financial matters. She's less of a planner than other girls, however, and often has trouble figuring out how to achieve her financial aspirations. If you can help in this regard, she'll rely on you and love you. It should be stressed that no man can call into question her big dreams. She prefers a guy who's willing to help her reach the stars because, after all, that's where she has set her sights.

The way to win her heart is to listen to her. This is a gal who loves to talk about herself more than other girls by a long shot. If you're thinking of becoming a psychotherapist, this is a great partner to practice on. She'll welcome the opportunity to talk about her family, her dreams, her problems, and anything else that's on her mind at the moment. This doesn't mean the younger sister of sisters has more psychological problems than other girls—in fact, she has fewer than most—it simply means she derives great pleasure in talking about her life and problems, and if you can be a big ear for her, that's what she's really going to appreciate. She'll fall in love with the man who listens to her best.

On a date, be prepared to pay for everything. Never ask her for financial help, or, if you do, promise you'll pay it back with interest. She'll find that funny, but she'll also really expect you to repay her—with interest. Take her to fancy places; she'll appreciate that. If you're cute, well dressed, come from a prominent family, and have a good education—all marks of social status—you'll do much better with her than if you're uncouth, sloppy, and struggling to make a mark in the world. Status and standing are important to her, and it's important for you to understand why. She grew up lastborn, competing against a bigger, smarter, stronger older sister. She's been playing catch-up all her life. You're going to have to help her continue the struggle because, believe me, it will *never* end. No matter how wealthy she becomes, no matter how financially secure she is, and no matter how good things seem to be going for her, she's got a

Comparison Chart
YOUNGER SISTER OF SISTERS
VERSUS OLDER SISTER OF SISTERS

Younger Sister of Sisters	Older Sister of Sisters
Friendly	Reserved
Easygoing	Driven
Relaxed	Type-A
Funny	Serious
Extroverted	Introverted
Impulsive	Measured
Approachable	Aloof
Trusting	Defensive
Accepting	Critical
Disorganized	Super Planner

chip on her shoulder. And she'll never rest. She'll always want more, better, bigger, faster. In many ways this is a good thing, because a girl like this will drive you to achieve the best in life as well. If you can play her game, you'll enjoy every second of it. If not, better bow out early and save yourself the challenge.

Advice for Breaking Up

It's rather easy to offend a younger sister of sisters. I've probably unintentionally offended her a half-dozen times already in this chapter, and I'm trying to be on my best behavior! The things she really can't stand are men who have no financial goals, men who can't plan, and men who are babyish. She'll initiate the breakup if she finds that you don't meet her expectations. She often has ambitions of financial success, so if she breaks up with you, it might help to write her off as a money-hungry, ambitious gold digger. The ambition of Lady Macbeth comes to mind in this context, although most younger sisters of sisters don't encourage their husbands to commit murder. They do, however, expect them to have ambitions of their own and to carry out those great plans and achieve something terrific in the world, especially financially.

If you wish to initiate the breakup yourself, you may find it easier than you think. The younger sister of sisters is often capricious and can set her sights just as easily on one man as another. Introduce her to one of your dashing rich friends, and she may make the breakup a simple matter. Or provoke a breakup by telling her you're going to quit your job. Beware that this girl may tell you she never wants to talk with you again, but if you can bow out gracefully, you may each find someone who's a better match.

Friendship and the Younger Sister of Sisters

It's easy to become friends with the younger sister of sisters. In fact, she has lots of friends because people enjoy her company. She meets people at work or in church, and they become good friends outside of this environment. Not infrequently she'll harbor a crush on someone and not say a word about it to anyone except a trusted girlfriend.

To remain friends with her, try to be a good listener. She loves to talk about herself, and if you can listen, she'll entertain you like no other girl. She's so creative and has such a flair for talking intimately that you'll find the hours whiz by while she's talking up a storm. If you have problems, she'll also be a good listener and give you some practical advice, especially about money matters.

Career

Sales is your strong point. You could sell the Brooklyn Bridge if you put your mind to it because you have a knack for making people trust you. This you accomplish by being observant and easygoing. You're so approachable and affable, people don't feel threatened by you. Men and women like talking with you, and they consider you a great friend. So when you go into sales you excel because you have a way of winning trust. Plus, you really do believe in the things you're selling, and you enjoy sharing what you know and creating enthusiasm in others. One of the most successful saleswomen of all time, Estée Lauder, was a younger sister of a sister. More about her in a moment.

Other careers in which you excel including acting (Cameron Diaz, Hilary Duff, Julia Roberts), singing (Ashlee Simpson), and being a news show host (Jules Asner, Katie Couric, Barbara Walters). You like working with people. In fact, you make a great assistant director. Your creative ability often leads to a career in writing, painting, music, interior design, cosmetology, or being a makeup artist. Because of your ability in sales, you're also good at selling the work of others as a literary agent or real estate broker. Often you have a secret life in which you dream of writing great operas and designing great buildings. If you could do all the things that float through your imagination on a typical day, you'd be a millionaire in no time at all.

○○○○●

Celebrity Case Study

ESTÉE LAUDER

Estée Lauder exemplifies all the chief characteristics of the younger sister of sisters, and her success in business and selling should inspire anyone from this birth order. Born in Queens, New York, to Hungarian Jewish immigrants, she was the youngest of nine children but grew up primarily influenced by a sister who was two years older.[1] Estée was embarrassed by her parents' accents,[2] and in many ways her life can be viewed as one heroic attempt to overcome her past and reach for a brighter future. Like many younger sisters, she had a keen ambition. This is often the result of having to compete with an older sister and dreaming of outshining that sister.

Her uncle was a chemist, and when he came to live with the family, he set up a shack in the backyard where he mixed chemicals. Young Estée was fascinated by his work. It seemed like magic to her, and it entered her head that if she could use some of that magic she might make some money. She began by introducing everyone in her family to her uncle's Six-in-One Cold Cream. Then she widened her social network and began selling his products in the stores of New York City.

Estée wanted the best for her products. She wasn't satisfied with selling them in drugstores or department stores like Gimbels. She wanted to sell them in upscale shops like Saks Fifth Avenue because she believed that would add sheen to the product and make it more desirable in the eyes of customers. At first Saks wasn't interested. They told her there was no demand for her products. Rising to the challenge, she told Robert Fiske, the store's cosmetics buyer, that there *was* a demand and that she would prove it to him. Shortly thereafter she gave away more than eighty sets of lipstick to a party held at the Waldorf-Astoria Hotel. The people at the party noticed that these lipsticks were in gold cases and had a creamy texture. When the party ended, women marched into Saks asking for the new product. Fiske quickly realized that there was a demand, and he placed an order for eight hundred sets of lipstick.[3] Estée Lauder was off to a roaring start, and she never looked back.

She used her friendliness and family contacts to rise in the business world. One technique she mastered was touching a potential customer while talking. By doing so she formed an instant bond that usually led to a sale. She used this tactic on Florence Morris, the owner of a new beauty salon, by massaging samples of beauty cream into the surprised woman's arm. The procedure worked, and Florence gave her a small counter in the new store where Estée could sell her products.[4] Using her interpersonal skills to the max, she quickly won major accounts in classy stores and watched her business grow to be a multimillion-dollar company within years.

She actually divorced her husband because she felt he wasn't interested enough in her business ventures. A few years later, she remarried him. To the younger sister of sisters, business ventures are very important matters indeed!

8

○○○○●

Younger Sister of Brothers

A re you sitting down? I sure hope so.

The reason I ask is that you're not going to believe this. You may laugh, you may get red in the face, you may get dizzy and come close to fainting, and I want to be sure you're going to make it through this chapter okay. But the plain and simple truth is that, when it comes to attracting men, you, the younger sister of brothers, are the luckiest creature alive.

Yes, you heard right. You're lucky, you're blessed, you're the recipient of a great and wonderful gift based on your birth order. Girls who grow up with older brothers are lucky because they get practice interacting with boys on a daily basis during their formative years. I know, I know, I can hear you saying it now, "My brother was bossy, he was brutal, he was sarcastic. . . ." I grant you that. I know all about it. And you know what?

Doesn't matter.

Sometimes your older brothers were bossy, and sometimes they were considerate, so you learned to cope with all kinds of male moods. This makes you quite capable of dealing with guys in the adult world. To your surprise, you may find that men consider you easy to relate to as well.

Because you couldn't physically win fights with your bigger and stronger older brother, you usually dealt with him by becoming funny, charming, and adaptable.[1] You also became extraordinarily sensitive to his state of mind. One of the most successful coping mechanisms learned by younger siblings, and especially younger sisters of brothers, is empathy.

Empathy

Why is it that very few women can empathize with a man the way you can? Part of the reason stems from the fact that you learned, as a matter of necessity, how to deal with your older brother's capricious and often tyrannical ways. A key part of the equation is that little sisters have to deal with brothers who, by virtue of being a few years older, are more advanced in many skills (physical, mental, and social), so she must learn to adapt herself to his preferences.

"My older brother was a monster," says one college senior. This comment is only half made in jest. There's an undercurrent of real rivalry between such siblings. Younger sisters who've had to deal with an older, stronger, and more verbally adept brother develop strategies that ultimately make them more wily, flexible, and creative than their brothers. The bottom line is that you learned to listen, empathize, and interact with males better than anyone else.

But rivalry and childhood squabbles aren't the only interactions that occur between younger sisters and older brothers. Almost all big brothers *sometimes* act in a considerate way toward their younger sisters, even in the same family in which bullying occurs. As Carolyn Lieberg points out in her delightful book *Little Sisters*, girls can remember countless times when an older brother helped with homework, for example, or recommended a good book for her to read, or played games with her. "My big brother protected me from bullies in the neighborhood," says one woman whose brother was three years older. "He used to let me borrow his toys and sometimes he even played with me," says another girl who has a brother one year older. "I remember we used to sleep in the same bed and take baths together until we were six or seven," says a girl whose brother is one and a half years older. She and her brother still enjoy a great relationship and talk a few times a week now that they're in their thirties.

Friendly big brothers teach little sisters that it's okay to trust men. When a big brother takes the time to help, or shares a toy, he's subtly guiding you in the ways of the masculine mind. Maybe this is why you seem to have, as one younger sister put it, "an almost magical ability to read the mind of a man."

You also love the spotlight. Girls who grow up with older brothers have to make them laugh to entertain them. They transfer this childhood skill into their adult life and become great comedians, storytellers, and conversationalists. Examples of younger sisters of brothers include Marilyn Monroe, Elizabeth Taylor, and Audrey Hepburn.

Like most lastborns, you have multiple interests and an openness to experience that includes being drawn toward the arts and culture. Because your brothers were more conservative, you carved out your niche by being liberal. This distinguishes you from your brother in your parents' eyes and gets you more parental attention. Little sisters often grow up to be rebels, freethinkers, or Democrats.

You're romantic, and you like your men to be romantic and attentive too. You believe love can solve most of your problems. Many younger sisters get into relationships with troubled men and then hope that sheer love and commitment will help them work out their difficulties. Family members may become concerned over your poor choice of a marriage partner. Such objections get your back up. You may marry him just to prove you have a mind of your own. "The more they criticize me," says one younger sister, "the more strongly I want to go out with him despite his problems, just to prove I'm right. It's ironic because if they *welcomed* him and his drinking problems and unemployment, I'd probably stop and think twice about continuing to date him!"

Best Match

You would think that with all you've got going for you, you'd have an easy time with love. But it's not true, not by a long shot. You sweat, squirm, and struggle just like the rest of us because you've felt heartache many times over. In fact, since you attract so many men and get into so many deep and troubled relationships with them, you've probably got more horror stories to tell than just about any

Janet Jackson

Janet Jackson grew up with six older brothers, including Michael Jackson, who's eight years older. She fits the pattern of a younger sister of brothers in many ways. Creative and artistic, she loves the spotlight. She has a playful, rebellious temperament. Her charisma and charm are characteristic of lastborn girls with older brothers.

other group of women. And yet, the younger sister of brothers has an advantage over other girls. No other birth order attracts men so pervasively and unfailingly as the younger sister of brothers.[2]

Your best match is the **older brother of sisters**. More than other girls, you're aware of what you need in a man and you tend to find it.[3] The older brother of sisters has a similar ability to sense what's best for him, so it's no surprise that the two often feel an uncanny attraction that blossoms into love. Another good match is a **middle boy** who has one or more younger sisters. You'll relate best to those aspects of his personality that are characteristic of the older brother of sisters: being charming, considerate, and chivalrous.

Your next best match is an **older brother of brothers**, but keep in mind that this relationship is better for *him* than for you. He's getting a partner who's willing to be led. You're getting the leader you need, but you're not getting the kind of deep understanding of your feminine nature that you prefer in a man.

A **younger brother of sisters** could also be a potentially satisfying match because you would understand each other, each of you having grown up with a member of the opposite sex. But a problem could be that neither of you bring to the relationship the kind of organization and guidance that's often necessary in a marriage. You would have lots of fun together—something lastborns are quite good at—but when it comes time to pay the bills, make plans for educating the children, or do long-range planning, you might very well feel a need for outside help.

A male **twin** could be a good match provided he had a twin sister. Your main difficulty would arise from his feeling that you didn't give him enough closeness and understanding, but overall this would be a favorable match, especially if you also shared career interests.[4]

Worst Match

A relatively poor match would be a **younger brother of brothers**. With him you'd suffer both rank and sex conflict. You would be irked by his inability to demonstrate a deep understanding of your inner self, and you would miss the leadership and romantic qualities you desire in a partner. He would miss the kind of big-brother competition and guidance he was used to as a youngster. It would help if the boy's father had younger sisters since a son learns how to deal with women from his father and he would have learned to take a leadership role with women. This relationship could also be helped if you have friends or family members who can give you guidance on matters that require long-range planning. As suggested by the research of Frank Sulloway, this relationship might also work in times of political and philosophical upheaval, during which two lastborns would be expected to bond together to achieve common radical goals.[5]

Your worst match is with a male **only child**. He's too career-focused and self-indulgent, and he wants too much attention. This match is made worse if his father was also an only child or a younger brother.[6] A male only child whose father had younger sisters, however, would be a better match. Still, an only child is the least favorable match because in a sense you're both lastborns, and he doesn't understand you the way you expect to be understood by a man. The short-lived affair between Marilyn Monroe and Frank Sinatra, an only child, illustrates the fragility of such relationships.

Advice for Dating the Younger Sister of Brothers

Younger sisters of brothers expect to be pampered and babied by the men in their lives—especially their dates. Watch for frequent displays of "help me" behavior, which elicit just this kind of caring attention from men. She's the star of the show, and she expects to be treated like one. She wants her boyfriends to take the helm and be romantic and to intuitively sense her needs. A playful approach is best. Tease her in a friendly, loving way.

Romance is the name of the game if you're pursuing a younger sister of brothers. You can't be too romantic with her. Flowers on her birthday, poems written on the spur of the moment, chocolates, even songs sung to serenade her will be appreciated. She may laugh and blush, but she's in heaven with this type of attention. She wants to be the center of your world, and if you have a romantic streak, this is a good match for you as well.

Never forget that she's critical by nature, so don't take too seriously all her negative remarks about the gifts you give her. She's naturally critical because when growing up she was constantly subject to the will of older people, especially her brothers, and she rarely had a chance to get things her way. She can find fault with the best restaurant, the perfect opera, the most beautiful beach. Just laugh off her critiques and tell her she'd make a great movie critic. The younger sister has a marvelous sense of humor. What matters most is that you really care for her, and she has piercing intuition about whether you do.

Examine your own heart before you talk with her. If you really love her, if you're drawn to her like a magnet, then let your feelings be your guide. She'll respond to that. If she selects you as a partner, consider yourself lucky, especially if you're an older brother, because this could be the perfect match.

Emotionally, the younger sister of brothers tends to keep her anger hidden. She may get upset at injustices done to herself or to others, but she typically keeps these feelings concealed. Sometimes she doesn't even know she's feeling anger, she does such a good job keeping it bottled up. When dating her, it may help to ask her how she feels now and then. If you can get her to confide in you, she'll enjoy venting about all the things she feels are wrong with the world.

Age Gaps

How do age gaps between siblings affect personality? In general, the closer you and your sibling(s) are in age, the more birth order applies. If your brother is only **one year older**, you're a super lastborn. You were influenced by him more pervasively during your formative years, and as a result you have more lastborn qualities. Girls with a small age gap are sociable, open to new experiences, and interested in the arts. They grew up having generally friendly relations with their brothers and typically fought less with them than other girls. You have a special ability to meld with a man's mind. You can use that power to the fullest by working with men, secure in the knowledge of your special ability to get along with them.

Girls with a **two-year age gap** fight slightly more with their brothers during childhood, which gives them a playful and teasing character as adults. They have a good ability to use sarcasm to poke fun at men. They like to form very close romantic relationships to replicate the closeness they felt as children. Angelina Jolie's brother is two years older, and she's vocal about how close her relationship with him is.

Girls with a **three-year age gap** are more conscious of the conflicts they had with their brothers, and they can perceive their brothers as separate from themselves more easily than girls with closer age gaps. This gives them a greater desire for independence. They may enjoy teasing a man more, and they may become masters of sarcastic humor, all in a playful manner. Elizabeth Taylor falls into this category. Famous for having close relationships with many men, she also had an equally caustic wit, which was often directed at Richard Burton, to whom she was married twice.

Girls with **four- to five-year age gaps** had somewhat less interaction with their brothers and have some of the independence and ambition of only children. Girls with even **larger age gaps** are functional only children[7] yet still possess many of the positive characteristics of younger sisters, such as sociability, friendliness, and the ability to relate well to men.

Advice for Breaking Up

Cupid himself might have difficulties breaking up with her! Men have a more difficult time breaking up with the younger sister of brothers than with any other girl simply because her ability to bond with them is so intense. The best way to make a break is to maintain a friendship, if you possibly can, especially during the first few months or years. Often she'll be willing to do that.

If you're devastated by the breakup—if she's the one who instigated it—then one tactic that sometimes works is to try to immediately find another younger sister of brothers to transfer your affection to, at least temporarily. You may not wind up with this new girl, but she can help heal the wounds inflicted in the battle of love, and this may be just the solace you need.

Friendship and the Younger Sisters of Brothers

She tends to have a few close friends, and more often than not they're male. Female friends typically feel threatened by her success with men. Male friends come from school, work, or social contacts through other people. It's not uncommon for her to make friends with her husband's buddies. Before long she's better friends with them than *he* is.

Her male friends may secretly be in love with her. She often senses this and uses their infatuation to cement the relationship. She does a good job of keeping these men at bay by playing them off one another. At times she leads men on, letting them think a romantic relationship is imminent. If she is pursued seriously by one of these men, she may stir up his resentment when he learns that what she wants is friendship, nothing more. But usually she's tactful, and she does a better job than other girls in avoiding bruising a male's ego.

Sometimes she's befriended by older sisters of sisters because they find her a good role model; they learn lessons from her in how to deal with men. Younger sisters of sisters identify with her and can become good friends, although they may become jealous of their friend's success with men.

She usually has a number of male mentors. Often these are teachers or men who are competent in a particular field. Not uncommonly they're older. She looks to them for guidance and advice in her personal life.

Career

While the younger sister of brothers has fewer career preferences than others, you do have one characteristic that makes your career choice easier—you work better with men than anyone. You seek a working relationship in which you can function as a junior assistant to a male in the same way you might have helped an older brother when he was engaged in some household task. For this reason you enjoy being an assistant to a male executive or the companion to a male explorer, artist, or scientist.

To understand your skill in this regard, consider the life of Lou Andreas Salome, who charmed and influenced many of the most notable artists, poets, and philosophers of the late nineteenth and early twentieth centuries. Lou had five older brothers and was not especially beautiful, but she had an inner radiance that more than made up for that. Freud said of her that she was the most intelligent woman he had ever met. German poet Rainer Maria Rilke praised her, saying that she was "one of the most wonderful people who have come my way. . . . Without the influence of this extraordinary woman my whole development would not have been able to take the paths that have led to many things." Nietzsche fell in love with her. So did author Paul Ree.

Why do you have this magical potential to draw men to you, to inspire them, to make them fall in love with you? It all comes from the first few years of your life when you were growing up with an older brother who dunned into you (without even being aware that he was doing it) the necessity of charming men and making them love you—it was the only way you could survive! This psychological profile becomes your modus operandi, and you excel at it.

You're the quintessential muse, model, or inspiration for male artists. But you often have great creative potential of your own and can do wonderful things, especially if helped and encouraged by the men in your life. You can become a great writer (novelist George

Sand, journalist Martha Gellhorn), athlete (skater Nancy Kerrigan, swimmer Lynne Cox), entertainer (singer Janet Jackson), or actress (Jane March, Marilyn Monroe, Elizabeth Taylor).

How to Learn by Studying Younger Sisters

Whatever your birth order, you can always benefit from studying the little sister. The more carefully you observe younger sisters of brothers, the more you'll develop and strengthen your most alluring traits. With each thing you learn, you'll become increasingly fascinating to men. Before long you may have more men interested in you than you know what to do with. That's the typical problem of the younger sister.

If you're lucky enough to be a younger sister, enjoy your power. But have a little pity on other women too. Try to teach them to follow in your footsteps. (Don't worry, they'll almost never be able to steal good men away from you.)

And if you're not a younger sister, don't despair. There are plenty of guys out there with older sisters who'd be more compatible with an *older* or *middle* sister like yourself. Find a guy like that, and you'll be happy.

So next time you meet a younger sister of brothers, take note of how she acts. She's giving you a free flirtation lesson just by being who she is. Notice the way she talks, the way she holds eye contact with guys, the way she appears comfortable around men. Before long you'll absorb all these little habits, and you'll be doing the same things yourself.

And if you find, as a consequence, that you have more guys becoming infatuated with you, if you discover that you're more popular than ever, if you wake up one morning to discover that you've received a batch of love letters from men you hardly know, if the opposite sex starts doting on you, paying more attention to you, calling you sweetie, telling you with their eyes, their words, and their actions that they're delighted to be with you, well, you can chalk it all up to experience, or you can thank your lucky stars that you learned a few things from one of the chosen few—one of those eternal objects of infatuation, those bold and brassy, funny and charming, sometimes considerate, and often bewitchingly narcissistic younger sisters.

○○○○●

Celebrity Case Study

MARILYN MONROE

Marilyn Monroe grew up with a number of older foster brothers who affected her as if they were full brothers, so it's not surprising that she exhibits many of the romantic patterns we've been discussing. Like many younger sisters, she had negative memories of her childhood. "They were terribly strict," she said of her foster parents in later years. "They didn't mean any harm . . . it was their religion. They brought me up harshly."

Look at almost any picture of her, and you'll see the typical flirtatious demeanor of the younger sister. Marilyn had a lot of male admirers. She married a number of times too. Sometimes younger sisters don't find their ideal match right away, and they go through one relationship after another, searching for the man who will make them feel loved and secure. Her first marriage was to Jim Dougherty, her second, to Joe DiMaggio. She met the baseball player in early 1952 when she was twenty-five and he was thirty-seven.

"I was surprised to be so crazy about Joe," she said. "I expected a flashy New York sports type, and instead I met this reserved guy who didn't make a pass at me right away! He treated me like something special. Joe is a very decent man, and he makes other people feel decent, too!" Career conflicts led to their separation in the fall of 1954, and shortly thereafter they divorced.

Marilyn went on a USO tour of Korea in February to entertain the troops for four days. During the tour she entertained over 60,000 soldiers. She recalled, "Standing in the snowfall facing the yelling soldiers, I felt for the first time in my life no fear of anything, I felt only happy." Like a typical younger sister, it was when she was surrounded by admiring men that she felt best about herself. Being at ease in the presence of men is one of the hallmarks of the younger sister of brothers.

Her beauty was only part of the reason for her success. Her charm, typical of the younger sister of brothers, was the other important part of the equation. The roles she usually starred in typify the personality of the younger sister of brothers—alluring, friendly, and comfortable in the company of men.

Part 3

Only Children, Twins, and Middle Children

The Male Only Child

You're one of the most creative, interesting, driven, successful, conscientious, friendly, and focused people on the planet. But don't worry, I'm not trying to flatter you. Everything I'm saying is based on the fact that you have characteristics of both firstborns and lastborns. If all of this sounds too good to be true, just keep in mind that you also have your little quirks. Perhaps it's some special way of eating or some little ritual you must follow before you go to bed. Small price to pay for all those positives, though.

The male only child enjoys a privileged position all his life. In some ways he fancies himself the most important person in the world, and he acts like he's a prince among men. He knows more, deserves more, and should get more of everything, including praise, attention, and accolades. In school you court the teacher's favor almost unconsciously by how attentive and conscientious you appear. You relate to people in authority better than anyone, and that includes firstborns, because you grew up surrounded by authority figures without any peers to distract you. In adult life you use your ability to relate to powerful people to pull yourself up by your bootstraps and get into positions of power yourself.

Tyler is an only child, and as a high school student he worked as a congressional page in Washington DC. His boss was Tip O'Neill. Despite Tyler's youth, he struck the former Speaker of the House as very mature. O'Neill invited Tyler to stay at his house and would joke with him like he was one of his friends. "A noise woke me up one night," remembers Tyler, "and I looked down the stairs and saw Tip O'Neill in front of the refrigerator, a huge sub in one hand, a bottle of milk in the other. 'Sh!' he whispered. 'Don't let my wife know.'" Tyler had such a good relationship with the Speaker that they joked about the incident for years.

Because Tyler relates well to men in authority, he was accepted as a friend by one of the most powerful men in the country. You have a similar ability to make career moves based on your uncanny rapport with those in power. Shortly after graduating from law school, Tyler was arguing a case before a state judge in a real estate matter. During the discussion of a tricky technical issue, he stopped and turned to the judge. "I'm sorry, your honor, I'm not sure about this one," he said with a straight face. "I only got a 'C' in property law." The judge laughed and ruled in his favor.

Tom Wolfe

The protagonist of *The Bonfire of the Vanities*, Sherman McCoy, is described as "Master of the Universe"—clearly a projection straight from the mind of only child Tom Wolfe. Male only children see themselves as great, omnipotent, and godlike. Wolfe, by the way, exemplifies many other characteristics of the male only child. As far as quirkiness goes, during his undergraduate years he wore a Civil War uniform to campus. As an adult, it was the perennial white suit. But these quirks don't alienate people from him; on the contrary, they endear him to fans. As a writer who also possesses plenty of lastborn traits, he has creativity to spare, along with drive and determination. He's also admitted that his novelistic insight into women was a bit shaky at the start, but given time and effort, he made up for it with *I Am Charlotte Simmons*, written from a female point of view.

Male only children take time to focus on improving their weaknesses, and that's one reason you'll have greater success in your work than your competitors.

Tyler's ability to relate to men in authority made his transition into practicing law an easy matter. Don't be afraid to use *your* skill with powerful people to move ahead in your chosen field. People in high places like you, and they want you to do well.

Kevin Leman has done more to point out the perfectionism of the firstborn than any other psychologist.[1] His insights are right on target, especially for the male only child, who grows up with a very highly developed conscience. You take things personally, and if something isn't to your satisfaction, you'll redo it until you get it right.

Josh is a comedian from New York City. He spends an hour rehearsing before going onstage to a forty-minute set. Even though he's reached the pinnacle of success as an artist—with a year-round tour schedule so packed it would exhaust most performers—he still takes a video camera to each show and records it. "I want to see if there's anything I can improve," he says. "I listen to it and note where the laughs come. Then if a joke isn't working I drop it. I'm constantly making the act better." Talk about perfectionism!

But perfectionism has two sides. The good side is that it helps you get things right. There are times when you want a perfectionist in your life; for example, your doctor. If your doctor is a firstborn or an only child, you're going to have a very careful person who will most likely obsess about a diagnosis until it's solved. When you're going in for surgery, you want this kind of perfectionism.

The bad side of perfectionism is the stress. Too much worrying about doing things right can ruin your day, not to mention your ability to get a good night's sleep. If you're a perfectionist firstborn or only child, you need to find ways to lighten up and calm down. Forgive yourself for not getting everything right, take time to meditate or go for a walk through the park. Each day do something to reduce stress.[2]

Best Match

Because you're both a firstborn *and* a lastborn, you have more relationship potential than the average guy, and you actually have *two* best matches: one for your *first*born personality and the other for your *last*born personality.

For your lastborn personality, your best match is an **older sister of brothers** because she'll complement your lastborn traits and be the kind of maternal caretaker you need to help you in your career as well as in your personal life. An older sister of brothers, though, is usually happiest with a guy who has older sisters, and she'll also have an advantage over you since she grew up with an opposite-sex sibling.

Many male only children find the **older sister of sisters** their best match. In this case, neither of you has an advantage because neither has opposite-sex siblings. She's also got the kind of strong personality that can help you relax about household tasks (because she's handling them so well) and pursue your career. If you arrange your lives properly by letting her take care of certain administrative matters in the relationship, you'll find you have all the time you need to pursue your work dreams—which is an all-important part of your life.

Anthony was an only child, and he married Cindy when he was in graduate school. He earned his PhD and became a professor of chemistry at a large university. Cindy took care of the house, the bills, the checkbook, the shopping, the family matters . . . and Anthony went on to gain academic honors, write books, and attend conferences. Despite the many opportunities he had to flirt with students or meet women at conferences in faraway cities, he never strayed and remained faithful to his wife through all their many years of marriage. Their sex life was also dynamic and exciting, even after they had their only child, a boy. They subscribed to sex magazines, rented racy movies, and kept the flames of passion alive. Anthony wasn't a particularly romantic guy and Cindy wasn't an especially romantic woman, yet they felt a continuous attraction that matured into a steadfast love. In fact, their sex life and marriage could be rated higher than average because they were so well matched.

What about the best match for your *first*born personality? As I mentioned, you've got both first- *and* lastborn traits. For your first-born persona, your best match would be a woman who has older

Jean-Paul Sartre

Sartre never married Simone de Beauvoir, but they had one of the most highly publicized relationships of the twentieth century. Simone grew up with one younger sister, who was two years younger, making Simone a super firstborn with all the dynamic, forceful, dominant traits of the older sister of sisters. She and Sartre enjoyed a tempestuous and romantic relationship that also included other lovers, much to Simone's dismay. But almost to make up for the fact that Sartre was involved with other women, Simone had a long-standing affair with Nelson Algren, an American writer. In many ways, Simone and Sartre were perfectly matched. Both philosophers, Simone helped Sartre with his writing and supported him in all his career moves. Their relationship is an instructive example of how well the male only child gets along with the older sister of sisters.

brothers or sisters. But since you can't have *two* wives, the most important question you've got to ask yourself is: "Should I satisfy my firstborn or my lastborn needs when looking for a romantic partner?"

In my opinion, based on observing many relationships involving male only children, you'll do better satisfying your lastborn persona in a romantic relationship, which means dating a firstborn girl. This is because you're so career focused that you need and deserve someone in your life who will support you while you work, and an older sister is best in this capacity. While a younger sister of brothers is the best muse a man can have, firstborn older sisters are the best caretakers, editors, publicists, and motivators for a successful partner. She'll understand you and look to you for great accomplishments. Like Simone de Beauvoir and Sartre, she'll help you do your best work.

But whether you date a firstborn or a lastborn, you must avoid women who don't express an avid interest in your career. You won't be happy for long unless your life partner shares your all-important career dreams.

Worst Match

Your worst match is another **only child**. The older sister of sisters respects you as a godlike figure, a father substitute—especially if you become successful in your chosen field—but an only child may have difficulty relating to you this way, unless her mother was an older sister of sisters. The one other exception is a marriage where two only children feel a narcissistic attraction. This can work, and indeed is the basis of many successful marriages. Just remember that if you marry another singleton, you'll want to have firstborn platonic female friends to keep your life balanced and provide you with the cheerleading you'll relish in your career.

Advice for Dating a Male Only Child

Two challenges face any woman dating a male only child. First, he's so career focused, even as a young man, that he'll constantly neglect you. Understand him and his need to succeed, and you'll have a lifelong friend and lover. He needs women who can support his dreams and help him achieve them. If he's into politics, help him with his campaigns. If he's a scientist, help him do research. If he's into sports, go to the gym with him. If you share his work, you'll share his life. Even if you can't follow him into the boardroom, into the laboratory, or onto the basketball court, you can tell him you understand and listen to him when he talks about work. Most crucially, give him the space he needs to do his job. It's important to him, and if you respect *that* he'll think you're heads and shoulders above other girls. After all, few people care as much about his work as he does, so if you show that you're different, he'll start to think of you as someone very important in his life.

An example of this strategy can be seen in the relationship of Hillary Clinton (an older sister of two brothers) and Bill Clinton (a functional only child). She supported him and stood by him as he ran for governor of Arkansas and for president, and he was drawn to her because of that support. Some say she stood by him through too many shenanigans, but the principle is clearly illustrated in their lives. Stand by the male only child, support him in his career, and he will love you for it.

The other problem you'll run into is his mother. She's got only one child. Mothers and sons have a tight bond, but the bond between a mother and a male only child is closer than any other. She'll be jealous of you throughout your dating years and even after you're married. Deal with that as diplomatically as possible, and you'll score big points with him. Don't talk negatively about his parents even when *he* does—and he *will*, since only children have more conflict with parents than other children.[3] Always be respectful of his parents, and he'll respect *you*.

Advice for Breaking Up

The male only child is one of the easiest people to break up with. He's so polite and conscientious that he'll put all the blame for the breakup on himself. You may feel guilty about it, but he won't try to make you feel guilty. He'll take it like a man.

If he's the one initiating the breakup, it will help you deal with your sense of loss if you can share your feelings with a male who is better matched with you. If you're a firstborn, start associating with a lastborn boy, especially one who has older sisters. If you're a lastborn, associate with an older brother of sisters. If you're a singleton yourself, realize that you're leaving a narcissistic relationship and seek out boys with younger sisters for a taste of what an interactive relationship can do for your sense of worth. In this way, you'll quickly be on the mend, and you'll find you can love again in no time at all.

Friendship and the Male Only Child

The male only child is an excellent friend. He's thoughtful, intelligent, focused, and enthusiastic. When spending time with him, you'll notice some of his quirky obsessions. Jerry, an only child, began collecting expensive watches and cigarette lighters in his teens.

When visiting friends, he would produce a gold Dunhill lighter and extol its virtues. Later on in life, he would show you his Rolex, invite you to take a drive in his BMW, and tell you about a $2.7 million condo he was renting. Status and doing things correctly was important to him, but he had many friends, and they enjoyed his company immensely.

You may find that the male only child cultivates *your* friendship. Kurt was a college student yet had the demeanor of an adult, a characteristic that came from associating with adults rather than children during his developmental years. He was good friends with the security guards at our college, somewhat unusual for a student, I thought. They always waved to him and said hello, and he frequently stopped to exchange a few words. Most other students and faculty ignored the guards. "Why is it that this security guard knows you so well?" I asked. He laughed. "I gave him a six-pack of beer last week. Every once in a while, I give him something." I was flabbergasted. "No, it's great," Kurt insisted. "It's always a smart idea to be on good terms with these people." Later that semester there was a snowstorm and parking wasn't permitted in the upper campus, but when we pulled into the driveway where other cars were being turned away, the security guard smiled and waved us in. Kurt threw me a knowing smile. Right away I realized his foresight. His friendship had paid off.

Career

Famous male only children include Quentin Tarantino, Robin Williams, Jean-Paul Sartre, William Shatner, Cary Grant, Frank Sinatra, and Franklin Delano Roosevelt. All had terrific career focus, and so do you.

Garth is a male only child and a millionaire. He inherited half his money; the other half he earned. A large part of his success came from his careful attention to detail. He has a program that lets him analyze the stock market on his computer, and he obsesses over it for hours on end. Of course, he's less attentive to his wife. But this is normal for the male only child.

Whatever career you select, you'll do well at it because you'll devote more time and energy to it than other men do to theirs. You'll also strive to rise to the top of the hierarchy no matter what corporation or organization you enter.[4] Like other firstborns, you want to be number one. But you don't pursue this goal with the ruthless zeal of the older brother of brothers. You maintain a friendly demeanor and don't usually walk all over those who are under you.

Garth jokes that when he goes into a restaurant he thinks of the waiters as his servants. Like other only children, he's supremely self-focused, but his philosophy, which reflects a deep egotism, isn't abrasive. He would never demean anyone to their face or try to humiliate anyone. He just knows he's number one, and nothing can shake him from that worldview. In fact, it's this great confidence that helps him succeed.

How does your powerful career focus impact your relationships? Be aware that your wife will often feel neglected because of your ability to put in long hours on the job. Take the time to focus on *her* now and then. And choose a partner who will support you in your career dreams. In this way you can maximize your accomplishments while maintaining a romantic base of support at home.

○○●○○

Celebrity Case Study

FRANK SINATRA

Frank Sinatra had an almost manic degree of focus. Even after he became successful, he honed his craft, studying opera to perfect his breath control. "For all his playboy antics, Frank Sinatra was dead serious about his career, which he placed above everything else," says one biographer.[5]

His marriages and relationships were less successful than the average man's due in large part, probably, to the fact that fame threw him together with some relatively unstable stars, including Ava Gardner, Lauren Bacall, Juliet Prowse, and Mia Farrow. Sinatra was friends with Ronald Reagan and other authority figures, not only due to the fact that he himself was a celebrity but also because, as an only child, he had a great rapport with people in high places.

A "ruthless perfectionist" when it came to music,[6] Sinatra brought the same sense of perfection to his search for a romantic partner. After his unsuccessful marriage to childhood sweetheart Nancy Barbato, he agonized over an unsuccessful relationship with Ava Gardner. A lastborn with two older brothers and four older sisters, she exerted a strong hold on his imagination. Sinatra spent many nights alone since he couldn't find anyone who matched her in his mind.[7] For a while he tried to forget his woes by pursuing Lauren Bacall. This romance was in 1957, after the death of her husband, Humphrey Bogart. But the Sinatra/Bacall relationship illustrates the issue of narcissistic attraction since both were only children. Although he proposed to her, he was erratic in his romantic behavior. According to Bacall, he got annoyed when she told him to do anything. "Don't tell me—suggest," he would demand.[8] Like most singletons, he didn't like being told what to do, but most importantly, he didn't feel the connection he needed, the kind of connection with a woman who would continue to help him in his career and support him through thick and thin.

Three things make Sinatra a model for the male only child: first, his ability to focus on work above all else; second, his ability to get along with those in authority; and third, his need for a woman who would support him in his career. Failing to find her, he spent the final years of his life alone. The message for any male only child is clear: seek a partner who can be both a romantic equal as well as a career enthusiast. When you find such a woman, stay with her because she'll bring you the kind of dual connection you need.

10

○○●○○

The Female Only Child

Let's clear up some misconceptions right from the outset. You are *not* spoiled just because you're an only child. Nor are you likely to turn out socially inept simply because you don't have siblings. The good news for all singletons is that being an only child does *not*—contrary to common belief—make you selfish, egotistical, dependent, lonely, or unsociable. As one group of investigators put it, "Research on young children has in general failed to find such characteristics related to only-child status."[1]

That's the good news.

Here's the bad news. (Don't worry, it's not *that* bad!) Only children have more conflict with their *parents* than do children with siblings. This finding may be explained by the fact that brothers and sisters fight among themselves, leaving less time to direct hostilities at parents. It's also more dangerous to fight with a parent when there are siblings, since parental investment in you may be lessened in favor of your more compliant brothers and sisters.[2]

So, the picture we're painting looks like this: you get along with your friends, but you fight with your parents. Does this sound like you? If so, relax. You're a normal only child.

Your Greatest Strength

Your greatest strength is that you get along famously with those in authority. You thus might seem to be a defender of the status quo, but really you're just trying to find what's valuable and good in the world; if someone has come along before you and found it, what use is there in trying to overturn the way things are? This attitude makes you the darling of those in power, and you would be well advised to locate a wealthy patron who can help you in your day-to-day dealings with everything.

Another characteristic that may confuse some people about you is your mercurial nature. You have both lastborn and firstborn traits and score somewhere in the middle range, although closer to the firstborn, when it comes to openness to experience. As Sulloway points out, this is because you "tend to identify with parents and authority."[3] As a result, you may strike people as having more firstborn than lastborn characteristics, including being conscientious, having feelings of guilt when you don't live up to your own expectations, being a perfectionist, and getting angry more quickly than others do when things don't go your way.

You are powerfully influenced by your mother's sibling position, more so than other girls. This is to be expected, since in the absence of siblings you only have your same-sex parent to teach you how to deal with the opposite sex. In this regard, you're more "likely to identify strongly with and emulate a mother who is an oldest or an only," and you may find you have "more trouble identifying with the playfulness and fun-loving attitude of a youngest."[4] If your mother is an only child, you'll become a super only, with strong female only characteristics: an ability to focus on the self, a desire to work with authority, and a need for patronage and financial support from your elders.

Imitation

Because of financial reasons, young Amanda couldn't be raised by her parents, so she was sent to live in Indonesia with her paternal grandmother and Ida, a crippled friend of the family. Having no money for a wheelchair, Ida usually got around by crawling across the floor on her hands and knees. By the time she was four years old, Amanda would imitate Ida by crawling on her hands and knees.

This wasn't done with cruel or heartless intent, it was simply the girl's way of playing with Ida.

Female only children are good mimics. You may have more imaginative power than you realize. Amanda's situation was similar to that of comedian Carol Burnett, who was raised by her grandmother. As a child, Burnett imitated Shirley Temple. She also fooled people into thinking she had a twin sister named Karen. Burnett says she "fooled the other boarders in the rooming house where we lived by frantically switching clothes and dashing in and out of the house by the fire escape and the front door. Then I became exhausted and Karen mysteriously vanished."[5]

Amanda had no playmates her own age. She played with men in their twenties, thirties, and fifties. If you met her, even though she was still a child, you would swear she was an adult. She acted and talked like an adult because the adult world was all she knew. Female only children have the demeanor of little adults when they're children. They strike people as psychologically old throughout their lives. They also act more mature than other students in school, which gives them an advantage when dealing with professors.

Like most firstborns, you stand out from other students because you're punctilious and conscientious. As a teacher, I noticed that female singletons often talked with me before or after class. If an assignment was going to be late, they notified me ahead of time. You strike your teachers, and adults in general, as being very well behaved.

Use your maturity and ability to be sober-minded and honest to your advantage. Teachers and those in authority will enjoy having you around to help with schoolwork, political work, or whatever task is at hand. Your temperament will win you a place in their administration and set you apart from others your age.

In the romantic arena, you'll find that older firstborn males who have good careers will find you attractive psychologically. They'll feel comfortable with you, and they'll learn to depend upon your assistance. This dependence can lead to a good working relationship, which can, in turn, lead to a romantic relationship. Lauren Bacall worked with Humphrey Bogart, who was twenty-five years older, before she married him.

More for *You*

During the 1970s China attempted to limit population growth by encouraging couples to have only one child. Couples in urban areas who had a second child were fined. Despite criticism from human rights advocacy groups around the world, the policy actually worked: couples reduced the number of children they raised, the population decreased, and China suddenly found itself with a large number of only children. An unintended outcome of the one-child policy is that it has provided an exceptional environment for testing theories about only children.

What has been discovered?

Although males were favored over females before the one-child policy was instituted, a recent study indicates that when a couple has a female only child they treat her just as well as if they had a male child. The authors of the study found "equally high educational aspirations and similar mathematical performance for male and female only children." They also found that "this gender equality in education is an unintended consequence of the one-child-per-family policy and that under China's current social and economic conditions, girls are better off living in one-child families in the big cities of modern China."[6]

This study has an important implication for female only children worldwide. When you grow up a female only child, the absence of brothers or sisters has an obvious benefit in affording *you* more parental investment. Consequently, vis-à-vis your friends and neighbors, you stand to have better economic and educational opportunities than others.

Your Greatest Weakness

Your greatest weakness is a tendency toward overreliance on benefactors, a trait you developed because of long years of dependence on your parents who let you be a child without pushing you to fend for yourself.

Rachel never had a real job. Her father left the family early in her life, and Rachel was raised by her mother and aunt. These adults weren't rich, but they had enough to provide for her. People referred to Rachel as the "little princess." She was very nice to everyone, and everyone was very nice to her—especially her mother and aunt, who paid for everything and took care of her well into her twenties.

Female only children, more than other girls, might rely on parents or guardians for financial and emotional support. If the family situation permits, they'll stay home and avoid working.

Rachel eventually got married and had two children, but she wasn't particularly fond of them. Her aunt and mother came to the house and looked after the children, as if they were Rachel's maids. Over the years, her aunt supplied her with everything, including food, money, and jewelry. Her mother and aunt would draw her bath, change the babies, and prepare food. In a sense, Rachel never grew up. When her husband began an affair with another woman, Rachel went back to live with her mother and aunt, bringing her young children along.

Although your greatest weakness is falling into a pattern of overreliance on your benefactors, this tendency can actually be turned into a tremendous advantage that can work wonders for your romantic life. You have the ability to elicit helping behavior from people, including potential suitors. To find a good match, you should *only* date men who respond to your childish need for a protector. These men will usually be your best romantic match.

Best Match

Your best match is the **older brother of sisters**. He can provide the romance and attention you desire in a relationship, but he's usually not content with your inability to relate to him in the playful way he's used to from his sisters. An example of this relationship working out beautifully, however, is the marriage of only child Lauren Bacall and older brother of sisters Humphrey Bogart. She may have gotten more out of the match than he did, for his best match would have been a younger sister of brothers; nevertheless, the onscreen chemistry between these two, especially in *To Have and Have Not* when they were first getting to know one another and not yet married, can provide inspiration for you.

Another potentially good match is the **older brother of brothers**, but he may strike you as too bossy. If his father had younger sisters it would make things easier since boys learn to deal with women from their same-sex parent.

A **younger brother of sisters** or a **younger brother of brothers** is another potential match that could work. In the former case, he would understand you since he grew up with a sister, but he might strike you as too easygoing, relaxed, and laid-back, especially about his career. In the latter case, you might feel he doesn't understand you, and he might feel that you aren't accepting enough of his need for adventure. But you'd certainly have fun with both these lastborns. In fact, they might be just what you need to lighten up your life after the overly serious demeanor of your parents, something from which you might be glad to escape—although you'll always have strong ties to home.

A **twin** could be a good match if he had a twin sister or if he also had a younger sister. If your mother had younger brothers, then a twin or a middle boy with older sisters might be your best match since you would have adopted many of your mother's older sister characteristics.

Worst Match

The male **only child** is your worst match because neither of you is used to peers of the opposite sex. Sometimes this relationship works, however, and when it does it's usually because of narcissistic attraction. In such a relationship be careful to allow yourself sufficient distance from your partner on occasion so that you can find your center apart from him. Otherwise you may tend to meld into him so completely that you *become* him.

No matter who you eventually wind up with, you may run into

conflict if your partner starts to remind you too much of your father. Such a similarity has the potential to reawaken early parent-child conflict, and you may find yourself resisting his suggestions and ideas simply because they remind you of the orders you received from your parents. The best way to resolve this problem is to become conscious of the underlying feelings that are causing it and to remind yourself that your partner is a unique individual with strengths and weaknesses of his own.

Advice for Dating a Female Only Child

The key point to remember is that she's got issues with authority that you can't begin to fathom, so be careful of criticizing her parents. Let *her* do that. And she will, guaranteed. She'll talk negatively about them every opportunity she gets, but she doesn't want *you* to agree. She just wants someone to listen. You can listen, but don't agree when she tells you how horribly they treated her. Deep down, she really loves them and is just venting. In a way they were like her big brother and sister, but since they were also her parents, the issue becomes complicated. She has conflict with them, but she also relied on them throughout her childhood, and she'll *continue* to rely on them all during your marriage! You have to get used to her ambivalent relationship with her parents and to the importance of her parents in her psychological life if you want to understand her.

You're also going to have to prove yourself to her. This is a test all female only children will put you through. You're going to have to measure up to her own father. She idolizes him, even though she also criticizes him and his many foibles publicly. In reality she needs you to be Big Daddy for her, and she wants you to prove that you can do that, both financially and emotionally. Support her in her trials and tribulations and stand by her when things appear bleak. She's looking for signs that you can do this—even on your first few dates together. Be strong, tell her you understand, and give her evidence of your trustworthiness. If you do, she'll reward you with the unconditional loyalty she directed at her parents.

Advice for Breaking Up

You may find breaking up with the female only child a difficult process, especially if you're a firstborn or have younger sisters. The difficulty stems less from your own feelings and emotions of loss and more from your concern over *her* welfare. Female only children have an uncanny ability to elicit caring and parental behavior from men, so you may discover that you feel guilty about breaking up with her and worried about how she'll fare without your help and guidance. Even if she was the one to initiate the breakup, you may still harbor these feelings of guilt and concern for her welfare and safety. To make life easier for you, and for her, encourage her to go back to her parents—or to the other guardians she may have found helpful in the past—so that you can get on with your life and she can start anew.

Friendship and Female Only Children

Compared to male only children, female only children are less successful, significantly less career driven, and have a much harder time defining themselves and knowing what they want in the world of work. According to Walter Toman this is because our society values men's careers more highly than women's. He also attributes the female singleton's problems to the fact that, more than other women, she desires a patron to help with her career.[7] Other researchers have suggested that during the developmental years the female only child is more protected than the male only child, which may lead her to founder as an adult when similar protection is not forthcoming as she seeks to make her way in the world.[8]

Quite a catalog of difficulties! But how does this help you befriend the female only child? The answer is that by providing the same kind of helpful and guiding support that was provided by her parents early in life, you can win her trust, friendship, and loyalty. In fact, the female only child thrives on relationships with those in authority who can befriend her, help her, and guide her. This kind of friendship is somewhat less egalitarian than other kinds of friendship since the relationship requires you to be a kind of godlike figure to her; but if that fits your temperament—and those of you who match this description know who you are—then you may even want to seek out female only children for friends. She'll look up to you, expect you to have wonderful insights into the world, and she'll listen to your advice as if it were the pronouncement of an oracle. In return, she'll give you the benefit of her quick wit, her loyalty, and her cheery friendship.

Career

Famous female only children include Condoleezza Rice, Lauren Bacall, and Tipper Gore. You do well in jobs where an elderly patron supports you financially, emotionally, or artistically.[9] A good career would be working as a writer or artist under the patronage of a wealthy benefactor. English art critic Myfanwy Piper had numerous older male artists virtually hold her hand and help her succeed. Another example is early twentieth-century still life artist Blondelle Octavia Edwards Malone, who one reviewer described as having "spent much of her life living a romanticized artist's existence. Financially supported by her parents, she traveled around Europe painting the gardens of dignitaries and wealthy aristocrats."[10] Both female singletons found the benefactors they needed, and when they did, their careers thrived.

You're happiest when the attention of older authority figures is focused on you. This desire leads you to seek out careers where you can be admired or revered, including stage actress, movie star, model, and voice-over artist. Working alongside college and university deans, governors, political officials, or presidents and CEOs of corporations is also to your liking and gives you the sense of security you desire in a job. For this reason, you can find satisfaction as an executive secretary, political aide, and assistant director on a film set.

Another career in which you'll excel is as a biographer. Into this work you will pour your soul, and you will come to adore your subjects as if they were a projection of the archetypical parental figures who are such a large part of your life. You could also work as a Web page developer, especially one focused on celebrities or historical figures.

○○●○○

Celebrity Case Study

BROOKE SHIELDS

Brooke Shields's career has been guided by her mother almost every step of the way. This is typical of the female only child, for whom a patron is often behind the scenes making sure that her career goes in the right direction.

Descended from royalty, Brooke is the granddaughter of an Italian princess.[11] A female only child could ask for no better family situation. Since she relies so much on her roots, it's nice to know they involve kings and queens.

When she was twelve, Brooke was selected by Louis Malle to star in the film *Pretty Baby*. The role of a child prostitute catapulted her to stardom, but later roles, even such prominent ones as co-starring in *Blue Lagoon*, didn't lead to a film career. Instead, she got sidetracked into other things, such as romances with various famous politicians and movie stars, including John F. Kennedy Jr., Michael Bolton, Prince Albert II of Monaco, and Michael Jackson. This is where the female only child differs markedly from the typical male only child, who will not let anything deter him from career aspirations.

From 1997 to 1999, Brooke was married to tennis star Andre Agassi. The marriage seemed to be under a cloud from the start, however, and tabloids hinted that the couple had serious problems. Quite likely their problems could be attributed to the fact that she was married to a lastborn. Agassi, who has two older sisters and an older brother, would have been seeking in a mate the kind of guidance, leadership, and support that a female only child is herself seeking from *her* mate. Yet according to *The Sun*, Brooke said, "Andre was the most compassionate, perfect person for me for those years when I really didn't know what I was going to do with my life." She added, "He was the first person who gracefully helped me to individualize. The love I have for him now is the same now as it was when we got married. It is truly profound."[12] Does this sound like narcissistic attraction to you? Certainly the girl who played the lead in *Pretty Baby* had a lot of the child in her, and her attraction for lastborn Agassi is perhaps not surprising after all.

Brooke's career illustrates how successful you can be when you click with your special older benefactors. She worked well with her mother, and she mesmerized Louis Malle, the director who jumpstarted her career.

You don't need to be a film star to see that the *pattern* in her life can also work for you. Keep looking for those elder benefactors. Whether they're senators, executives, or older employers and mentors, they'll help you and guide you in a way that will make you feel comfortable expressing your creative potential.

11

○○●○○

Twins

You know you're special, you've always known it! Ever since you were a baby people have been giving you attention just because you're a twin. Still, I bet you sometimes wonder whether you *deserve* all this attention, all the fuss that's been made over you.

Rest assured about one thing: you actually *do* have a special power and ability simply because you're a twin. Your special power is your ability to form close relationships, including romantic relationships, with others. You feel a deep connection and an intuitive understanding of your twin that's greater than the rapport felt by other brothers and sisters.[1] You're used to this high degree of connectivity, and if it's absent from a relationship you feel that something vital is missing. Whenever you're in a relationship, you seek to replicate this close connection, which is why you excel at fostering and nurturing interpersonal harmony.

The point is so important it bears repeating. You are better than most people at forming close interpersonal relationships. And that's something no one will ever be able to take away from you.

Closeness

Twins grow up helping one another more than other brothers and sisters. At times you may argue with your twin, but usually those arguments are minor in nature.[2] You help each other more than other brothers and sisters because, in helping your twin, you're

121

Fraternal versus Identical Twins

Fraternal twins develop together in the womb but share no more genetic similarity than any other brothers or sisters—only half their genes are the same. Like any other siblings, they might look different, or they might look quite similar.

Identical twins have exactly the same genetic makeup. They look so much alike that even their parents have trouble telling them apart.

There's no difference between fraternal and identical twins when it comes to romantic ability. Whether you're a fraternal or an identical twin, you have a special ability to form close interpersonal relationships. This ability comes from the fact that you grew up with a sibling who is so close in age. Other brothers and sisters, even those who are only eight or nine months apart, can't match you in this special power.

helping yourself. "An identical twin may not have all the answers to his or her co-twin's questions," says psychologist Nancy Segal. "On balance, however, an identical twin may be the best source for most types of assistance for which we would normally rely on other people, such as emotional sustenance or investment decisions. This is because, genetically speaking, helping an identical twin is like helping oneself, i.e., helping one's own genes to survive."[3]

Your propensity for mutual assistance is transferred into your romantic relationships and leads you to be caring and helpful, even with those who aren't your twin. When you begin to date, you look for the same kind of closeness you experienced while growing up. As Segal explains, "Twins may, thus, come closer than anyone else to achieving the coordinated, harmonious relations for which we all strive."[4] The important point is that twins learn to transfer their skill at interpersonal relationships into their adult relationships, and anyone who dates you will be the beneficiary of this unique sharing and closeness.

Boy-Girl versus Same-Sex Twins

Same-sex twins grow up with no peers of the opposite sex, unless they have other opposite-sex siblings, so they're subject to sex conflict with their partners. On the other hand, boy-girl twins suffer no such handicap, and they're preeminently prepared for relationships with the opposite sex.

The Bush twins are a good example of the problems same-sex twins sometimes run into. Jenna and Barbara Bush (b. 1981), the twin daughters of President George W. Bush, have no other siblings. They seem to have a slightly anti-authoritarian streak, running afoul of the law a number of times. Most of their offenses involved underage drinking or misrepresenting their age while trying to buy alcoholic drinks. In their college years, the Bush twins got into more trouble with alcohol than with boys.

Compare the behavior of the Bush twins with that of Aaron Carter, who has a twin sister, and you get an entirely different picture. He seems to be very well adapted to the opposite sex. He's already dated Lindsay Lohan and Hilary Duff, stirring up jealous fights between the two. He also went out with Paris Hilton while she was still dating his older brother, Nick! In fact, the two brothers had a very public dispute about the date on their reality TV show. It's no surprise that a guy who grew up with a twin sister finds himself quickly enmeshed in the world of romance and all the intrigues that go along with it.

Boy-girl twins have an uncanny ability to be successful in romantic relationships. As mentioned above, they often show a preference for partners who are either twins themselves or who have siblings close in age. Interestingly, the contrary is also true, that is, people who grow up with siblings close in age are often drawn to twins and find dating a twin to be a very comfortable experience.

Arianna, a beautiful young lastborn whose brother is seventeen months older, began dating a twin when she was only fourteen. This boy had a twin sister and was very romantic and attentive. Arianna wrote endlessly in her diary about him. Although her family was displeased, she talked about marrying him. When she was in college, she spent a year abroad in Germany. While there, she met a music student, Jan, and fell in love almost immediately. As it turns out, Jan also had a twin sister. "I feel like I'm in heaven when I'm with him," she wrote in her diary. "How am I ever going to leave this country and say good-bye to him?" Although she didn't end up marrying either twin, to this day she maintains that they were two of the best matches of her romantic life. Asked to describe similarities the young men shared, she thought for only a moment before saying that they were "comfortable with women." This comfortableness with the opposite sex is the hallmark of boy-girl twins.

Best Match

Your best match is another **twin**. Marrying another twin provides a sense of continuity and keeps you in your comfort zone.[5] Growing up a twin is kind of like being a celebrity. People come to see the twin babies, and relatives and friends give you special attention. When you become an adult, you may miss the attention you received by virtue of being a twin. Marrying a twin rekindles some of that special status and can keep you feeling like a twin celebrity for the rest of your life.[6]

Your next best match is someone who has a sibling very *close* in age. The best match for a boy-girl twin is someone who has an opposite-sex sibling. This is because you've grown up with someone of the opposite sex and are used to the experience. Marriage to someone who has an opposite-sex sibling, preferably one close in age, will replicate the kind of intuitive connection you had while growing up.

The best match for a boy-boy twin who has no other siblings is a twin from a boy-girl pair. But this girl may not be as happy with you; she may long for the kind of twin she grew up with, and she may not relate as well to your relative lack of insight into her feminine nature.

The best match for a girl-girl twin who has no other siblings is a twin from a boy-girl pair, but the same considerations we discussed regarding the boy-boy twin apply. You also do well with a boy who has a younger sister, although he would tend to feel that you didn't understand him sufficiently. The closeness you provided, however, might easily make up for your lack of experience with peers of the opposite sex.

If you're a same-sex twin who has other opposite-sex siblings, those siblings are critical for figuring out your best match, especially when they're close in age to you. A same-sex twin boy develops last-born traits if he has an older sister, and everything we discussed in the chapter on younger brothers of sisters applies. Similarly, he develops traits of the older brother of sisters if he has a younger sister.

Having additional opposite-sex siblings is an important consideration even for boy-girl twins. Aaron Carter, for example, has a twin sister, but he also has two older sisters, one of whom is only a year older. This older sister is very important for predicting who Aaron Carter will be compatible with. Since he has a twin sister, his best match would be a twin girl from a boy-girl pair, but since he also has an older sister very close in age, his next best match would be a firstborn or middle girl who has a younger brother. The closer in age the girl's brother, the better for Aaron.[7]

Worst Match

Your worst match is an **only child** whose same-sex parent is also an only child. In this case, the only child's traits would be reinforced to such a degree that he or she would become a super singleton with very pronounced traits of an only child.

A relatively unfavorable match would be a partner whose siblings are six or more years older or younger, since this individual would be a functional singleton. The reason you would be unhappy in such a matchup has to do with the sense of isolation you'd likely feel. Having grown up with a sibling identical in age, you respond best to the same closeness in a romantic relationship.

Twins who have other siblings must be analyzed based on those family constellations. So, for example, twin girls who also have a younger sister would find themselves mismatched with an older

THE BIRTH ORDER BOOK OF LOVE

brother of brothers for the same reason that the older sister of sisters is mismatched with such a partner.

Advice for Dating a Twin

If you possibly can, you'd be wise to date a twin at least once in your life. Dating a twin lets you see what an ideal relationship can be—and once you experience that extraordinary closeness, you may never want to date anyone else.

Keep in mind that twins have a special need for personal space. While growing up they typically shared a room, toys, and even a wardrobe. Many of them felt that they were in danger of losing their identity. "I resented being dressed the same," says a twin who had to wear the same clothes as his twin brother.[8] This theme of needing their personal space is echoed by nearly every twin who has been studied.[9]

Because twins need their space, you must respect this wish if you hope to have a good relationship. This means that when dating a twin it's going to be important to balance closeness with the personal space they also need.

Although they need personal space, a twin's desire for closeness is the more important drive, and a twin will do anything to achieve this kind of deep intimate connection in a romantic relationship. They fall into patterns of sharing and bonding much easier than others do, and they expect their partner to reciprocate. "You see, twins can't be alone," says Amy, who has a twin sister. "They always have to have one person very close to them. When you have a boyfriend, he has to be as close to you as your twin was because you are used to a very close relationship."

"So your husband or boyfriend replaces the twin that you've left," says Ann, Amy's twin sister.[10]

Twins sometimes feel that they have telepathic powers, at least when it comes to their twin. Alanis Morissette claims that she's in telepathic contact with her twin brother. When you're with a twin, you may find that they're trying to read *your* mind. You should feel

126

flattered by this. What could be nicer than having someone so keenly interested that they wish they could know what you're thinking!

Advice for Breaking Up

Breaking up with a twin can be an especially difficult experience. If you wish to break up with a twin boy, the best thing you can do to ease the pain for him would be to introduce him to a twin girl. The affinity twins feel for one another will make your separation easier, since he'll start to bond with her. If you wish to break up with a twin girl, the same strategy will work if you introduce her to a twin boy or even to a boy who has a sister close in age.

Twins may need more time than usual to adjust to the idea of being separated, so you may wish to remain friends to ease the transition. In fact, this is often the best way to separate from a twin.

Non-twins who break up with twins may feel a curious sense of liberation after they're apart, especially if they were the ones instigating the breakup. After all, sometimes twins can be stifling in their demand for closeness. Twins, of course, are used to that kind of closeness, but non-twins can find themselves worn out by the intimacy demands of dating a twin.

Twins who break up with twins will have the worst time of all. This is due to the close interconnection they'll have experienced in the relationship. The best strategy is to take some time off to get your bearings, then look for another twin.

Friendship and Twins

The curious thing about being friends with a twin is the conflicting feelings you'll have. On the one hand, you'll feel a sense of closeness and kindness radiating from the twin. They can surprise you with their considerateness. They're often able to do things for you that you wouldn't have expected. This will feel very friendly. But on the other hand, you'll never be able to match the twin for considerateness, unless you're also a twin. Don't get caught in the trap of feeling guilty when you sense that the twin is so much nicer to you than you are to him or her. You'll sometimes feel that you're playing second fiddle to your friend's twin, but no matter what you do or how nice you act, you'll never equal the closeness he has with his twin, so don't even worry about it.

Twins naturally enjoy friendships that replicate the closeness of their bond with their twin. At the same time, twins will readily acknowledge that, as much as they enjoy friendships with schoolmates or colleagues, those friendships pale in comparison to the closeness they feel with their twin. When growing up, twins often spend more time with each other than they do with their mother, and as a result they get used to being with their twin. In school and out, they may prefer playing with their twin to playing with other classmates. They may, indeed, need a respite from contact with others, and they can find themselves drawn into contact with their twin as a means of recharging their batteries and enabling them to go back into the world of their friends.

Boy-girl twins often develop intense platonic relationships with overtones of romantic love. Montgomery Clift, for example, who had a twin sister, was very close friends with Elizabeth Taylor. Don't be surprised if you find yourself falling in love with your twin friends.

Career

If you're a twin, look for careers in which you're working with people, especially your own twin. Try to find employment in a field where people are important, because you excel at doing things as a team. This would include careers such as figure-skating, coauthoring books, tennis doubles, and exploring.

Mary-Kate and Ashley Olsen found the perfect career—acting together on TV and in movies. When twins work alone, they prefer jobs that allow them to do things that are intensely people-oriented. In other words, they enjoy careers like photography, detective work, sound engineering, news reporting, and speech-writing.

Twins often discover that they're drawn to the same career as their twin. Mario Andretti and his brother both started working as race-car drivers. The Keiths cofounded a center to study twins. The

Gills worked together as photographers. You make excellent business partners and often excel at fighting off the competition, something you do naturally as twins.

○○●○○

Celebrity Case Study

MARY-KATE AND ASHLEY OLSEN

Mary-Kate and Ashley Olsen are fraternal twins who look so similar that many people mistakenly believe they're identical. They began their media conquests early, starring in the TV show *Full House* when they were just five months old. They each took turns playing the character Michelle Tanner. During the initial episodes, viewers didn't know the character was played by two different people on alternate days.

These twins associate more with each other than with anybody else. They do this even though they've become so famous that they've parleyed their celebrity status into multiple fields. The girls have terrific closeness and bonding skills; in fact, they're so nice that, according to those who work with them, they don't even act like famous celebrities.

Not surprisingly, they also have difficulty ending relationships. Mary-Kate's breakup with billionaire Stavros Niarchos III was especially traumatic because he started dating Mary-Kate's good friend Paris Hilton—while still dating Mary-Kate. The gut-wrenching pain of the separation is clear in Mary-Kate's comments on the breakup, which she clearly found hard to talk about. "I miss him and I love him and I don't speak with him anymore," she told *W* magazine. "It's a hurtful and painful subject. I've pretty much been with someone my whole life, so this is a hard time for me."[11]

Like most twins, the Olsens received attention merely by being twins. At only five months old, they were signed to act in a TV show simply because they were twins. They've continued banking on their twin status to land roles because fans like to see them together in movies and on TV.

Mary-Kate and Ashley got a lot of attention as youngsters, but as they have matured into adults, they may have experienced more difficulties than the average non-twin. A large part of a twin's identity comes from being together and being perceived as special by virtue of being a twin. When twins grow up and face the challenges of the adult world, they're sometimes surprised at the lack of attention they get when they're not with their twin.

The special challenge for you as a twin is to make your own way in the world after you have been uniquely prepared for living in close proximity with another person. This is why finding the right romantic relationship will be one of the most important, and most satisfying, things you'll ever do.

oo●oo

Middle Children

Lucky the middle child of a family! So said renowned psychologist Alfred Adler, himself a middle child. And it was with good reason that he believed you have certain advantages. Middle children are unique among all the birth orders in one crucial respect: they have the greatest potential for adaptability and multiple personality roles. No, this doesn't mean you're schizophrenic or that you have multiple personalities! It does mean, however, that you, more than anyone else, can adapt to the situation, roll with the punches, go with the flow, and come out a winner in the game of love. Now, with a potential like that, I'd have to say middle is the place to be.

If you're a middleborn, you may have felt confused about your place in the family. After all, firstborns are usually the do-gooders and are closely allied with parents, so they have their niche, dominating and controlling their younger siblings. And lastborns are perpetually coddled and protected and almost invariably enjoy a special place of privilege in a family. But middle children are, more often than not, left to wonder where they fit into the picture of the happy home. Are you supposed to challenge the older ones and try to surpass them? Or are you supposed to take charge of your younger siblings and be nurturing and protective?

In the final analysis, all these possibilities and capabilities are your special birthright. The fact that you can wear many hats means that you've got greater adaptability and more potential for change.

It also means that you have a better chance of finding a good match, especially if you know how to use your special multi-persona talents in the realm of love.

Switch Hitters

In baseball, switch hitters are players who can hit from the right or the left side of the plate. They're more adaptable and can change batting styles to strategically confound right-handed or left-handed pitchers. As a middle child, you've got a similar natural ability. You're a switch hitter with your *personality*. That's right, you can change your temperament and play the part of the firstborn when that's appropriate, or the role of the lastborn when that's more to your advantage.

Annie has an older brother and a younger sister. She thus has two potential birth orders: she possesses the psychological qualities of a younger sister of brothers—creativity, diverse interests, a Siren-like ability to charm men—as well as the psychological qualities of an older sister of sisters—dominance, drive, and determination, together with the older sister of sister's natural ability to relate well to men in authority. Annie has both these profiles, and anyone who describes her as just one or the other is missing half the story.

What does this mean in practical terms?

Well, it means that Annie has the power to switch from one profile to the other, reacting like a younger sister when that's to her advantage (such as when flirting with a man), or switching things around and acting like the older sister when that's more advantageous for her (such as when dealing with students in a classroom environment).

How do middle children make the switch? Most do it automatically, without even thinking. Some middles, however, have become aware of their multiple personas, and they make the shift consciously, just like driving a car with standard transmission where you engage the clutch and shift gears manually. It doesn't really matter whether you make the shift consciously or unconsciously, as long as you change gears, so to speak, to fit the situation.

Being a switch hitter is one of the greatest advantages that a middle child has over those from distal positions—firstborns and lastborns. Middle children have multiple potentials for making good matches, especially if they have older and younger opposite-sex siblings. For example, Tom Cruise has two older sisters and one younger sister, so he'd be compatible with any girl who has a brother. (Katie Holmes has one.)

Age Gaps

Let's talk about one of the most important factors influencing your romantic potential—the age gaps between siblings. The logic behind considering age gaps is intuitive, compelling, and easy to understand.

If you've got huge age gaps between you and your siblings, their effect on you is going to be diminished. It stands to reason, doesn't it? If your older brother is sixteen years older, he won't have been around much during your formative years. You will not have played together, shared toys, or even talked much, because by the time you were three or four, he was in college, working, or even out of the house and on his own. So the first principle to understand is that *big age gaps diminish influence*. In fact, if the age gap is six or more years, the influence is usually negligible.[1]

Janice has an older brother seven years her senior and a younger brother two years her junior. What can you say about her personality? Is she likely to be more like a younger sister or an older sister? In this case, she's much more likely to have the characteristics of the older sister. This is a crucial determination for her love life. And it's equally important for you to consider the age gaps between you and your siblings when trying to fathom your personality and who would be your best match.

If you're a girl with brothers who are both older and younger, it's going to be extremely important to consider the age gaps between you. If your closest-in-age older brother is *two* years older, and your closet-in-age younger brother is *seven* years younger, you can virtually ignore the influence of the younger brother—the age gap is too large. The close age gap with your older brother, however, is the key to your personality. He would have been in your face throughout childhood, molding your personality, playing with you, teasing you, taking your toys, influencing you profoundly without your even being aware of it—and turning you into a younger sister of brothers. (Lucky you!)

See how relevant age gaps are? Don't forget to factor in this issue.

Number of Siblings

Almost as important as the age gap between you and your siblings is the *number* of your older and younger siblings. It's common sense, isn't it? If you have a huge number of older siblings, you'll be more like a lastborn. If you have six or seven younger siblings, you'll be more like a firstborn.

The legendary explorer Ernest Shackleton had one older sibling and *eight* younger siblings. Knowing that, what can you say about his personality? Would you expect him to be a leader or a follower?

The answer is that with eight younger siblings Shackleton naturally developed many more firstborn traits—his leadership and commanding personality inspired scores of explorers to follow him to the ends of the earth on numerous Antarctic expeditions. Certainly his older sister contributed *something* to his personality, making him a natural magnet to women and giving him boldness and courage, but the eight younger siblings were the decisive force shaping his personality. Although he was a middle child, you could confidently predict that he would be more like a firstborn because of the large number of younger siblings.

Gender of Siblings

Here's where Cupid really gets involved! Knowing the *gender* of a middle child's siblings is the single most important factor to consider when looking at their potential for romantic happiness. Let me prove this to you with a famous example.

Princess Diana had two older sisters and one younger brother. It's also relevant that these siblings were close in age. The sisters were four and six years older, the brother, three years younger. Knowing this, what can you tell me about her personality and romantic potential?

The answer to this question is easy. The first thing you want to do is to look at her *opposite-sex* siblings when considering romantic potential. So in this case we're interested in the fact that Princess Diana had a younger *brother*. That's a hundred times more relevant than the fact that she had older sisters. The older sisters aren't totally irrelevant for her personality, but they're much less important than her brother when considering romantic potential. Remember, it would be her younger brother who taught her, as a child, how to deal with the opposite sex. The experience of growing up with a younger brother makes a girl develop qualities of the older sister. That's the vital point for understanding Princess Diana's romantic life. From that simple fact flows all our analysis of her best match (a younger brother of sisters) and our prediction that she would have rank conflict with any man who had younger sisters (including Prince Charles!).

See? Once you know the sex of a middle child's siblings, you can say a lot about their romantic potential.

Compromise and Negotiation

I bet it's no surprise to learn that you're the great negotiator. This skill served you well as you grew up surrounded by warring parties, namely your older and younger siblings. Just as a politician has to bring hostile factions to the peace table to resolve conflicts, you had to find ways to get your irate siblings to calm down and stop fighting, if only so that you could get some peace and quiet at home. For this reason, you have very good negotiating skills, and you often make a good lawyer or diplomat.

Middle children excel at finding compromises, and more than others they seek nonviolent methods of reaching consensus.[2] Martin Luther King Jr., who was a middle child, illustrates the nonviolent approach to compromise. The skill of the middle child in this regard is uncanny, as the following story illustrates.

John is a world-famous gourmet chef, and at eighty-two years of age, he's still sought out by businesses for special events. In the last ten years, however, he has become rather short-tempered. Recently he got into a big argument with one of his customers, who was so offended by his attitude that she refused to pay. John, a firstborn, immediately called his agent, Harold. A middle child, Harold is a very savvy negotiator. Not only did Harold calm the client down, he convinced John, a very proud person, to write an apology note, which resulted in a partial payment—a much better outcome than they had expected.

Recognize your negotiating skills and use them to your advantage. You can even employ this skill in matters of romance, negotiating for a better table in a restaurant, improving relations with your partner's family, and working in many other ways to have a more comfortable relationship with less fights and arguments than your friends and neighbors.

Smack Dab in the Middle—And Confused

Are you often confused about who to go out with? Do you find that you're frequently torn between two potentially good partners? Is it difficult for you to decide which person would be better for you?

Relax, you're a normal middle child! If you weren't confused, something would be wrong. Difficulty deciding between two potentially good mates is a common middleborn dilemma. And it has a relatively easy solution, which I'll get to in a moment. First let me explain why you're so indecisive.

Having contradictory romantic feelings is par for the course for you because you grew up with older and younger siblings. A girl with older and younger brothers is going to be attracted to big brothers *and* little brothers. She'll need both in her romantic life. On the one hand, she needs the leadership a firstborn can provide, but on the other hand, she responds to the fun-loving, easygoing, laid-back babyishness that only a lastborn is capable of.

What's a girl to do?

First, try to narrow your choice to one or the other based on the age gap between you and your siblings. For example, if your older brother is only *one* year older while your younger brother is *six* years younger, your best match is going to be with firstborn men. This is because you are more of a younger sister, the proximity of your older brother having made you a super laterborn.

The second solution applies when you're equidistant from older and younger siblings. In this case, you're smack dab in the middle, and you really do need both men equally. Best suggestion is to choose one, and keep the other as a platonic friend. In this way you'll have both in your life.

Best Match

Your best match depends first and foremost on *whether you have older or younger opposite-sex siblings*. It's also important to consider the *number* of siblings you have, as well as the *age gaps* separating you.

We'll illustrate this with a look at the best match for Britney Spears.

Britney Spears grew up with one older brother, four years older, and one younger sister, ten years younger. Like all middle children, she has two sides to her personality that must be considered when figuring out her romantic potential. The best match for her younger-sister side is an older brother of sisters. The best match for her older-sister side is a younger brother of sisters. In making this analysis, it's important to keep in mind that, as pointed out earlier, her *opposite-sex* sibling is the key to computing romantic potential. Based on the gender and number of her siblings, we thus conclude that her best match is an older brother of sisters.

Finally, we factor in the age gaps issue. Her brother is much closer in age than her sister. In fact, her sister is so much younger that we can essentially rule her out as a significant influence. Because Britney's brother is only four years older, his influence on her personality would be the pivotal factor for her compatibility with a man. Her best match consequently should be an older brother of sisters.[3]

Worst Match

Your worst match depends almost entirely on whether you have older or younger opposite-sex siblings. It's also necessary to consider the number of siblings you have, as well as the age gaps separating you from them.

Let's illustrate with an analysis of Tom Cruise.

Middleborn Cruise grew up with two older sisters, one and three years older. He also has a younger sister one year younger. Because his sisters are so close in age to him, they would have had a profound impact on his personality, causing him to have super firstborn traits as well as super lastborn traits. So he has two potential worst matches. On the one hand, because he has a younger sister and likes to lead, his worst match would be an older sister of sisters.[4] On the other hand, because he has two older sisters and has a babyish lastborn quality, his worst match would be an only child.

Let's look at another example, which takes into account the *number* of siblings.

Helen has four younger brothers: two, three, five, and seven years younger. She's also got an older brother six years older. Knowing this, what's her worst match?

In this case, the fact that she has a large number of younger brothers means she'll be much more like an older sister than a younger sister. Additionally, the fact that two of her younger brothers are very close in age (two- and three-year age gaps) means she's got super firstborn traits. The worst match for the older sister of brothers is the older brother of brothers. In this situation, we can stop the analysis here, because Helen's older brother can be ruled out based on the fact that he's significantly older. As a result, we conclude that Helen should be on her guard if she finds herself in a romantic match with the older brother of brothers. They'll both want to be in the driver's seat, and Helen may also complain that her husband doesn't understand her sufficiently.

Advice for Dating a Middle Child

Before dating a middle child, it's a good idea to find out whether he has any opposite-sex siblings, the most important factor for understanding his romantic potential. The next most important matter is to find out how many siblings he has, as well as the age gap separating him from them. The following example illustrates how to analyze a middle child for dating potential.

Todd, a middle child, has three siblings: a sister four years older, a brother two years older, and a brother two years younger. The first thing to notice is that he has only one opposite-sex sibling, an older sister. This is the key factor to keep in mind because it makes him have laterborn traits. You know that younger brothers are creative, they have diverse interests, and they're easy to get along with. This quality is doubled in Todd because he's also got an older brother, so he should have twice as many laterborn traits. Keeping this in mind, you'll want to engage Todd in discussions about his creative pursuits. If he plays the drums or sings, ask whether you can attend one of his band rehearsals. Knowing he has diverse interests, press him to reveal other hobbies and avocations he may have. You can expect to find talking with him fun and enjoyable.

But don't forget that Todd also has a younger brother. This, too, is an important part of his personality, and it can't be neglected if you want a full picture of his psychological nature. As you know from reading the profile of the older brother of brothers, men with younger brothers like to lead, they're dominant, and they can be quite helpful if you have a problem. Keeping these qualities in mind, you might want to ask Todd for help with something you're working on, or listen to him give suggestions about life, something firstborns, and males in general, love to do.

Finally, you've got to get a composite portrait. Remember, you're dealing with a middle child here, not a firstborn or a lastborn. In putting the two profiles together, it's critical that you become sensitive to when Todd makes the switch from one to the other. If you're observant, you'll notice that he shifts from giving you advice about things (his firstborn persona) to smiling, laughing easily, and waiting for you to set the direction of the conversation (a lastborn trait).

A large part of the fun of going out with a middle child is in watching him make this switch between firstborn and lastborn personality, and in the process you'll get both interactive and narcissistic pleasure from the date.

Advice for Breaking Up

Breaking up with a middle child is usually more difficult than breaking up with a firstborn or lastborn because middle children have more complex ways of relating to people. For example, if you're breaking up with a middle girl who has older and younger sisters, she'll have related to you as both a firstborn and a lastborn. If you're a firstborn, you'll have enjoyed a strong interactive relationship with her lastborn persona. At the same time, you'll have had narcissistic attraction since she has a younger sister. For this reason, when breaking up with a middle child it's often helpful to talk about your reasons, which satisfies her firstborn need to verbalize and think logically about the situation. But it also helps to reassure her emotionally that you still care for her and wish to remain friends, which is what a laterborn needs more than anything—a continuing sense of emotional commitment and support.

If all goes well, you'll remain friends long after your breakup. But if you need to make a clean break, there's really no easy way to do it with a middle child. They have so much potential for relating to people, and their interaction style is so deep and long-lasting, that it may take years before you'll both be able to get used to the fact that you're no longer together.

Friendship and Middle Children

Always remember that middle children have the most friends. They're very popular, and everybody's going to want to be with them. This is because they have the ability to form lasting bonds of friendship with so many different types of people. You're always going to have to share your middleborn friend with others.

This doesn't mean you should worry about it. On the contrary, a middle child is a great friend because she can switch between two personas at a moment's notice. She can give you the relaxed, easy-going companionship that lastborns are famous for, and in the same afternoon provide you with the leadership and take-charge attitude of a firstborn. In fact, you'll often feel so comfortable with a middle child that you'll wish she would never go home. This is when you've got to be careful, because that middle child might start looking like a very good potential mate.

Career

As a middle child, you have more career options than others because you have both the creative lastborn traits we've discussed as well as many of the leadership and managerial skills of a firstborn. Jobs involving mediating, negotiating, and resolving conflict often appeal to you. These careers include being a lawyer, a diplomat, or a labor negotiator. In addition, careers in real estate, sales, and politics can be fulfilling because you'll work with many people and you'll need to find compromises.

At work you can expect to meet many individuals who will be attracted to you because they find you a good match. When going out with these people, keep in mind that you may have a preferred match based on the number and gender of your siblings.

For example, Bob, an insurance salesman, has an older sister two years older as well as a brother three years younger. Because he has a younger brother he's got a lot of leadership skills. Lastborn girls are attracted to him. But Bob realizes that his best match is an older sister of brothers because his only opposite-sex sibling is his older sister. For this reason, Bob keeps these younger sisters at bay, telling them that he's got other plans when they call him for dates. He's biding his time, waiting to meet the right woman. And when he does, he'll not only help her buy a great insurance policy, but he'll begin to exert his considerable younger brother charm.

Knowing that you have the potential to be attractive to many different kinds of people is flattering, of course. But knowing who you're a good match with is even more important. Remember to consider the gender and age gaps between you and your opposite-sex siblings when considering who to date. If you keep those things in mind, your middleborn charm will surely draw the perfect match to you before long.

Part 4

Common Problems and How to Overcome Them

Firstborn Rank Conflict

Who hasn't quailed at the endless parade of marriage mismatches? It's enough to make any young hopeful give up the chase, throw in the towel, and resign herself to being single. If so many beautiful, rich, privileged gods and goddesses can't find the right match—good grief! What hope is there for any of us?

As it turns out, there's more hope for us than you might think. By analyzing the types of conflict lovers routinely encounter, birth order theory helps us see how people can harmonize, in the best of cases, or how they can at least avoid getting on each other's nerves, in the worst of cases.

Some of the biggest relationship mistakes are made by people who aren't aware of the dynamics of conflict. At the outset of a relationship, lovers are on their best behavior, and conflict may not even be on their mind. But with marriage statistics so dismal,[1] it pays to think ahead about the types of conflict that might occur. What distinguishes good relationships from bad relationships is the degree and type of conflict present as well as the way that partners deal with it.

Rank Conflict

One of the most significant types of conflict you can experience is rank conflict.[2] Rank conflict can best be understood by imagining the presidents of two foreign nations in the same room. In this hypothetical example, they would each feel—presidential! Why should either defer to the other? Perhaps they might decide to work together on a mutually beneficial project, but even if they do, who is to set the direction and organize the proper approach to that problem? Who's to say when the problem is solved? And who's to direct their work? You can be sure that, no matter what they do or how they arrange their time together, they'll always feel the effects of rank conflict because they're both leaders.

Being firstborn is a lot like being president. You feel that you're in charge no matter where you go or what you do. At times when someone gives you directions, orders, or even advice, you wonder whether they've lost their mind. How dare they give orders to *the president!* There's a great feeling of entitlement that comes with being firstborn, but also an equally great fear of being undermined. At any moment, the opposing party—your younger siblings—may decide to launch a political attack upon the current president. This is why most firstborns are defensive.[3] And whenever you meet another firstborn, it's like meeting the president of another country. There's a moment of awkwardness, a struggle for power, and an underlying deep suspicion of the motives of the other person.

Now take two firstborns and put them into a romantic relationship. Just as with the two presidents, you're going to get conflict because, in most cases, two firstborns will fight over leadership issues.[4] They'll both want to be in the driver's seat when it comes to nearly every major issue a couple can encounter: Where should we live? What kind of car should we buy? What shall we name the kids? To put it in the simplest and most direct way possible: firstborns are control freaks. They like control so much that they often drive their partners batty. And why? Because they grew up ruling the roost over their younger siblings, and they're comfortable being the leader. It's all they know.

The rank conflict that we've described between two firstborns also occurs when you put two lastborns into a relationship, and we'll discuss lastborn rank conflict in the next chapter. Note that rank conflict can also occur between middle children. For example, if a boy with an older and a younger sister (like Tom Cruise) marries a girl with older and younger brothers, they'll have rank conflict because he'll want to be the boss (at least some of the time), and so will she.

Rank conflict is often hard to detect at the beginning of a relationship. This is particularly true when people are young and inexperienced at dating. The thrill of going out with someone new is so exciting that it clouds rational perception and makes underlying conflict difficult to perceive.

Ian and Irene are paramedics in their twenties. They're both firstborns, and they met on the job and discovered that they both liked going to museums. Before long they went to a museum together for their first date and everything seemed to be going well. The two young people had a lot in common, including the fact that their jobs were similar, they both liked modern art, and (something they joked about) they both had names starting with the same letter.[5] After dating for a few months, though, conflict started to become apparent. The underlying rank conflict wasn't strong enough to prevent them from initially being attracted to one another,[6] but after they began living together, that conflict came to the fore and proved difficult to deal with. They started arguing over power issues, such as who was going to decide what they would do, and six months later they broke up.

The moral of this story is that you need to be especially perceptive and sensitive to issues of rank conflict at the outset of a relationship. If you're a firstborn and dating another firstborn, no matter how physically attracted you are, or no matter how much you have in common, ask yourself whether you notice rank conflict bubbling up from beneath the surface. If you can feel it during the first few dates, it's likely to become even more pronounced later.

Professional Rank Conflict

Many doctors marry doctors, and lawyers often marry lawyers. Usually they meet in graduate school, fall in love, and get married soon thereafter. Since they have similar interests and career goals, they think it's a good match. But sometimes too much similarity can work against you in the form of firstborn rank conflict.

In many cases married doctors and lawyers are firstborns.

Firstborns tend to go further in their academic careers, so the higher you go in the academic world, the more likely you are to find that your classmates are firstborns. By the time you get to graduate and post-graduate programs, a large percentage of your classmates are going to be firstborns. When they become romantically involved, however, it may not be the best match.

Let's go back to the hypothetical about the two presidents. In some situations, they'll stop arguing and work together on a goal that's mutually beneficial. When they work together, there can be a lull in the conflict between them, especially when they're making progress toward some common goal or, as Sulloway has observed, during times of radical social revolution.[7] In a similar manner, two firstborns can temporarily bury the hatchet and work together side by side toward some common purpose. This is actually the best way for them to arrange their lives so that they don't fight. They turn their creative energies outward, and together they fight against some common enemy or work toward some common goal instead of fighting with each other. For example, two doctors may work together to open a clinic, develop a new drug treatment, or simply run a medical office. When they work side by side like this, their rank conflict will be less noticeable.

Firstborns Nick Lachey and Jessica Simpson did this to some extent, for example when they sang together on Simpson's 1999 album *Sweet Kisses*. This kind of side-by-side activity is the best way for firstborns to find peace and harmony.[8] The fact that they're similar in so many ways—both wanting to be in charge, for example—means that they'll be best when they work together on some project, such as recording a song or making a television show. But when they allow themselves to get contentious, they more often than not end up throwing lamps at one another . . . or finding that they just can't keep the relationship going.

Nick and Jessica

The breakup of Nick Lachey and Jessica Simpson may be the best thing that ever happened to *you* —if you're a firstborn. How's that possible?

Now I'll grant you that that may sound like a heartless thing to say, and it may be minimizing the angst the breakup certainly caused *them,* but the fact is that you can learn a lot about what *not* to do by considering their brief love affair and marriage. Let me describe their birth order, and let's see if you can spot the problem:

- Nick Lachey has numerous younger siblings of both sexes, the closest in age a brother, Drew, three years younger.
- Jessica Simpson has only one younger sister, Ashlee, four and a half years younger.

Wouldn't you say that these two were headed for firstborn rank conflict? Both firstborns, they were often at loggerheads over leadership issues. In fact, their marriage spats were aired on MTV for the world to see.

Not only were they both firstborns, but Nick was a super firstborn. The close age gap between Nick and his brother Drew, and the fact that he had numerous younger siblings, makes him have more firstborn characteristics than the average first child. He thus would be more controlling, more dominant, more critical than the average firstborn. Two firstborns often fight over leadership issues, so the fact that Nick and Jessica had many arguments shouldn't be surprising.

The lesson to be learned from their breakup is that firstborn rank conflict can be a kind of danger signal. It could mean that you'll find each other intolerable in the long run. Can you overcome these differences, or would it be better to call it quits and remain just friends?

Two Types of Temptation

After she began divorce proceedings with Nick, Jessica Simpson was spotted meeting occasionally in a coffee shop with a man who would have been a perfect match for her—Warren Beatty. Married for many years to actress Annette Bening, Beatty has a long history of relationships with beautiful women, including Madonna, Brigitte Bardot, Jackie Kennedy, Diane Keaton, Cher, Barbra Streisand, and others. But that's not why he'd be a perfect match for Simpson. When Beatty and Simpson meet for a chat, one could almost predict an instant rapport because she's a firstborn and he's a lastborn. (It would actually have been slightly better for *him* if Simpson had a younger *brother* instead of a younger sister.) Beatty, in fact, would be the *ideal* match for Simpson because he has a sister (actress Shirley MacLaine) three years older. This is precisely what a firstborn girl with a younger sisters needs—a lastborn boy with an older sister.[9] He was also sixty-eight, which is theoretically what Simpson should also be drawn to: an older man who can take the place of the father she looked up to all her life. Too bad he's already married, she must be thinking, because we get along *really* well.

All couples are vulnerable to temptation, but when two firstborns like Nick and Jessica are in a relationship, temptation usually comes from one almost irresistible source: lastborns, who have the uncanny ability to charm and win the hearts of firstborns, even when they're not trying to do so. This winning charm probably explains the fascination Simpson apparently had for Beatty. But in this case, temptation had another tentacle to snake around the forlorn older sister: Beatty was an older man.[10] As we discussed in Chapter 3, older sisters of sisters and older men are a dangerous mix.

When firstborn rank conflict rears its head in a relationship, be on your guard against these two types of temptation. Expect that both of you will be powerfully attracted to lastborns, and if one of you is an older sister of sisters, you can expect to have a thing for older male authority figures. Once you understand these two faces of temptation, you can consciously ward off the danger they pose to any relationship between two firstborns.

Kissing Conflict

Let me share an example of how firstborn rank conflict can go virtually unnoticed in a relationship, lurking underneath the surface to erupt when least expected. I've written several books on kissing and was holding a kissing seminar at a college, which involves directing four volunteer couples in kissing demonstrations in front of an audience. At this particular school, I was told by the director of student activities that all the participants were wonderful, loving couples. One couple in particular, Janet and Justin, were described as "beautiful." Indeed they were. Janet was a tall blonde who looked like a movie star. She had a cheerful, upbeat personality. Her partner looked like Paul Newman with blond hair. He had the same kind of smoldering good looks, but he lacked Newman's charm.[11] In fact I found him quiet, reserved, and almost shy. Typical of many elder brothers, he didn't enjoy being onstage.

During the show they had to do thirty different types of romantic kisses, including the upside-down kiss (where the boy leans over his partner and kisses her), the vacuum kiss (where he sucks the air out of her mouth during the kiss), and the French kiss. Most couples enjoy doing all of these demonstrations, and they usually get a kick out of performing them in front of a crowd of cheering classmates. But Justin never smiled once during the entire show. I was puzzled by this. Sure, he was a firstborn, but even firstborns loosen up sometimes and can have fun!

After the show I learned the reason for his demeanor. Janet confessed that she had told him, "Either you do this show with me, or we're through as a couple." In effect she had given him an ultimatum. She was exerting control over him by forcing him to participate in the kissing show, something she wanted to do because she had a theatrical flair and liked being in front of an audience. But Justin had no similar interest, and the only reason he agreed to do it was to keep the relationship alive.

Two firstborns can look happy to the world, but they may be suffering from a secret contest underneath the surface. Like Janet and Justin, one of them may be trying to exert control, and the other may be going along for the ride just to keep the relationship alive. They may look content on the outside, but in a situation like this, neither is really happy. Justin was sulking because he had to do something he hated. And Janet was suffering because her boyfriend was sullen and moody after the show, even though she had gotten her way and participated in the demonstration.

Teacher and Student

Many teachers are firstborns, especially at the college level. This is a natural result of the fact that firstborns go further in their academic careers than do other birth orders. In addition, students who appear most conscientious to their professors are often firstborns. This has been my experience in interacting with six thousand students over the past fifteen years. Especially attentive are older sisters, a reflection of the combination of gender and birth order effects: women are more compliant; firstborns, more conscientious. As a result, teachers will find that they have a natural affinity for firstborn students. And students, who often feel a transference effect when in a classroom, will feel a certain affinity for their teachers, a kind of unconscious attraction.[12] In not a few cases, this attraction can lead to romance in which firstborn rank conflict plays a part.

Angela was a bright student at a well-known California college. Henry was an associate professor in the sociology department. From the very first day of class, Angela felt an attraction toward her professor. As a result she was even more attentive than usual. She always sat in the first row, was on time with assignments, never missed a class, and frequently raised her hand to answer questions and participate in discussions. During breaks and after class, she frequently came to the front of the room to chat with Henry about the course, which she told him she found "fascinating." Before long Angela had developed a crush on her professor. Little did she realize it, but he felt the same way. During the semester Angela helped Henry work on an article he was writing, and after the class ended she continued to help him as a research assistant. By this time they were both in a stage of deep infatuation, and it would have been almost impossible to prevent them from dating. The university had a policy that prohibited dating students during the semester, but once a class was over, there was no bar to their going out together. Before long they were engaged, and within months they had become man and wife.

But as two firstborns, they had serious rank conflict. Within two years they were arguing so frequently that they often talked of separation or divorce. They didn't have children, which was another source of contention between them. Henry wanted children, but Angela did not—at least not right away. She was still in her mid-twenties, and she wanted to wait a few years. Henry, meanwhile, was in his late forties and wanted to start a family, even though he was having relationship problems with Angela. "The biggest problem was that once she stopped being my student, she no longer had a deferential demeanor around me. I really liked her when she was a student and a research assistant because she did what I asked," said Henry. A similar complaint troubled Angela. "I liked him when we were first dating because he never told me what to do except for the assignments and the research. But now he tells me when to cook, what to wear, and even when to have a baby! He's a monumental control freak, and I can't live with it." Within months of making these remarks, the two separated, and a year later their divorce was finalized. Angela subsequently began dating a number of middle children. Henry is currently married to another firstborn.

The fact that couples don't perceive firstborn rank conflict at the outset of a relationship means that they may be unpleasantly surprised after they begin dating or after they get married. It seems that birth order may not strongly affect marital choice, but it does impact marital satisfaction.[13] Consequently, at the beginning of a relationship it's important to be especially sensitive to issues of firstborn rank conflict. If you're dating a firstborn, ask yourself whether they're giving you the room you need to be yourself. Keep in mind that they're on their best behavior during these initial dates. Watch carefully for temperamental quirks that annoy you, such as telling you what to do, how to behave, and how to act. If it annoys you now, chances are that it will annoy you even more later on. As Angela and Henry discovered, initial attraction can be deceptive, and firstborn rank conflict can be the biggest stumbling block two firstborns experience, especially if they started out as student and teacher.

Searching

Recently I was a guest on a television show and had an opportunity to talk with two young women backstage. Both were knockouts.

They had been invited to the show to discuss their romantic life, so they were eager to talk about men, almost as practice for their segment. Both were firstborns, and neither had found the right match. One, the older sister of one sister, said, "My problem is that after a few weeks I fall in love with the guy, but as soon as I do he loses interest in me." I asked her what type of guy she had last been dating. What she said won't surprise you: "He was a firstborn, and we used to fight all the time." I explained to her that she might have been physically attracted to him but that he was a bad match. "Firstborns tend to want to always be in control," I said. As she listened, her eyes lit up. "You're right!" she said. "That's exactly what happened between us!"

The other girl had a younger brother and sister. "My problem is that I fell in love with this guy, but we broke up, and now I want to get back together with him." I asked why she wanted to get back together. "I just can't keep him out of my mind. I made a mistake by breaking up with him. He was just so much fun to be with." Naturally I asked what his birth order was, and what she said shouldn't surprise you: "He was a lastborn with one older sister." I told her that, all other things being equal, her relationship with him should be heaven on earth. She rolled her eyes and clapped her hands to her face in glee and hope. "Oh, if only we could get back together!" she said. "I felt that we had a great connection."

Both of these firstborn girls were searching for love. One appeared to be drawn to firstborn men, which was understandable. She was looking for the same strengths that she possesses. She admitted that people called her bossy and said she was demanding. But these same traits were also present in the guys she was dating—firstborn men. The other young woman was searching in the right direction and had found a good connection with a lastborn. I told the first to widen her net to include lastborn guys. "See how you enjoy their company," I suggested. "Compare them in your mind to the firstborn guys you've been dating. I bet you'll find that the lastborn men have a deeper rapport with you and that you enjoy their company a lot." She nodded thoughtfully. The other I urged to pursue the guy she had broken up with. "He's potentially a good match,"

I said. "Lastborn guys can be unpredictable, kooky, and creative. But that's just the kind of guy you need. You can keep him in line, and you'll enjoy doing it." She smiled, and once again I saw that I had hit the nail on the head. When you know what you're searching for, it makes the search that much easier. It can even make it fun.

How Sandra Bullock Avoided Rank Conflict— And How *You* Can Too

No birth order position is inherently better than any other—each has its positive and negative aspects. For many years it was thought that being firstborn was the best birth order position.[14] Research indicated that firstborns did better in school, were more conscientious, and gained higher academic degrees than laterborns.[15] Firstborns and only children also won more Nobel Prizes and were more likely than any other birth order to rise in a hierarchy, such as becoming president of the United States. Frank Sulloway's work has gone a long way toward reversing the way birth order theory favored firstborns, with *Born to Rebel* giving laterborns all the ammunition they need to argue that they're more creative, that they're more likely to come up with innovative ideas, and that they're the premiere original thinkers.[16]

Because each birth order has some negative aspects as well as some positive aspects, the prudent person compensates and tries to overcome the negatives. Probably no firstborn woman has done this better than Sandra Bullock. The first of two girls, she has consistently avoided rank conflict by dating lastborn men, including Ryan Gosling, Matthew McConaughey, and Tate Donovan. Of them all, the best match for her should have been Ryan Gosling because he had only one sibling, an older sister. Unfortunately he was much too young, so the match didn't last.

Sandra Bullock's husband, Jesse James (a distant descendant of the outlaw Jesse James), also has a sister, which ensures that the couple doesn't have total sex conflict. He's also got a reputation for being a bad boy (he hosts the Discovery Channel show *Monster Garage*)—just what a firstborn girl needs to keep her on her toes.

If you're dealing with firstborn rank conflict in a relationship, here are some suggestions on coping with the situation.

- Work side by side with your partner, like Nick and Jessica did when recording together. Those were their happiest days.

- Avoid open confrontation and power struggles.

- Try to see your partner's side of things.

- Realize that your partner will want to lead. Allow this in certain areas, and get consensus on which areas you'll each control.

- When children come along, let the wife care for the girls and the husband, the boys.

- Help your partner see the power struggle dynamics between you by talking about them. Don't let arguments fester and get worse.

The best way to avoid rank conflict is to look for a relationship with someone who's the opposite of yourself. The idea that opposites attract has a lot of validity, especially when it comes to birth order. Generally speaking, lastborns and firstborns tend to get along better than two firstborns in a romantic relationship. But if you're already attracted to a firstborn, or married to one, you can handle the situation if you keep in mind that *understanding* firstborn rank conflict is half the solution. Understanding your partner will help you cope with their natural bossiness and will ultimately allow you to get along much better.

CHAPTER 14

Lastborn Rank Conflict

What if you're a lastborn and you marry another lastborn—what lies ahead for you? The truth could be more alarming than you might think. . . .

So far we've looked at examples of rank conflict in the marriages of firstborns. But rank conflict is even more insidious when lastborns marry. In the case of two lastborns, you won't argue over who's in control or in charge of the situation. Instead, neither of you may spend too much time looking at or caring about the direction the relationship is going. You'll both like having a good time so much that you'll hardly ever get anything done. Lastborns are usually so laid-back, creative, and have so many diverse interests that you may never get organized enough to do the kinds of things that all married couples need to do to survive. The car insurance expired? So what, leave it till next week! The roof requires a new gutter? Who cares! My career could use some attention? Forget about it, I'll start a *new* career!

Good Vibrations

If you're like most people, you want good vibrations from a relationship. You want to feel that your partner is into you for all the right reasons. Naturally you want someone to be attracted to you physically, but beyond that there's emotional connection, a crucial element of any good relationship. Most girls know this better than guys. In fact guys can be overly focused on the physical, so much so that they often overlook emotional connection.

Ryan and Rhonda were both good-looking singers. They met while auditioning for a musical I was directing. During the first rehearsals they were often together. Ryan was a lastborn with one older sister, three years older. Rhonda was a lastborn with one older brother, four years older. The first thing to notice is that their names both start with the same letter and are two syllables long. This observation may sound irrelevant, but it actually has a scientific basis. People are drawn to others who have names that start with the same letter and have the same number of syllables, an unconscious narcissistic attraction.

Ryan was constantly flirting with Rhonda, trying to get her to date him, but she resisted just as ardently as he pursued. A model whose photos have appeared in major teen magazines, Rhonda was used to guys trying to date her. "Let's just say, I have no problem in that area," she says. "I've always been able to get dates. The question I've learned to ask myself is, 'Will I be happily matched with this guy?'" She had developed a system for weeding out guys, one more girls should use even if they aren't models. She'd ask herself not whether she was physically attracted to someone but whether she was emotionally attracted. Anyone who saw Ryan would admit that his looks were equal to hers; in fact, he had appeared on numerous TV soap operas and had the clean-cut good looks of a model himself. "I was attracted to him physically," admitted Rhonda. "It was just a matter of clicking. We got along fine on the set and were actually cast as husband and wife in numerous productions together. I just didn't feel a romantic connection."

Ryan told me, "She's one of the most beautiful women I've worked with, and I've worked with many attractive actresses." Once when they were cast in a musical together, he called me on the phone and begged me to write a new scene for him in which he would have to kiss Rhonda. I actually wrote the scene, but Rhonda dropped out of the production, and ironically he was compelled to kiss another actress, one he didn't like.

Lastborn rank conflict can account for much of Rhonda's disaffection. She was savvy enough to be able to step back from Ryan's hot pursuit and analyze whether she thought they were compatible. Ryan was never able to do this. He was always mesmerized by her beauty and charm. If they had gotten married, I suspect that they would have been divorced within a few years. Lastborns are personable and friendly, but when in a relationship together they often feel something missing. That missing element is the care and guidance they were used to from their older siblings.

Young Relationships

Jay and Christina felt they had the best relationship in the world. Both students at a Jesuit university, they went to parties together, worked on research projects as a team, and even performed in the same school plays. Jay had an older sister and brother, Christina had one older brother. Both lastborns, they were popular on campus. They had started dating in freshman year, and three years later they were still together and happier than ever.

Yet many relationships just like this run into rank conflict. . . . How can we explain this apparently happy couple?

Because they're both lastborns, Jay and Christina are going to be among the most agreeable and friendly people on campus. They're also going to be open to new experiences and have multiple interests. People are naturally drawn to agreeable people. And when Jay and Christina get together, their openness to new experiences leads them to explore the world together in new ways They join different clubs together, get involved in lots of extracurricular activities, and share new interests.

This usually works best for young couples during their school years, when financial responsibilities are at a minimum and the challenges of running a household aren't a factor. The likelihood that Jay and Christina will feel happy later in life is good, provided they can agree on how to handle the kinds of challenges that most couples face—buying a house, having children, and paying bills. Not that lastborns can't do these things, but in a relationship with two lastborns there's a tendency to expect your *partner* to handle such details.

This is a perfect time to point out a difference between firstborn and lastborn rank conflict. In the former, we're dealing with two people who, as a general rule, are more difficult to get along with, more stern, more neurotic, anxious, and judgmental. In the latter case, we're usually dealing with two party animals, friendly and personable individuals who everybody loves. The prognosis for two lastborns may look better than that for two firstborns, just because firstborns are so much more difficult to live with. But the difference is misleading because over time a relationship with two lastborns is more likely to run into subtle kinds of rank conflict problems.

While rank conflict between firstborns will lead to fights about who's in control, rank conflict between lastborns usually centers over who should be the one to relax while the other does the chores. A more insidious effect of lastborn rank conflict, which we'll deal with later, is that it can lead to temptation as the lastborn unconsciously yearns for a firstborn.

Who's the Star?

Admit it, you want to be the star in your relationship. You want to be the one who gets recognition for doing good, for being there when times are tough, for making the right moves and the smart choices. Everybody does.

But lastborns are used to the spotlight. They grew up with family attention focused on them. While firstborns are held up as models of good behavior and as the conscientious one who follows directions well, lastborns are often put in the middle of the living room and made to dance and sing for the amusement of friends and family. Laterborns have more of an audience (their older siblings) than firstborns while growing up. This is one reason they tend to become performers, comedians, singers, and stand-up comics more often than their older siblings.[1]

And it's also why they want to be the star in their relationships. They want to tell the funny stories, get the laughs, and have people applaud their antics.

"I went to a meeting recently," says Ryan, a lastborn, "and the host asked if there was anyone in the audience who wished to make a comment. Naturally I wanted to because I love being onstage. But I acted shy, as if I didn't want to say a word. I was hoping people would push me up there to get me to speak. And after a while, when no one else volunteered, I was delighted when they picked me to voice my concerns. I just loved it!"

This is typical lastborn thinking. Ryan is describing a feeling that most lastborns have—they like public attention and are comfortable when they're put on the spot. For this reason there's often a subtle struggle for attention with lastborn couples, which is quite different from firstborn rank conflict. Two lastborns may not openly fight for control, but they will think their partner is hogging the spotlight when he or she tells more jokes and gets more laughs at a family or social gathering.

The way to deal with this kind of lastborn rank conflict is to admit that your partner has things to contribute too. Let him or her tell stories. Then see if you can top them. Another approach to this problem is to see if you can learn anything by listening to your partner carry on. Sometimes you'll notice comedic skills that you yourself can employ next time you speak.

But sharing the stage with another lovable and funny lastborn can be challenging. If you suspect they're upstaging you, that's a natural reaction. That's one aspect of lastborn rank conflict—a subtle sense of loss in a relationship where two lastborns are both consciously or unconsciously vying for attention and feeling that their partner is stealing the show.

Is It a Deal Breaker?

Is lastborn rank conflict a make or break issue?

Three lines of evidence argue that it is, that lastborn rank conflict is indeed something to be *avoided* at all costs in a relationship. First is the theoretical argument that, all other things being equal, you'll be happier with someone who matches your siblings' birth rank.[2] Second are clinical studies on rank conflict, which suggest that you should avoid it.[3] And third is anecdotal evidence that last-born rank conflict creates problems in relationships.[4]

Are these arguments proof positive that lastborn relationships are the end of the earth? Certainly not. They merely suggest that there's a force at work in lastborn relationships which may prove troublesome for couples. Once we take into account the fact that lastborn rank conflict can pose a problem, we can look at successful lastborn relationships to see how some lucky and inventive couples get around the problems.

James and Pauline are two lastborn college students, and they work together on the student newspaper. They're happily dating. Although they're happy together on a daily basis, we must observe, however, that they're young and without the kinds of complex problems that often stymie more mature lastborn couples. In addition, they deal with the issue of lastborn conflict (albeit unconsciously) by having firstborn friends who provide them with the kind of guidance and planning capability they need in their lives. James is friendly with Emma, a firstborn who has a younger brother. She provides helpful editing advice and also suggestions for which stories he should cover. "She's like a mentor to me," says James. "I can always rely on her to give objective and insightful criticism. I need that kind of feedback in my life and career."

Pauline relies on Eric, the editor of the newspaper. "He's so grounded," says Pauline. Eric, who has a younger brother and sister, says he also enjoys working with Pauline. "She's one of the most creative people on the paper," he says. "We have a very professional relationship, but I also know that I can call her at any time of day or night and give her an emergency story. For example, when the water main broke on campus, I called her at 2:00 a.m. and she got out of bed and covered the emergency. It got her a first-page by-line too."

The case of James and Pauline illustrates how lastborn rank conflict can be ameliorated by having firstborn friends who provide the kind of working relationships and guidance that lastborns need but aren't getting from their partner. Couples without such support systems and social networks may have a more difficult time coping with the disorganization and chaos that lastborn rank conflict produces. But when such support networks are in place, two lastborns can enjoy their relationship to the fullest and also be tremendously creative and productive.

Some relationships, though, run into more difficulties with lastborn rank conflict than others. Consider the case of Liz Taylor and Richard Burton.

Taylor and Burton

Of all Elizabeth Taylor's many husbands (and there have been seven to date) none was as famous as Richard Burton. She married him twice and divorced him twice. There was something about Taylor and Burton that caught the public's imagination and set it on fire like none of her other husbands or companions. Maybe it was the way they looked together. Maybe it was the way they acted. But more probably it was the way they fought.

A friend of the family who visited them in their hotel said of the two, "They've been acting like a couple of kids in a playpen."[5] This sentiment often fairly characterizes the way two lastborns act together. Taylor and Burton were cast in the film version of Edward Albee's *Who's Afraid of Virginia Woolf*, and biographer C. David Heymann reports that "there were elements of similarity between the real and the screen couple."[6] In other words, they were constantly fighting about trivial things.

But to date no one has really tried to explain why Taylor and Burton fought so much. Both raised as lastborns, their interaction was probably the result of lastborn rank conflict.[7] The same pattern can be seen in many relationships between lastborns. They're used to living a carefree life, lolling about and being creative. Indeed, Taylor and Burton lived rather sloppily, even letting their dog sleep in the hotel bed with them so often that the smell permeated the mattress and caused management to add the cost of a new mattress to their bill. What a lastborn needs is an organized, agenda-toting, goal-oriented firstborn to keep him on track and give him the kind of attention and interaction that will make him feel loved. With

Taylor and Burton, however, one suspects that they both felt like kids again in the relationship. That can be fun for a while, but eventually, when you don't sense the kind of connection you need, you'll tend to react as Taylor and Burton did, by arguing and getting on each other's nerves.

Temptation and the Lastborn

When lastborn rank conflict is present in a relationship, both partners are more easily tempted by firstborns. The lastborn perceives the steady, planning, conscientious firstborn as a psychological safe haven and refuge from the chaos and childishness of his primary relationship.

Toward the end of his first marriage with Taylor, Burton went to Rome and stayed with Carlo Ponti in his fifty-room mansion. The Italian film producer was married to Sophia Loren, a firstborn with one younger sister. Loren felt an immediate attraction for Burton. During his stay, Burton and Loren, who was twenty-five years younger than Ponti, spent time alone together on many occasions. "They took long walks and drives in the country," says Taylor's biographer, "played Scrabble, and went swimming. He spent one weekend alone with her on the Ponti yacht."[8] Taylor soon arrived in Rome to keep an eye on her wayward husband, but their marriage had by this time been strained to the breaking point. As for Burton and Sophia Loren's relationship, one could easily see how they might be attracted to one another—between them there was no lastborn rank conflict as there was between Taylor and Burton.[9]

Two lastborns may be in love or may be attracted to each other, but in a relationship they're often at a loss for how to arrange their lives to achieve maximum compatibility. Like Taylor and Burton, they're each seeking something the other can't easily supply—the loving and guiding quality of leadership. Their dissatisfaction with their partner's personality and their lack of genuine interaction[10] more than likely was a major contributor to Taylor and Burton's divorce.

○○○○●

Celebrity Case Study

SARAH JESSICA PARKER AND ROBERT DOWNEY JR.

Ironically, Robert Downey Jr. and Sarah Jessica Parker—two lastborns—met while working on the film *Firstborn*. Within eight weeks Downey decided to move in with her. Little did they realize that they were setting themselves up for seven years of nonstop rank conflict.[11] Their relationship was a classic case of lastborn rank conflict; and the same pattern—chaos, childishness, and creativity—can be seen in many relationships between lastborns.

One major chaotic ingredient was the physical setup of their living quarters: their apartment was like a crash pad for young actors and creative people. In addition, during these years, they suffered from an absence of career direction and business sense. Both Downey and Parker took a hit-or-miss approach to work.[12]

The second major sign of lastborn rank conflict is the general naïveté that surrounds the relationships of lastborns. True to form, Downey and Parker drifted along, living like children. "The worst thing you can say about a few of us, myself included, is that we didn't fully grow up," says Kiefer Sutherland, who lived with the couple for a few years.[13] This free and easy collegiate-style living is typical of artists, but it's often problematic when both partners in the relationship fall into the same pattern.

The third hallmark of lastborn rank conflict is the clash of two unguided creative lives. Lastborns are often too focused on their own creative pursuits to take the time to relate well to their partner. True, lastborns are usually charming and affable, and Downey and Parker fit this description, but lastborn rank conflict leaves them each seeking something that the other can't supply—the loving and guiding quality of leadership. They especially need this leadership to guide them in their creative careers. Toman points out that a younger sister of brothers, like Parker, "would miss the sense of leadership and responsibility she is used to with her brothers."[14]

Although Downey's substance abuse is a separate problem from rank conflict, lastborns are more likely to do risky things[15] such as experiment with drugs. Parker claims that Downey's drug problems caused their breakup, but underneath such obvious difficulties was the much more intractable issue of rank conflict, leaving them both unfulfilled and unsatisfied. They broke up in 1991.

165

Avoiding Lastborn Rank Conflict

It's overly simplistic, of course, to claim that two lastborns or two firstborns can't be happy together. They certainly can be happy; however, it's important for them to remember that they'll inevitably experience rank conflict. Once lovers understand this dynamic, they can be more forgiving.

But if you're a single lastborn, it's best to seek out a firstborn. Let's say you have the same birth order as Sarah Jessica Parker—two older brothers and an older sister. (If you have only one older brother, the analysis is identical.) For the sake of compatibility, choose a guy who has one or more younger sisters. Your ideal match would be a firstborn, although a middle child who has one or more younger sisters would also be a good catch. If you marry another lastborn, you'll almost always experience some of the disquieting effects of lastborn rank conflict.[16] You might want to save yourself the emotional roller-coaster ride by selecting a compatible partner right from the start.

CHAPTER
15
○○●○○

Sex Conflict

Sex conflict . . . sounds like it might be a very interesting topic, and let me assure you that it *is*. But it's got nothing to do with *sexual* relations. Instead it has everything to do with *interpersonal* relations, and more specifically with how well people get along with and understand the opposite sex.

In the context of birth order and compatibility, sex conflict[1] refers to the communication and relationship problems that occur when a person grows up without opposite-sex siblings.[2] Individuals from single-sex sibling constellations have significantly less opportunity during their formative years to interact with peers of the opposite sex, so they generally encounter more trouble as adults understanding a spouse than do people who grow up with opposite-sex siblings.[3]

Partial sex conflict exists when only *one* partner in a relationship has no opposite-sex siblings. When sex conflict is partial, as in the marriage of Tom Cruise and Nicole Kidman, for example, only *one* of the partners experiences difficulty understanding the other. (In this case, it was Kidman, who has no brothers, who would have experienced the difficulty.)

Total sex conflict exists when *both* partners in a relationship lack opposite-sex siblings. Total sex conflict (as with J-Lo and Ben Affleck) is a more deep-rooted problem and should raise a warning flag for any couple. While it's not an insurmountable obstacle, there should be good reasons for a couple to stay together if total sex conflict exists. One benefit, however, that Walter Toman suggested might exist when both partners have no opposite-sex siblings is that neither would have the advantage over the other.[4] Perhaps this is why so many of these relationships *do* seem to work.

Examples of Sex Conflict

Let's look at two examples of how sex conflict worked to impair relationships.

Zachary grew up the last of three boys. His father died when he was in grade school, and he was raised by his mother and two critical older brothers. He was extremely intelligent, but his social skills were limited. He wore rumpled clothes, rarely combed his hair, and mumbled when speaking. After high school, he began a relationship with Alexis, a beautiful girl who had abundant social skills and who came from a middle-class family. Alexis had one younger sister, who was autistic. Her parents disapproved of Zachary, but the two were often together. Alexis and Zachary dated often and had sex frequently, but the two would not talk much. Within three months they began seeing other people.

Zachary began dating Victoria, who had a younger brother. She seemed to have a much better rapport with him than Alexis. On dates Victoria and Zachary often talked, and she was quite helpful to him, coming to his apartment and cleaning the kitchen. Meanwhile Alexis entered into a series of relationships with different men but never found one that satisfied her.

On analysis, the relationship of Zachary and Alexis appears to have ended largely because of total sex conflict. Lack of communication and understanding eventually caused them to break up. Although they had a good sexual relationship, ironically that wasn't enough to overcome their sex conflict—that is, their difficulty understanding each other.

Another example illustrates how even partial sex conflict can cause problems in a relationship.

Otis and Emily have no rank conflict: he's lastborn, she's firstborn. He grew up with an older sister and brother. She grew up with one younger sister. They met in college in the computer club. They dated for six years and seemed to be heading toward marriage. Everyone who knew them thought they had a lot in common: both were intellectuals, both liked computer programming, and both were interested in scientific careers. But increasingly they found that they had difficulty communicating. Emily would have tantrums and, according to Otis, would demand that he do certain things, such as drive slower or wear a certain shirt. "She didn't seem to understand me," says Otis. Emily was the one who eventually broke off the relationship. Their problems were less severe than the previous couple's (evidenced by the fact that they stayed together six years) because Otis and Emily didn't suffer from total sex conflict; the fact that Otis had an older sister meant that only Emily experienced sex conflict. But in this case it contributed to the difficulties between them because she had a hard time understanding Otis, who everyone else considered kind and easygoing. "She just didn't appreciate his great qualities," said a friend after their breakup.

Sex conflict doesn't mean that a relationship is impossible. It does mean, however, that those who have no opposite-sex siblings may have to work harder to understand their partners. It's difficult enough for people *with* opposite-sex siblings to understand their partners sometimes, so the challenge faced by someone with little or no experience living with peers of the opposite sex can be formidable.

And yet many relationships work despite sex conflict. What can account for this harmony?

How Sex Conflict Can Be Overcome

A number of mitigating factors can offset the problems posed by sex conflict. First, in the case of total sex conflict, neither partner has an advantage because both suffer from the same handicap. While total sex conflict is theoretically worse than partial sex conflict, it may in some cases work as an equalizing factor that smoothes over difficulties since both partners experience the same obstacle to understanding.

Bob and Amanda are from single-sex sibling constellations. Bob is a middle child with one younger and one older brother;

Amanda has one younger sister. Bob and Amanda are happily married, have three children, and report no conflict. "We get along fine," says Bob. "He's a wonderful man and a complement to the family," says Amanda's aunt, who knows them well.

In this relationship total sex conflict, which is typically a hindrance to understanding, actually seems to be working to foster equality and harmony. "We're very good together," says Bob. "I expect it has something to do with the fact that we're both logical and we like to talk out our problems instead of yelling at each other like some couples." The fact that they each have sex conflict may be an equalizing factor in this relationship. Their similar approach to logical discussion of problems is another helpful factor working to keep them happily married.

A second way that sex conflict can be mitigated is if one partner has more understanding by virtue of having grown up with cousins or friends of the opposite sex who substituted for opposite-sex siblings. When asking about families, it's important to inquire into who the person grew up with. If the family adopted a child, or a cousin came to live with the family, that adoptee or cousin becomes a functional sibling. Functional siblings, although not blood brothers or sisters, have a similar psychological effect on the developing child.

Yet a third way that sex conflict can be mitigated is by other factors taking precedence over sex conflict, such as the narcissistic attraction of two firstborns or the shared goals of two people in the same career. An example of the former situation would be an older brother of brothers dating an older sister of sisters. Both firstborns, they might feel a keen understanding of one another and identify so strongly that narcissistic attraction becomes the glue keeping them together. Two people sharing the same career goals can sometimes live side by side and be so career-focused that sex conflict poses less of a problem than it otherwise would. An example of such a relationship is the marriage of Nick Lachey and Jessica Simpson. During their first year together they both worked on their singing so that their partial sex conflict (Jessica Simpson has no brothers) was less problematic.

Friendship and Sex Conflict

Sex conflict also operates in non-romantic relationships, such as between friends or roommates. Sex conflict has been shown to impair the ability of same-sex college roommates to get along. Roommates who have sex conflict experience greater friction than those who do not. For example, older sisters of sisters are generally more compatible with younger sister of sisters than they are with older sisters of brothers.[5] In the latter case, there is partial sex conflict because the older sister of brothers isn't used to living with girls.

Ironically, then, the sex conflict that people from single-sex sibling constellations experience in their romantic relationships is *not* present in their friendships with persons of the same sex. In other words, a younger brother of brothers, who would experience sex conflict in romantic relationships with women, would *not* experience it in friendships with men.[6] This has important implications for dealing with sex conflict in romantic relationships. If you're going out with a person from a single-sex sibling constellation, it's a good idea to allow your partner free time to associate with his same-sex friends.

The Dynamics of Sex Conflict

Looking at sex conflict can give us insights into the dynamics of relationships that aren't readily available using other measures of compatibility. For this reason, calculating the amount of sex conflict that you'll potentially experience is an important consideration for anyone starting a relationship. The following points may help when considering a relationship in which sex conflict is present.

- In some cases, you may prefer a relationship with sex conflict. Samantha, the older of two girls, appeared to have deeper insights into Jonathan, a musician, than other potential partners, even women with brothers. Because of her education, upbringing, and life experiences, she had developed keen insights into artistic men. In such a case, a relationship with Samantha may prove to be more satisfying for Jonathan than a relationship with a woman who has no sex conflict.

• If you have sex conflict (you grew up in a single-sex sibling constellation or you're an only child), you may wish to minimize the advantage of a potential partner by selecting someone who *also* has sex conflict. In such a situation, neither of you may have keen insights into one another. Sometimes this can be an interesting type of relationship because your partner will always possess a sense of mystery and there will always be something new to discover. This dynamic can also add to the romantic fun of a relationship. The relationship of Bob and Amanda, described earlier in this chapter, fits this pattern.

• You may prefer a partner who has sex conflict because you find him or her sexier. Persons with sex conflict are often more stereotypically male or female.[7] As one writer put it, "the 'masculine male' and the 'feminine female' may be the most socially desirable, in that they conform to normative expectations."[8] Sean Connery, the older brother of a brother, who was James Bond in seven films, and Brigitte Bardot, the older sister of a sister, who was an international sex symbol, are two examples from the cinema of stereotypically male and female superstars with sex conflict. If you prefer a partner who is more stereotypically male or female, then you may actually seek out a person *with* sex conflict. The one exception to this pattern is the older sister of sisters, who often has instrumental or masculine traits. But younger sisters of sisters are exceptionally feminine,[9] and older brothers of brothers as well as younger brothers of brothers are very masculine.[10]

• You may prefer a partner with sex conflict in the hope that you'll argue less. Levinger and Sonnheim suggest that growing up with opposite-sex siblings might "set up certain obstacles to subsequent adult functioning."[11] In other words, individuals who have sex conflict might be *more* suited to romantic relationships because persons from single-sex sibships won't bring childhood opposite-sex sibling squabbles into a new relationship. Instead, they will treat partners as adults to be respected and related to in a mature way. If this dynamic is the controlling one in your relationship, then your choice of a person from a same-sex sibling constellation might result in fewer arguments. Erica had a younger sister and brother, but her boyfriend, Patrick, the older of two boys, had sex conflict. Yet they almost never argued. Patrick had no childhood experience arguing with a sister, so he never got into arguments with Erica. She found it odd, but once she got used to it she liked the "peaceful and calm" nature of their relationship. Because of the partial sex conflict, there was less understanding between them, but that was acceptable to her because of the reduced arguing.

- You may prefer a partner without sex conflict in the hope that you'll argue *more*. This may sound paradoxical, but stay with me because it's an important point. People without sex conflict (that is, people who have opposite-sex siblings) are often well versed in the give and take of sibling arguments, and they may relish a good argument with opposite-sex partners. Such arguments are not heated and angry discussions but may be intimate exchanges of opinion, friendly banter, or playful cajoling. Tom was enamored of a married woman, Arlene, who had an older brother who was three years older. During her childhood, Arlene learned to argue with her brother in a playful way. When she was with Tom, she flirted with him by getting into playful arguments about inconsequential matters. "I love talking with her," says Tom. "She can talk about anything. She even likes to arm wrestle when we talk. I think she's flirting with me, and I'd love to have a relationship with someone like that. Just knowing her has taught me a lot about the kind of girl I want to marry." Not long afterward, Tom met Raquel, who has two older brothers. "Raquel has the same kind of arguing skills as Arlene," says Tom, "and it's really fun to talk with her because she never gives up in a debate. Sometimes it can get to be too much, but usually it's wonderful. I can't imagine that we'll ever run out of things to talk—and *argue*—about!" The playful interactions between them are the glue keeping them together.

Despite the above scenarios, in most cases it can be expected that you'll prefer a partner who has no sex conflict. Even Toman's severest critics, Levinger and Sonnheim, admit that "there may be clear-cut advantages in having had intimate opposite-sex exposure as a child."[12] You thus would be opting to select a relationship without sex conflict in hopes of having more understanding and better communication.

If you have no opposite-sex siblings, you may relish the added attention and understanding that you'll get from a partner who does *not* have sex conflict. Ashley, a gourmet cook and an only child, enjoyed her relationship with Oliver, a lastborn with an older sister. They seemed to click from the first moment she met him. "He's fun to be with and he's considerate," she says. "I like him and we get along fine." Oliver's side of the story is different. In his opinion the relationship is somewhat less than ideal. "She doesn't really listen very well," he says. "It's a good and loving marriage, but I do miss the warmth I had from Carly [his former girlfriend, who had two younger brothers]. My wife doesn't ask about my work much, whereas Carly always did." In this relationship, sex conflict is at work, but it's having a different effect for both partners. From Ashley's point of view, the fact that Oliver has *no* sex conflict is working to her advantage since Oliver is very understanding and attentive. From Oliver's point of view, the fact that Ashley *does* have sex conflict is working against him since his wife doesn't care for him as much as other partners did. The sex conflict issue isn't *ruining* their marriage, but it is affecting it in subtle ways, causing a slight dissatisfaction for Oliver and a slight buzz of warmth for Ashley.

The lesson to be learned from this relationship is that if you have sex conflict and you select a partner who *doesn't,* you can expect to be understood and loved, but you should be aware that your partner may experience a subtle sense of dissatisfaction. Try to make this up to him in some way. Ashley is careful to make elaborate meals for her husband because she wants to, in effect, pay him back for his understanding. The one thing she can do, because she's a gourmet cook, is to satisfy his desire to eat well. In many cases the dynamics of sex conflict can be worked out to everyone's mutual satisfaction, but it sometimes takes a little thinking and planning to make it an equal equation.

It's prudent to consider the issue of sex conflict carefully before making a commitment to any particular partner. During the dating phase of a relationship, you'll get a chance to discover how sex conflict affects your relationship. If you're like most people, you'll want to avoid or reduce sex conflict by choosing a partner who has an opposite-sex sibling. But, as in some of the examples above, you may wish to choose a partner who *has* sex conflict, either because they appear more masculine or feminine, because they'll have less of an advantage over you, or because they are, by virtue of their education, experience, and temperament, more understanding of you and your career goals than other individuals. Whatever your preference, knowing *how* sex conflict can affect the dynamics of a relationship will give *you* the advantage.

How to Deal with Sex Conflict

Chances are that you'll encounter sex conflict in many of your romantic relationships. The following are some techniques you can use to defuse potential problems.

- Allow your husband to go out with the boys or your wife to go out with the girls. They'll appreciate the time spent with their same-sex friends.

- Encourage your partner to talk about what's wrong. Ben Affleck had the right idea when arguing with J-Lo. Getting the differences out on the table always helps.

- Be extra considerate in explaining your motives, thinking, and feelings to a romantic partner who has no opposite-sex siblings. They may have a difficult time understanding where you're coming from, and your explanations will help them feel closer to you.

- Become friends with your partner's siblings. By looking at the dynamics of your partner's relationships with his same-sex siblings, you can learn a lot about how he'll relate to *you*.

Remember that sex conflict isn't an insurmountable problem. If you're already in a relationship or marriage, understanding the potential problems will really help you deal with them. You can actually make relationships work that have stumped celebrities because understanding the problem is half the solution.

If you're not yet in a relationship, the best thing to do is to avoid sex conflict, or at least consider its implications whenever you can, especially during the dating phase. You and your partner will both be happier if you make a wise choice at the outset and select someone with whom you're highly compatible.

16
○○●○○

Communication Problems

Why do some couples who seem to have it all break up? Usually the individuals involved don't even realize what the difficulty is, but *you* will when you discover the secret to good relationships based on birth order differences in communication style. You'll be able to predict which couples will last and which won't. You'll also discover how communication problems caused by birth order can, in some cases, be overcome.

Most communication problems stem from the tendency of people to replicate their early life experiences at a time when this isn't appropriate. Firstborns and lastborns have different childhood experiences dealing with siblings, and consequently they wind up with different communication styles as adults. The basic issue in communication difficulties is knowing how people with different birth orders approach speaking and listening. Firstborns and lastborns often have different expectations of what a conversation should mean and achieve. Deborah Tannen has done a brilliant job of describing gender-based communication differences in her book *You Just Don't Understand: Women and Men in Conversation,* which I highly recommend. But conversational styles also differ based on birth order. In fact, gender and birth order effects interact to produce some of the most difficult communication problems.

Lastborn Communication Style

In most families, a lastborn is subject to both doting love as well as contentious bullying. Lastborns thus grow up with a variety of skills reflecting this varied experience. On the one hand, they know how to interact gracefully and bask in the limelight of attention; on the other hand, they know how to withstand criticism and attack better than firstborns. These skills contribute to their greater agreeableness, but a lastborn's communication strategies can nevertheless lead to conflict and problems, especially for those who don't know how to deal with this type of communicator.

Depending on whether their older siblings are boys or girls, there are striking differences in how lastborns communicate.

The younger brother of brothers loves conversations that meander here and there, touching upon all the intricacies of a subject. He is quick to sidestep a verbal attack and often hotheaded in his approach to argumentation, bullying forward as if he were fighting a big brother. When provoked, he can boil over into anger, although he's less likely to reach this critical point than firstborns because he's had to weather years of insults and taunting from older brothers, and he's more used to it and better able to deal with it in a friendly way. When talking with a younger brother of brothers, challenge him on every turn. He likes to fight in conversation; he actually enjoys the give and take of debate. Don't be afraid to contradict what he says and challenge it. This is the kind of talk he enjoys.

Younger brothers of sisters expect to receive attention from women. They tend to be babyish and boyish, waiting for girls to dote on them. By being charming, they can often get girls to do things for them. As the first male of the family, they also display masculine bravado and like to be considered macho, even though they're often quite sensitive and empathetic because of their close relationship with their sisters.

When talking with a younger sister of sisters you can go in any direction you wish. She'll follow your lead better than a hound on the track of a fox. Switch topics at will, bring in irrelevant side points, digress to your heart's content—you won't throw her for a loop. She has the wonderful ability to be distracted easily and talk about anything. But make her feel that you care about her point of view. And finally, let her talk about herself. She yearns to be understood.[1] But the younger sister has a flip side: because her older sisters were often bullying and critical, the younger sister has a competitive nature and likes to work toward some goal. For this reason she's great when it comes to talking business strategy.

Younger sisters of brothers enjoy teasing and flirting, something they did with their big brothers. They also enjoy hearing stories. You don't have to be another Shakespeare to keep the younger sister of brothers enthralled. Just keep piling on the emotional and feeling details, things like: "And then he raised his voice and seemed to be exasperated when he was saying . . ." or, "He seemed upset about the situation, but I don't know why." That last one is a sure winner with her because she loves a good mystery and will try to analyze the interpersonal situation for you.

By understanding these different conversational styles, you'll be better prepared to avoid conflict and get along with lastborns.

Only Child Communication Style

Male only children are such confident speakers that they strike other people as boastful. Rudy Giuliani, former mayor of New York, is a good example. A male only child's confidence comes from growing up the darling of his parents. As a result he does very well in academic and business environments. Because he has no younger siblings, he also has many of the agreeable characteristics of lastborns. He can be quite friendly and amusing as a conversationalist. Of course, *his* comments will be the most important. The way to enjoy a conversation with a male only child is to realize that he'll orient himself toward praise like a magnet lining up with magnetic north.

Female only children are much less verbal than their male counterparts. They typically take a listening role in conversations and try to avoid arguments. If they have mothers who are firstborns, they adopt firstborn characteristics and interrupt people. The way to have a good conversation with a female only child is to talk about her heroes. She also responds well to praise, like the male only child, but she has less self-confidence and is more liable to doubt kind words and suspect flattery.

Firstborn Communication Style

Firstborns like to give information and instructions. They grew up doing this, and they continue the practice as adults. This is a masculine modality, but even firstborn women tend to slip into this commanding and preachy style when they become managers or are in other positions of authority. Another firstborn conversational ploy consists in cutting off other speakers. This, too, is a masculine tactic,[2] but one that is also employed by firstborn women. Overall, firstborns are more suspicious of the motives of other people and are more neurotic, traits that make their communication style more quirky, defensive, and domineering than that of lastborns.

Older brothers of brothers like to control the direction and topics of conversations more than others. They also use bullying and self-praise more than lastborns. A typical example of firstborn hubris is talkmeister Don Imus,[3] whose sarcasm led to his dismissal from his job at CBS.[4] But older brothers of brothers also have a kind and considerate side. At times they had to care for their younger brother, so they learned to be helpful. They can listen especially well to men's problems, and they can offer solutions that often turn out to be excellent.

Older brothers of sisters are exceptional listeners. As youngsters they learned to be considerate of the opposite sex. As adults they act with kindness and courtesy toward both men and women. Examples of firstborn listening skills include Sigmund Freud and Carl Jung, both of whom turned listening into a profession.

Older sisters of brothers are empathetic listeners when the speaker is a male. They learned this skill from listening to their younger brothers. They can also take a very dominant role in a conversation. When they're in positions of authority, they take charge verbally and can be demanding. Their maternal side is always present in their conversations. They can be solicitous and offer suggestions. A good way to enjoy a conversation with an older sister of brothers is to ask for advice.

Older sisters of sisters can be as dominant as older brothers of brothers. Even as teenagers these young women are little Amazons, with the confidence and conversational strength of firstborn males. They can easily bully others in conversations and cut them off.[5] Their helpful side comes out when they use their inherent ability to guide others, a skill they developed while helping their younger sisters.

Understanding these communication styles can help you get along better with firstborns. When there's a firstborn you wish to impress, listen carefully to his comments and let him talk himself out. He'll have so many things to tell you and so many instructions that you may laugh to yourself at how controlling he sounds. By allowing him to have his say, you can win his loyalty. Then you can get in a few words edgewise and set him straight about things he may know nothing about.

Middleborn Communication Style

Middleborns have two conversational styles: bossy firstborn style, and laid-back lastborn style. Knowing this can help you communicate with them.

You begin by waiting for a middle child to slip into her bossy firstborn role. She'll raise her voice and badger and beleaguer you with pleas to do things her way. Just keep your cool and wait patiently until she calms down. At this point she's apt to switch into her much more accommodating younger sibling role, which means that the two of you can talk reasonably about the subject. Not only that, but she'll be amazed that you didn't get into an argument with her. Most people fight fire with fire, and when she's in her older sister role, she's like a tiger and provokes aggressive verbal banter from coworkers, friends, and family. But if you see through all that and you're calm and collected, she'll think you're an angel.

Once you understand middleborn changeableness, you may be able to communicate with middle children better than their friends and family members, who are usually puzzled by their temperamental personality. Just wait until they switch into their younger sibling role, and then you're sure to find that communication becomes much easier and more pleasant.

Lastborn Communication Problems

Although lastborns are, as a general rule, more pleasant in conversations, their communication styles can lead to problems when people don't realize where they're coming from or what their intentions are. These problems can occur whether it's another lastborn or a firstborn who is talking with them.

Steven is a lastborn and a very successful actor. On dates he sits in his girlfriend Heather's living room and talks about how many push-ups he can do or what he's going to accomplish in Hollywood. Heather listened patiently at first, waiting for him to say something nice about her hair or her cooking—or anything. But Steven never did. "He talked about himself so much and in such an egotistical way that I never felt he loved me," says Heather, who is also a lastborn. It wasn't that Steven lacked romance. In fact he was a very loving, caring person. I had seen him in tears during an audition, and I knew he was capable of deep emotional expression. It was just that he felt his life revolved around himself and he didn't care what was going through Heather's mind. When he was growing up, his older sister was very controlling, and he had developed an independent streak that taught him to talk about himself but not to listen. Subconsciously what Steven was doing was waiting for Heather to take a doting big-sister role toward him in which she would listen to his rambling talk and rein him in, even guiding the conversation. But Heather, being a lastborn, never reacted this way.

Heather preferred being with Tommy, who was a photographer and a firstborn with two younger sisters. Eventually she began seeing Tommy on a regular basis, which drove a wedge into her relationship with Steven. Tommy happened to have a totally different conversational style. "He's a listener," says Heather. "He's like a sponge. Everything I say goes into his ears, and he responds to it. He shows that he's interested by being attentive." Tommy is very comfortable with Heather. "I'm curious about her," he says. "I like hearing what's on her mind. Sometimes she goes on and on about emotional issues, and it can be a bit tiring. But usually she entertains me with the funny things she says."

Heather and Steven broke up after three months, and Heather began dating Tommy. Clearly Heather needed someone who was less egotistical than Steven. This is not to say that lastborns are more egotistical than firstborns; in fact, many are very selfless. It's just that Steven's early life experiences with his older sister caused him to magnify the lastborn trait of babyishness and prevented him from being a good listener the way Tommy was.

Only Child Communication Problems

Like the diva in an opera, both male and female only children want to be the center of attention. This desire originates in their early years, when they were the world to their parents. Keep in mind that every only child still yearns to return to that primal time when they were the only one who mattered.

The main difficulty only children have when it comes to communicating with a partner is a reluctance to give up their birthright as only children. The male only child still wants to be considered God's gift to the world, and his wife better pamper him and treat him with tender loving care. She may get angry when he barks orders, demands compliance, and whines like a child. In her opinion, he's acting immature, as if he expects a maternal figure to materialize and take care of everything. Because of his needy personality, his best match is often the older sister of sisters. She has the high level of competence he requires of a partner. In such a relationship he may actually calm down and feel loved, and of all the female birth orders, she may understand him best.

Art, an only child, and Heather, an older sister of a sister, have a terrific relationship. He's a retired biochemist, and she's a socialite with an abiding interest in singing. "At the outset of our relationship," Heather recalls, "Art would demand this and that, but he quickly saw how there was no need to adopt a whining tone with me." For his part, Art claims that he never whined. "I just told her what I wanted, and that was her interpretation. But the great thing was when I discovered that she was different from all the other girls I had been dating who thought I was demanding. Heather is competent and loving, and as soon as I saw that she could take care of things just as well as I could, I began to calm down."

A Freudian might say he had found his mother substitute. A birth order expert would say they had resolved their communication problems because Heather was responsive to Art's singleton demands and needs.

Female only children often suffer from somewhat similar communication problems, but instead of demanding and whining, they tend to regress and become dependent. When things go sour in her relationship, Arlene becomes withdrawn. Nick, a lastborn, didn't understand at first. "I thought she was depressed," said Nick. "But I learned that her withdrawing was simply a signal to me that she needed to be babied. She wasn't depressed at all, she just wanted attention."

Luckily Nick was able to resolve the difficulty posed by Arlene's unusual reaction to stress. Most people never realize that a female only child is prone to regress to a babyish state when things get difficult. What Arlene really needed was the loving and guiding understanding of her mother. If you happened to be Arlene's romantic partner, you would need to be gentle and kind, and if you gave her some time and space, you'd find that she would come out of her shell.

The point to be made about only children is that they communicate with adults and partners in many of the same ways that they communicated with their parents as children. If you understand this about them, you can avoid most communication problems and develop strong ties and great dialogue. If you can mimic the communication pattern of their parents, you'll be in heaven with an only child.

Firstborn Communication Problems

Firstborns are less agreeable and more neurotic than other children, and as a result they encounter more communication problems. They compensate for this by being dominant during conversations, which is a natural extension of their greater drive to control. This control is primarily achieved through verbal means, and as a result they develop sophisticated linguistic skills. Sometimes, however, their very skill with words gets them into trouble.

Ronald and Robin worked together as codirectors of a dance studio in New York. Both firstborns, they were excellent managers. Ronald had a younger sister, and Robin had a younger brother. There was no sex conflict between them. Everyone thought Ronald was charming and chivalrous. He was soft-spoken, enthusiastic, and friendly. Tall and bearded, he reminded people of Abraham Lincoln except that his hair was red. Robin was short and attractive, and she also had a pleasant personality; in fact, everyone liked working with both of them. Before long they were dating. They lived in separate apartments but frequently stayed overnight in the other's so that they could be together. Occasionally they talked about moving in together, but Robin, who was more sensitive to the nuances of the relationship, didn't want to make such a commitment.

One day I overheard Robin talking with Lori, the public relations manager. "He told me to use birth control pills," Robin was saying. "Why?" said Lori in surprise. "Because I don't want to get pregnant, and he thinks we should have sex more often, and he's concerned that my current method of contraception isn't going to be safe enough. But I don't want to go on the pill." Lori seemed to understand this, and the two women continued their discussion, characterizing Ronald as insensitive and unable to see Robin's point of view.

Robin and Ronald had a lot in common—they worked together, loved dance, and were both excellent managers. But before long they had stopped their relationship and drifted apart emotionally. The rift between them stemmed from their communication problems. Although Ronald was a good listener at work, he had a rather controlling personality. "He wants to tell me what to do," Robin told Lori. In fact Ronald listened to her only to the extent of knowing what her wishes were so that he could express his viewpoint about issues he considered important. "He doesn't put himself in my shoes," she said.

Their relationship could have been saved if they had each realized that their communication problems stemmed from the fact that Ronald was a good listener but that he had a subtext in his mind—a subtext that said he needed to control Robin. This is why he was a good manager: he knew how to get people to do what he wanted. Ronald could have realized this aspect about himself if he had known what to look for, namely, firstborn controlling tendencies. When he tried to control Robin's choice of contraceptives, he displayed a classic firstborn trait. This is something that Robin could also have dealt with if she had realized that her boyfriend was not being critical of her as a woman or a lover. He *did* like her; in fact, he wanted to continue the relationship. His problem was that he didn't put a check on his managerial skills when dealing with his lover. If he had lightened up and relaxed about the choices that Robin had made, she would have sensed more of a connection with him.

The point for firstborns is to realize that you have a streak of the manager in you and that it will impact your listening and speaking skills. Having managerial skills is a good thing in moderation. But when you bring that managerial skill home, you've got to watch yourself more carefully than you do on the job. You're going to be perceived as controlling and unfeeling unless you check yourself and give others freedom to do things their way.

If you're firstborn, it might not be easy to let your partner do things her own way. You'll want to give instruction and information, especially when your partner doesn't do things *your* way. But by becoming conscious of the problem, you'll gain control of your domineering temperament. And if you can check yourself, your partner will appreciate it more than she'll say. She'll stop resenting you and begin responding to you as a person rather than as a boss. And then in those (hopefully) rare instances when you *do* need to make a suggestion, you'll find that she's more than willing to listen.

Middleborn Communication Problems

The biggest communication problem you'll encounter with middle-borns is getting used to their changeable style, which, as discussed earlier, involves switching back and forth between their firstborn and lastborn personas. The middleborn may not even realize that they strike people as having two different personalities. But if you watch for it, you'll notice what I'm describing. It's really quite clear to see once you know what to look for. It's even a little funny to see how they shift back and forth.

Samantha is an athletic middleborn with an older brother and younger sister. She's dating Larry, a laid-back lastborn. Larry grew up in an artistic environment, and his hobbies include painting, reading, and meditating. One of the things he and Samantha share is an interest in tarot. "My favorite card is the Moon," said Larry. "It signifies that something is emerging out of the unconscious. Samantha shares some of my interests, but when we started dating there were times when she would become demanding and order me to stop reading or to forget what I was focusing on. That annoyed and puzzled me, so I tried to meditate to understand the problem I was having communicating with her." Despite his attempts to improve communication with Samantha, Larry didn't fully understand his girlfriend's dual nature. Samantha's lastborn persona was what attracted him initially, her creative, open-minded side; but her first-born persona surprised and irritated him. "She's entirely too bossy at times," he observed.

After a few months Larry became acutely sensitive to Samantha's moods, as he called them. They really weren't moods; her different communication styles are more appropriately referred to as manifestations of her dual middleborn nature. "So now when she gets irritated at me and tells me what to do," said Larry, "I realize that she's just morphed into her wild woman side. If I wait a few minutes, she usually calms down and becomes a sweetie again." This "wild woman" side is actually the firstborn component of Samantha's personality. Unknowingly, Larry stumbled upon a way to cope with his girlfriend's dual nature: when she gets demanding, he

187

steps back and lets her talk herself out. An important lesson can be learned from Larry's experience with Samantha. Once you adapt to their changeable nature, you'll find yourself, like Larry, communicating much better with middle children.

Twin Communication

As we discussed in Chapter 11, twins have an enhanced ability to form bonds of friendship and love. That's the key to understanding their communication style. When they deal with others, they naturally seek connection, so they're genuinely sensitive, good listeners, and observant. They're looking for kindness and consideration from everyone they meet. In actuality, what they're unconsciously seeking is the affection they experienced with their twin. But no non-twin can ever give them this level of connectedness, so twins will always feel a bit let down and disappointed in their relationships with non-twins.

When dating a twin, the biggest communication problem you'll run into (if you're not a twin yourself) is the lingering suspicion that the twin is disappointed in you. This disappointment is apparent in most of the deep conversations the twin will attempt to have with you. They never want to hang up the phone; they want to know every last detail of an interaction when you tell them a story; they examine your every word, and to them every word has heightened significance. "Why doesn't he let up?" you're thinking to yourself. "I'd like to relax and do something else right now." The twin, however, is never able to completely relax when it comes to emotional connection because twins live and breathe connectedness. This is something non-twins find hard to understand. But certain sensitive souls, like Arianna, who dated two twins, really like that about the personality of twins. "I loved the two twins I dated," she said. "They were the most considerate people I ever met."

The best way to deal with the intimate twin communication style is to become resigned to the fact that it's really a lost cause. Put more simply, you're never going to equal a twin in intimacy and connectedness, so don't even try; you'll just feel frustrated. Learn to accept the fact that a twin will expect more from you in a relationship than any human can give, unless you happen to be another twin. But don't despair! It's perfectly okay to have a relationship with a twin, and you don't even have to *be* a twin to get along with one. Become used to the fact that they need a great deal of closeness, and try to enjoy their heightened ability to be intimate with you. It's really *very* nice once you get used to it.

17

○○●○○

Conflicting Values

Your partner has values, some of which are hidden and unknown to you. Not everyone goes around telling others what their personal, political, and moral values are. Indeed most of us don't consciously think of our *own* value system. Of course, if the guy you're dating wears a t-shirt saying STOP THE WAR! he's advertising some of his political values. But values are often more submerged and invisible—and there are many *types* of value systems. Just because you know his political values doesn't mean you understand his economic, moral, or relationship values (such as who should express love, how often, and in what manner). The bottom line is that any potential partner is liable to have many value systems that are invisible to you, and these values *can* erupt into major conflicts between people.

Let me give you an example.

J. D. Salinger became a recluse in 1959, moving to New Hampshire after *The Catcher in the Rye* was published. He let it be known that he wanted no media interviews. His value system placed a high priority on individual privacy. A lastborn with an older sister, Salinger married a lastborn with an older brother. Shortly after he got married, he built a small concrete bunker a quarter mile from his home, and he would retire there to write, sometimes staying away from his wife and kids for up to two weeks at a time.[1] This behavior got on his wife's nerves, and she filed for divorce, claiming that his actions amounted to mental cruelty.

In this case, the value of privacy, which Salinger prized so dearly, caused a rift in his marriage. You can see a similar clash of values in many relationships. Conflicting values can lead to problems, especially when one is unaware of a partner's values—or of how to deal with such conflict.

Values in Conflict

Henry is a middle child with a younger brother. He has an older brother, but there's such a large age gap between them (nine years) that he can be considered a functional firstborn. His girlfriend, Shelly, is a lastborn with two older brothers and an older sister. Henry and Shelly have no rank conflict to speak of, but they do have conflicting *values*. Like most firstborns, Henry is conservative. He consistently votes Republican. Shelly is a staunch Democrat. Her parents are Democrats, and her father even ran for local office, so she wasn't about to change her party affiliation. During her relationship with Henry, she often got into heated debates over political issues. The two were like warring politicians, especially around election time when politics was the topic of the day.

"I don't know how I wound up with a Republican," Shelly told her amused girlfriends.

But the conflicting values in their life didn't stop there. Henry also put great stock in orderliness and accounting. A typical firstborn perfectionist, he liked everything to be measured, metered, recorded, and controlled. Shelly, in stark contrast, was laid-back about keeping financial records. Henry would lecture her repeatedly about keeping better track of her expenses, all to no avail.

Eventually they broke up, but then got back together a few months later. "I really love her," says Henry. "It's just that we argue so much I thought the relationship was doomed." Shelly expresses similar sentiments. "He's a good man," she says. "If only he could lighten up on the accounting issue—and vote Democrat once in a while." She smiles and explains that they love one another, but that they *do* have issues.[2]

When I spoke with this couple, I told Shelly to realize that Henry's strictness was due to his firstborn tendency to want control and order in his life. I also told Henry that Shelly's laid-back accounting style was typical of lastborns. He shouldn't expect her to change anytime soon. Once they realized that they weren't likely to change their partner, they began to work at accepting one another's differences. "I think it's our differences that brought us together," Shelley says. Indeed she may be right, since firstborns and lastborns are often a good match. In this case, values in conflict, which threatened to destroy the relationship, stopped being such a problem when they each understood where their partner was coming from.

Understanding Another's Values

Anne is a successful interior designer. The first of seven children, she grew up with three younger brothers. Her husband, Chad, is an only child and a millionaire. He inherited his money. To this day his focus is on money, and money has been his lifelong hobby and passion. He spends hours each morning and afternoon on the computer and the phone, monitoring and overseeing his many investments.

Before meeting Chad I was warned that he was egotistical, spoiled, and self-focused. "He's arrogant and closed-minded," his brother-in-law said. "He can't tolerate any opinion other than his own." The brother-in-law told me he didn't expect the marriage to last.

When I entered their home I was impressed by its beauty. Anne greeted us first and was charming and personable. Later Chad appeared, talking in a loud voice and spouting opinions on everything from how to treat waiters in a restaurant to how to relax on vacation ("I consider hotel staff to be put on earth to serve me!"). The funny thing, though, was that he too was charming in his own way. His remarks were actually humorous after you understood where he was coming from.

His brother-in-law took me aside and asked whether I had had enough and wanted to leave. "On the contrary," I said. "I find him immensely likable and amusing, and I'd like to stay for dinner."

As I observed Anne and Chad together, I immediately saw that Anne had learned to deal with her husband's boastful ways. She smiled graciously when Chad made grandiose statements. People in the family all wondered how long the marriage would last, but I saw that it would last forever. She had the secret—she knew what motivated her husband. Instinctively she realized that he was a big baby, that he was harmless, and that she could manage him by humoring him.

Indeed, after dinner Chad went up to his wife and kissed her and put his arm around her. "We're inseparable," he said, smiling.

"Yes," added Anne, "when you're not on your computer!"

Everyone laughed at her little joke. But the point of this story should be clear: if you understand the value system of your partner, you can avoid conflict. In this case, a man who others thought insufferable had been tamed by the loving understanding of a perceptive wife. The older sister of three brothers, Anne had the right birth order for a good match with an only child. But more than the right birth order is needed. You must also understand the temperament and value system of your partner. Anne apparently knew that Chad was basically a good man who had a limited range of social skills. He needed to be right in most conversations, he had loud opinions that he liked to air, and he wanted time to focus on his investments. All these traits are common to male only children. Anne understood her husband perfectly. She treated him with respect, but she also had a sense of humor about him, and it was obvious that she didn't take his pronouncements too seriously. She also gave him space to focus on his investment hobby, which was tantamount to a career for him.

When you understand your partner's value system like this, a relationship is possible with a person who the rest of the world might consider a bore. In actuality, Anne and Chad are very happily married to this day, due in large part to Anne's understanding of her husband's value systems.

The point to be taken away from these examples is that you don't need to be a mind reader or a philosopher to understand a person's temperament. All it takes is a basic understanding of how birth order affects a person's value system. Once you understand someone's value system, you can actually predict how they'll behave, what they'll consider appropriate, and most importantly what they'll want and need in a romantic relationship.

Birth Order and Romantic Values

Because knowing a person's values can help you get along with even the most difficult people, it's worth keeping in mind a few guidelines about the birth orders and the romantic values they live and love by. The following profiles are based on observations of thousands of individuals, as well as the research of many experts in the field.

Firstborns. Expect them to be dominant, conservative, and religious. They're perfectionists, and they have strict rules. They value timeliness and faithfulness. They will often interrupt you during conversations, but don't be put off by this tactic—it's their way of exerting control. It really suggests a fundamental insecurity. (All firstborns, remember, were unseated as king or queen by their younger siblings, which is why they have underlying insecurities and need to assert their dominance.) They'll pontificate and try to play the know-it-all more often than not. They'll give orders and expect to be obeyed. The way to get along with them is to enjoy their orderliness and try to bring out their fun side. Even firstborns like to relax and have fun, and you can help them do it, especially if you know they're more anxious and neurotic than most people. Get them talking about their favorite philosophy or belief system, and you'll make fast friends. If you can listen to some of their advice, they'll love you for it. You might even benefit from some of their suggestions.

In matters of love, they're initiators. They like to set the pace and know the direction a relationship is taking. It helps if they can direct you in some way, by suggesting things to do, places to go, or topics to discuss. They like being in control. When it comes to sex, they're more conservative than lastborns and may have certain hang-ups and rules that can't be broken.

Lastborns. They value freedom, abhor the status quo, and put high value on doing things their way. Don't try to change them on

Predicting Birth Order

While I was working on this book, I happened to be on the West Coast for a few days, and one of my friends invited me to a screenplay reading in Santa Monica at a posh beachfront apartment where one of the actors lived. When I arrived I was introduced to the director, an attractive young woman. I found her slightly annoying. I couldn't say exactly why, except that she struck me as bossy. Being a firstborn with an annoying bossy streak myself, I wondered if we might be suffering from rank conflict. I put the thought out of my mind, however, and sat down to enjoy the play.

After the reading, while people were having wine and cheese, I struck up a conversation with the director, and I mentioned the book I was writing.

"Can you guess my birth order?" she said.

I can often tell a person's birth order based on the way they behave and speak, but it helps if I can see them interacting with others. In this case, I had only talked with her for a minute or two before the reading, and I had seen her interacting with members of the cast— two male actors. Nevertheless I felt I could do a good job of predicting her birth order based on my initial impression when talking with her. The bossy edge in her voice told me she had at least one younger sibling.

Then I used a technique that I learned from Kevin Leman. I looked at her clothes. According to Leman, if a person dresses nattily they're likely to be a firstborn. She was wearing a gold corduroy jacket and gold hoop earrings, but when I looked down at her legs, the coordinated impression was marred by a casual pair of blue jeans and scruffy moccasins.

"You're not a firstborn," I said.

Her eyebrows went up. "That's right!"

"You have one younger sibling, and I'm sure it's a brother."

"Right again!"

"I haven't seen you interacting with too many people," I said. "But as far as your older sibling, I'm convinced it's also a brother."

"Amazing!" She was beaming. "How on earth did you do it?" Her boyfriend came by to see what she was so excited about, and she turned to him. "He just told me my birth order, and that I have an older and a younger brother after talking with me for just two minutes!" Then she gave me an inquisitive look. "How did you do it?"

"You have a bossy streak," I said, "which is typical of people who have younger siblings. I'm also a firstborn [I have three younger siblings] and people are always complaining that I'm bossy." She laughed at this, and I knew I had hit the nail on the head. I continued: "You directed a play with two men, and you were very comfortable talking with them before and after the reading. That suggested to me that you have a younger brother. You're used to directing men because you grew up giving your younger brother directions." She was smiling as if I had read her mind. I launched into my final point: "As to your older brother, I know that girls who have older brothers are very good at interacting with men, and when you were talking with me, your eyes held mine in that rather seductive way girls with older brothers have." She burst into laughter. Her boyfriend didn't look too happy. So I said it had been nice talking with them, and I excused myself.

Predicting a person's birth order isn't magic. It's something that you can often do once you begin to observe people and notice how they behave. You'll see patterns similar to those I've outlined in this book. And you'll find that once you know a person's birth order you'll get along better because you understand their value systems. Once I realized that the director was a middle child with two brothers, I felt more comfortable talking with her and I was no longer bothered by her bossiness. Although we had partial rank conflict (since she has a younger brother and I have a younger sister), I was able to respect her older sibling persona when she switched into it. No longer bothered by her pushy interpersonal style, I could enjoy interacting with her.

Knowing a person's birth order is going to give you a similar advantage in any social situation, especially a romantic relationship. Once you know what to expect from the various birth orders, you'll be able to handle the most dominant firstborn as well as the most off-the-wall lastborn, and everyone in between!

this issue because they'll just rebel and resent your intrusiveness. More than other children, they'll be relaxed and easygoing, social and agreeable. At a party they'll be easy to talk with and funny. They may get lost in conversations and need some guidance on which topic to tackle next, but once you get them going, they can be passionate about their beliefs. They're fun in a debate or argument, and they won't hold it against you if you contradict their beliefs. In fact, one of the joys of talking with a lastborn is challenging them and arguing with them. Unlike firstborns who get very defensive and paranoid if you attack their beliefs, lastborns are more able to enjoy the give-and-take of heated discussion.

When it comes to love, lastborns are classic counterpunchers, reacting rather than initiating, waiting for contact from you rather than moving toward their partner. But be prepared for your advances to be met with ardor and enthusiasm, for they're the most creative of all lovers. More than others, they're likely to experiment with unusual sexual practices and ideas, and it's hard to startle them. They may have religious beliefs, but instead of adopting a strict firstborn approach, they're more likely to be nondenominational and spiritual and to think for themselves instead of following the rules of an orthodox faith. For this reason, they're likely to be open-minded about things to do on a date, places to go, and sights to see. They're also more willing to travel for adventure—and for love.

Middle children. They value conflict resolution. If their younger siblings are close in age, they may have more firstborn traits. Be aware that they may shift value systems since middleborns are switch hitters. They can baffle you with their changeableness. But the key to enjoying their company is finding out how you're compatible with them and then focusing on *that* element of their personality. For example, if a girl has both older and younger brothers, but you have just one older sister, you're going to enjoy your partner's *older* sister persona more than her *younger* sister persona. When you're with her, you'll naturally encourage her to play the role of the big sister. When she does switch into her little-sister role, you can also get a narcissistic thrill. This is why middle children are often very popular—they have so many possibilities when it comes to interpersonal relationships since they offer interactive *and* narcissistic pleasure to firstborns and lastborns alike.

Pay particular attention to how many opposite-sex siblings a middleborn has and whether these siblings are older or younger. That's the key to understanding a middle child's romantic relationships. For example, a girl with older sisters and younger brothers is going to play the role of the big sister with her male partners. That's what she knows best.

Another example: A boy with both older and younger sisters will be compatible with any girl who has a brother. This boy will be especially comfortable in romantic relationships. He may be a little confused, however, over whether he should be the leader or the follower in the relationship. Knowing he has both older and younger sisters, however, can allow *you* to elicit the kind of behavior you need from him. For example, if you're a lastborn with older brothers, you'll want to encourage him to take a leadership role with you. If you're a firstborn with younger brothers, you'll probably enjoy it more if he takes a junior role.

Only children. Male only children value the freedom to pursue their career. Above family, above friends, above everything comes the pursuit of excellence and job success. Once you understand this, you can work with him, live with him, and love him more easily. Be patient with his career obsession and he'll respect you and love you in return.

The best example of this obsession is the life of Jean-Paul Sartre. A fierce believer in freedom, he was even more passionate about his career. It came first, above family and friends. On many occasions he alienated his brilliant wife, Simone de Beauvoir, with his intense dedication to his work. The success of their legendary relationship was due, in large part, to the way de Beauvoir understood her famous partner and the way she allowed him to focus on his writing.

Female only children are almost the exact opposite of their male counterparts. Career means almost nothing to them. They may have careers, of course, but above all they value love. They're much more family-focused than male only children. Female only children also value great men and women more than the other birth orders, with the exception of the older sister of sisters, who nearly worships male authority figures. The female only child likes to place her trust in doctors, philosophers, religious leaders, and other authorities, be they male or female. In reality these great men and women are archetypes from her unconscious—in other words, substitute parents—and the devotion she has toward these historical figures mimics the devotion the little girl had toward her parents.

Understanding the value systems of male and female only children can help you relate to them as friends, coworkers, and lovers. Remember to give the male singleton space to work and you'll get along much better. If you don't nag him about the long hours he spends slaving away at his chosen profession, he might even occasionally bring home a vase of flowers for you. And try to be patient when the female only child talks in glowing terms about her favorite author, saint, or world leader. If you act wise and all-knowing around her, she may come to view *you* as her hero too.

Twins. The value system of twins is not hard to figure out based on what we know about their early life experiences. Above all there is the twin in their life. Everything else is secondary in importance. Whether they have a same-sex or an opposite-sex twin, you'll be expected to be as close and intimate as their twin when you begin to date. Realize that you can never give such intimacy, and bask in the warmth of the twin's closeness toward you.

If you watch twins with this value system in mind, you'll quickly discover how solicitous they can be, and how loving. They seek to transfer their affection to other twins, but they'll also fall in love with *you* if you act like one. This entails being attentive, listening, and understanding. Above all, empathy is the name of the game. Twins will want to know how you feel, what you desire, and most importantly, what you think.

Relationships with twins can be empowering in many ways, not the least of which is in showing you what a good relationship can feel like. Once you date a twin, you'll see how close two people can be and how intense a loving relationship can become. But always remember that twins also value their space. Give them the intimacy they desire and the space they occasionally need, and you'll be on the road to an extremely enriching and rewarding relationship.

Values work invisibly to affect everything we say and do, and as we've seen, they exert some of their strongest influence on romantic behavior. Birth order directly impacts a person's values—making firstborns conservative, lastborns rebellious, middleborns changeable, and so on—so it should come as no surprise that knowing the basics of birth order theory can give you a real advantage in the dating game. Once you understand how birth order works, you'll be able to predict, with a good deal of accuracy, what a potential date's values are and, consequently, what they'll respond to romantically. And *that's* the kind of knowledge any lover would love to have.

18

○○●○○

Loss of a Parent or Sibling

Successful relationships are much more likely if you know yourself and your partner thoroughly. If an early loss of a parent or sibling occurred, it's tremendously important to know this about your partner since it can influence the capacity to form permanent bonds of love and commitment. You don't have to take my word for it that this event would be important. Leading researchers in the field have confirmed that early loss has a pivotal impact on sexual orientation,[1] psychological makeup,[2] and capacity to love.[3] Joel learned the hard way when a good relationship suddenly crumbled because he didn't understand the impact of loss.

Joel was intelligent, enthusiastic, and romantic. He worked in the admissions office of a small college in Ohio, and it was there that he met a young woman who changed his world. Ramona was twenty-two, and when she walked into Joel's office one morning and said she wanted to go back to school, he was mesmerized. He suggested that she take a look at the campus before applying. It just so happened that there was no one else there that day to give her a tour, so Joel and Ramona strolled around the grounds of the college together, then made an appointment to meet the next day to discuss Ramona's college plans.

That night Joel ran through the entire afternoon in his mind. Ramona had told him that her parents divorced when she was thirteen and that her older brother had died when she was seventeen. She had another older brother, three younger brothers, and one younger sister. Ramona had experienced tragic loss in her life, and Joel wanted to help her. He also felt she was perfect for him. On the basis of talking with her for only a few hours, he had fallen in love.

Joel was overlooking one thing, however. He had heard about the losses Ramona had sustained, but he didn't know how they had affected her. Over the next two months, Joel got to know Ramona better because she consulted with him throughout her application process. This was not unusual, for Joel helped many young people complete their applications. But in this case it was more a labor of love. Before long they were dating and becoming very much more than just friends.

When the director of admissions denied Ramona's application on the basis of poor high school grades and low SAT scores, Joel was devastated, much more so than Ramona. Joel even went so far as to talk with the director of admissions about Ramona, pleading her case and asking the director to give her another chance. But he couldn't change the director's mind, and eventually he had to accept the fact that she wouldn't be admitted.

They continued their relationship, however, and had many dates over the next few months. Joel seemed to be in another world when he was with Ramona, and it never occurred to him that he was really seeing only one side of her. In fact, she was simultaneously dating another young man. Even though her brother had warned Joel about this possibility the first time they had met, Joel had put it out of his mind, believing that she would drop the other young man in favor of him.

One day, Ramona suddenly announced that she was pregnant by this other man and that she was going to marry him. Devastated, Joel went home and tried to make sense of what had happened. The next day when he showed up with a bouquet of flowers, Ramona wasn't there. Her brother met Joel at the door. "Do you know," he said, "that you remind me of my older brother, Larry, who passed away six years ago? Ramona mentioned to me, when she first met you, that you reminded her of Larry. You sound a lot like him. Maybe you can be a friend of the family."

Reeling from the shock of the breakup, Joel tried to understand. But what he was hearing was too upsetting. It actually took months before he got over the heartache. When he did, he had learned an important lesson about loss. A person who loses a parent or a sibling, through death, divorce, or separation, experiences a void that needs to be filled. One way to fill that void is by relocating the lost person's love in a *current* relationship in an attempt to master the trauma.

Ramona had lost a father *and* a brother. The father was still alive, but divorce had torn her family apart, and she rarely saw him. That event had happened when she was only thirteen. Then three years later, her older brother died. That shock left another psychological void—one that was filled by Joel. When she met Joel, he reminded her so much of her brother Larry that she commented on the similarity to her other brother. In this case, the resemblance was so striking that even the other brother noted the similarity.

A person who experiences a loss may relive it in some way, which Ramona did with Joel. Unfortunately for Joel, the way Ramona relived the loss was by manipulating things so that she had to break up with him. When they separated, it was like another death—but this one was easier to deal with because she was older and Joel never really died; he just stopped seeing her. What appeared to be a perfect relationship suddenly ended, and he never saw it coming, although the clues were there.

The Impact of Loss

Understanding a partner has been made easier now that social scientists have helped explain the way that death or divorce of parents affects personality. Researchers at the University of Chicago, Johns Hopkins University, and the London School of Economics studied young people touched by divorce and discovered that the risk of serious emotional disorders increased in these children. Children of divorce are also more likely to develop psychological problems later in life.[4] One of the largest research projects on this topic, at the Danish Epidemiology Science Center in Copenhagen, Denmark, studied 2 million 18- to 49-year-old Danes and discovered that early loss or death of a parent caused a greater than average likelihood of homosexuality.[5] In 2007, scientists at the Tel Aviv Souraski Medical Center in Israel made the remarkable announcement that they had uncovered a link between early parental divorce and negative physiological changes in a child's HPA axis.[6] The HPA axis (hypothalamic-pituitary-adrenal axis) is a set of feedback interactions between the hypothalamus, the pituitary, and the adrenal glands that, among other functions, regulates mood and sexuality.[7] The point is that *early loss can have a profound and measurable impact on adult romantic behavior.*

When you're dating a person who experienced early loss, either through the death of a parent or sibling or through divorce or separation, be aware that things may be happening below the surface that are causing your partner to act differently from the norm. Such an individual may need to test you repeatedly before he'll feel comfortable in a relationship. Or he may need to leave you or cause *you* to leave him to relive the trauma of his early loss. He may even need to act out sexually. The bottom line is that you should look out for unusual behavior when with a person who experienced early loss. In some cases he may have learned to cope with the loss, but in other instances you'll be in for a few surprises as a result of his childhood traumas.

Brandy is a firstborn of second-generation Irish immigrants who divorced when she was ten. She and her younger brother, who is three years younger, became very close in the aftermath of the divorce. They lived with their mother, who never remarried. In school, Brandy was an average student. Energetic and attractive, she was somewhat of a loner, and although she had girlfriends she rarely called them or went to their homes to play. Most of her free time was spent caring for her younger brother.

In high school Brandy went through many relationships with classmates. In college she had problems concentrating, and after a year she dropped out and became an office administrator. Bored with this job, she began searching for other work. In the process of doing so, she met Mark, also a firstborn. Mark was a sales manager in a clothes company, and he helped Brandy get started as a sales-woman. Before long they were dating. Throughout their courtship, Brandy was worried that she would repeat the pattern she had established with all her previous boyfriends: a quick romance followed by a breakup that she initiated. Mark, a perceptive individual, sensed her anxiety but didn't know exactly why she was less enthusiastic than he was about their impending marriage. Eventually he asked her to go into couples therapy with him.

During the course of therapy, Mark learned about Brandy's ambivalent feelings toward marriage, how those feelings were caused by the early divorce of her parents, and how she feared the same thing would happen to her if she got married. It was this realization that helped Mark change his manner toward Brandy. He became more reassuring and finally convinced her that he would never leave. At this point Brandy felt she could stop therapy. She believed that she had finally found a man who would love her forever, something that had not happened in the case of her parents.

Throughout their relationship, Mark sensed that Brandy was always one step away from breaking up with him. He thus encouraged her to talk about her feelings with other therapists and with him. In this way he kept the marriage alive. One of the most successful techniques Mark adopted was a weekly meeting in which he and Brandy sat down for half an hour and took the time to talk about their expectations, fears, and hopes for the future. "I know she's still worried about the past," he says. "But when we talk about it, I get a chance to reassure her, and it helps."

You can have the same good results with a child of divorce. For starters, it's the perceptive acknowledgment of the psychological impact of divorce that can help you move in the right direction. Get your partner to talk about feelings that lie below the surface. And keep in mind that the insights you gain from these discussions will not only help you understand her, they'll also enable her to trust *you* more.

The effects of early parental divorce can persist throughout the lifetime of an individual, but people are having success despite these traumatic childhood experiences. *Knowing* how divorce has made your partner cautious about trusting others and fearful of a divorce in his or her own life can help you cope and move on to a brighter future together.

Honorary Laterborns

One of the most insightful discoveries in the field of birth order is the finding by Frank Sulloway that *firstborns who experience significant conflict with a parent are likely to exhibit lastborn traits.*[8] If you seriously want to take a relationship to the next level with a firstborn who experienced parental conflict, you must understand the implications of this insight. The only way to fully understand such a firstborn is to realize that he's going to have many laterborn traits, such as agreeableness, openness to experience, and diverse interests, even though at the core he'll always be a firstborn with visions of leadership, dominance, and control dancing in his head.

Remember that this applies only to firstborns who experienced *significant* conflict with one or both parents. Significant conflict is defined as more conflict than four out of five people had with their parents. The reason this strife has such a topsy-turvy effect on firstborns is that, under normal circumstances, firstborns identify with parents and become little parental figures themselves: conservative, religious, and one-track minded, with a focus on a single career. Excessive conflict with a parent, however, makes firstborns develop quite differently. In families where firstborns don't identify with their parents because of significant conflict, those firstborns acquire many lastborn traits, including greater openness to experience, diverse interests, and agreeableness.[9]

There are simply too many variables in human behavior to expect that you can understand a person completely; in fact, most people don't even understand themselves well. But if you get your mind around this important discovery about honorary laterborns, you'll have a keen insight into firstborns who experienced significant parental conflict. This kind of conflict with one or both parents is a type of loss—it amounts to a loss of the normal connection that a firstborn feels with his parents. The parent becomes, in effect, a monstrous big brother or big sister, causing the firstborn to develop into what Frank Sulloway calls an honorary laterborn.

The top three things you need to know about a firstborn are whether he experienced significant conflict with a parent, whether he has male or female younger siblings, and whether those younger brothers and sisters are close in age (one to five years). With this knowledge, you can make confident predictions about his personality, and you'll know how to get along better with him, even if he has experienced loss.

○○●○○

Celebrity Case Study

KURT COBAIN AND COURTNEY LOVE

The issue of loss and honorary laterborns is clearly illustrated by the story of Courtney Love and Kurt Cobain. Both firstborns, they were also both honorary laterborns. Cobain's parents divorced when he was only seven. His mother recalled that he changed radically after that and became very withdrawn. He certainly didn't follow a firstborn career, instead becoming interested in music and art and also becoming quite rebellious in school, a typical laterborn trait.

Courtney Love had an even more difficult childhood. Her parents divorced when she was only four. After the divorce she lived in numerous foster homes and developed a classic laterborn personality. She traveled widely and had a consuming interest in art. As a teenager she taught herself to play guitar and joined one band after another, but her personality was so jarring, dominant, and neurotic that she was ejected from most of them. In her case, you can clearly see the remnants of the firstborn persona coming to the fore, including bossiness, defensiveness, and dominance.[10]

Courtney and Kurt met in 1991 and married the next year. Both talented songwriters and musicians, they seemed to have a great future ahead of them in the music world. Unfortunately, this idyllic future was disrupted by Cobain's mental deterioration in 1994.

Courtney Love reported that her husband made a suicide attempt in March 1994 in Rome, purposefully overdosing on a sedative. He made another suicide attempt in Seattle later that month. Finally on April 8, Cobain was found dead from a self-inflicted shotgun blast to the head in his Lake Washington home.

The troubled lives and careers of Courtney Love and Kurt Cobain are easier to comprehend once we realize that they were both motivated by the same forces that tear any honorary lastborn apart. On the one hand, they had a core of firstborn traits, including the desire to be a leader, the need to dominate, and the sense of destiny that most firstborns possess. On the other hand, because of their experience of early loss and parental conflict, they each had a vast array of lastborn traits, including creativity, a need for self-expression through the arts, and diverse interests. Both were also risk-takers, much more so than typical firstborns.

In Cobain's case the results were tragic. As study after study indicates, children who experience early loss grow up with significantly more problems than those who don't. The message from their lives is clear. When entering into a relationship with someone who experienced such trauma and loss, it is important to try to understand the impact it has had on the person you're dating. Failing to do so could cause surprises down the line. But if you allow yourself time to gain the needed understanding and appreciation for how loss has affected your partner, you're much more likely to make relationships work that have stumped the stars.

Tips for Dealing with Loss

- Get your partner to talk about any early losses.

- Find out the details of early loss. For example, did it involve a parent, a sibling, a death, a divorce?

- Ascertain the age at which your partner experienced the loss. If before age seventeen it's likely to have far-reaching impact on personality. Conversely, the older he was, the less impact he'll have felt.

- Don't expect your partner to be totally over the experience even if the effects seem to be invisible to you.

- Be on the lookout for situations where a partner puts you into the role of a missing parent or sibling. Be understanding of such mental substitutions; they're to be expected.

- Ask your partner to tell you about the emotional impact that the loss had on him. Often getting him to open up like this will bring you closer together and lead to a happier resolution of his difficulties.

Narcissistic Attraction

Everyone knows people like this. They're cute. They're sexy. They're in love. But they're the same! In other words, they're so similar you could almost be looking into a mirror. Not necessarily *physically* similar—although that can happen too—but psychologically similar. When you look into the psychological mirror, they're identical, or so nearly identical that it's apparent that something out of the ordinary is going on.

Take Don and Pamela, for example. Just looking at them you know they're a couple: Don's a tall, good-looking professor of physics at a Connecticut university; his wife, Pamela, is a tall, good-looking executive secretary at the same school. Don has blonde hair and is in his early forties. Pamela has blonde hair and is in her late thirties. When Don talks, his voice booms stridently, and behind his back people say he loves the sound of his own voice. Pamela's voice is confident, measured, and slightly droning, as if she were reciting a memorized speech. Don is a firstborn with one younger sister three years his junior. Pamela is a firstborn with one younger brother two and a half years her junior.

Is it just coincidence that these two wound up with each other? Or is it possible that their very similarities drew them together?

"From the first time I met her, I was attracted," says Don.

"We got along famously from day one," says Pamela.

Their friends and family all agree—they're a perfect, loving couple. They have two kids, live in a nice house in the suburbs, and enjoy their time together, rarely arguing.

The happy marriage of Don and Pamela supports the *homogamy theory* of relationships. According to this theory, two firstborns should be great together, as should two lastborns. The problem with firstborn-lastborn couples is that they're apt to experience the same rivalries they had to deal with as children, and as a result their marriages are filled with reawakened conflict that mimics the relationships they had with their siblings. On the other hand, two firstborns, like Don and Pamela, or two lastborns, would avoid such reawakened childhood conflicts and have a more harmonious relationship.[1]

Although the homogamy theory sounds good on paper, and although we all know couples like Don and Pamela, a more careful examination of the theory reveals that it's based on narcissistic attraction.[2] Narcissus was the Greek god who fell in love with his own reflection. Everyone is narcissistic to some degree, and healthy narcissism is perfectly normal. Narcissistic attraction involves being attracted to people who resemble yourself. Don and Pamela are alike in many superficial ways (their looks and the way they talk, for example) and also in many psychological traits (they're both dominant, extroverted, and commanding personalities). Their relationship is primarily based upon narcissistic attraction: they like in each other what they like about themselves.

Freud made a distinction between narcissistic relationships and interactive relationships. Narcissistic relationships represent an early stage of psychic development, an infantile stage in which you love yourself and cannot relate to others except through your own needs and primitive desires. As a child develops, he realizes that others exist—first his mother comes into the picture as an object of his affection. This object love, as Freud termed it, represents a more mature and satisfying relationship.[3] As we grow and learn about others, we develop object relationships with people who are different from ourselves, and these relationships are based mostly on interacting with people rather than living with them side by side.

In narcissistic relationships, you *identify* with your partner, whereas in object relationships you *interact* with your partner. In narcissistic relationships you perceive your partner as an extension of yourself, in fact in such a relationship you may treat your partner almost like a clone of yourself. You'll expect your partner to do the same things that you do, and to do them in the same way. For example, Don expects Pamela to drive the way he drives and to take care of the house and yard the way he takes care of them. (She does.) In narcissistic relationships, the love object reminds you of yourself. Don sees many similarities between himself and Pamela. In effect he loves what's best in himself—his fair hair, his tallness, his commanding voice—in his wife, Pamela, who also possesses these traits.

In object relationships, on the other hand, you perceive your partner as different from yourself in significant ways. In such a relationship you're more likely to feel that your partner complements you, filling needs and deficiencies that you have. An interactive relationship is one in which you share the tasks of the marriage in different ways. For example, you do lawn work, your partner does housework; you drive the car, your partner reads the map; you decide where to go, your partner provides the weather report for your excursion; you initiate some action, your partner responds to your idea—all in a playful, fun, and complementary manner. There's a light-hearted and enjoyable give-and-take in the interchanges between you and your partner even when you're disagreeing about something.[4] That's the beauty of the interactive relationship, and that's why it can be so satisfying and rewarding on many levels: physical, sexual, and psychic.

This isn't to say that narcissistic relationships don't have their pleasures too. They certainly do, and many people can go a lifetime with narcissistic love driving their relationship. Just look at Don and Pamela. I'm sure you can come up with other examples from your friends and relatives. Simply think of any two firstborns or two lastborns who are a couple, and you've got narcissistic love at work.

As Walter Toman points out, however, every relationship has some element of narcissistic love as well as some element of object love. For example, even though it's primarily narcissistic, the relationship of Don and Pamela has some degree of interaction and give-and-take, which is object love at work. Similarly, in even the best object relationships, there's always some element of narcissism

Narcissistic versus Object Relationships

NARCISSISTIC RELATIONSHIPS	OBJECT RELATIONSHIPS
• Relationships of identification.	• Relationships of interaction.
• Partners value similarities.	• Partners value differences.
• You work side by side doing the same chore	• You work as a team, each doing different chores.
• You enjoy discovering similarities in your partner.	• You enjoy discovering differences in your partner.
• The relationship as a whole tends to be less mature.	• The relationship as a whole tends to be more mature.
• Celebrity example: firstborns Nick Lachey and Jessica Simpson.	• Celebrity example: firstborn Brad Pitt and lastborn Angelina Jolie.

The major differences between **narcissistic** and **object relationships** are outlined in the table above. Notice that narcissistic relationships occur when persons from the same birth order marry (two firstborns, for example, or two lastborns). Object relationships occur when persons from opposite birth orders marry (a firstborn and a lastborn).

present. Even in people who are quite dissimilar there are some traits that are the same, and some hobbies and interests can be shared in a narcissistic way.

Picture two people on a roller coaster, screaming with joy and fear as they go down a big drop—that's a narcissistic encounter since they're both the *same* in that primal moment of emotion. They're not interacting because they can't talk over the roar of the roller coaster; all they can do is hold on tight and scream with pleasure and apprehension. When two people are like a mirror image of one another, they're in a narcissistic mode.

In narcissistic relationships the predominant feeling is one of identification with your partner, whereas in object relationships the predominant feeling is one of interacting. I'm not saying that narcissistic relationships are bad, in fact they can be a lot of fun at times, as the example of the two people on the roller coaster illustrates.

The point I'm making is that narcissistic relationships are significantly *different* from object relationships, and understanding and being sensitive to those differences can help you double your romantic fun, as I'll explain in a moment.

Narcissistic Relationships

Wesley, a moving company supervisor, and Brooke, a lab technician, are both lastborns. Wesley's sisters are two and a half and four years older. Brooke's brother is two years older. The two met in college and signed up together for a course I taught. They seemed like a very happy couple, although in class they didn't associate with one another, perhaps because they were trying to hide their relationship from others After graduation they continued dating and were more open about their involvement. I worked with them on an acting project when Wesley was twenty-six and Brooke was twenty-three. They got along fine but tended to be very socially oriented, often going out to clubs and dancing into the wee hours. They talked about marriage and were seriously considering that possibility. Brooke claimed that she had a lot of fun with Wesley. In fact she said, "He's the only guy I have fun with! Everyone else I've dated has been too serious." Wesley had similar positive comments to make about the relationship, although he was less verbal about his feelings.

Everything was going fine, and eventually they married. Wesley is now in his early thirties and says the marriage is a perfect match. Brooke, however, is more sensitive to the nuances of their relationship. "I'm happy to be with him," she says. "But I'd say we have about a 20 percent incompatibility." When I draw her out on this point, she admits that Wesley is frequently difficult to talk with. He doesn't express himself well. "He's good at writing, but I need someone who I can talk with on a daily basis," she says.

What's happening here is that the narcissistic element in their relationship has reached a saturation point. Wesley isn't inarticulate, but he's reserved and not verbally expressive. However, if Brooke could see him with Dana, one of his former classmates, she would be surprised at how talkative he can be. When he's with

Dana, who has a younger sister, Wesley seems to opens up, relax, and become a little showman. He talks, tells jokes, and acts like a little kid. I asked Wesley about this different behavior with Dana, and he said that he just felt comfortable with her. It was a different feeling than he had with his wife. He said he had no intention of starting an affair with Dana, that was the furthest thing from his mind, but he did enjoy her company.

My analysis is that Wesley enjoyed his time with Dana in a different way than he enjoyed being with Brooke. He and Brooke were so similar they had almost burned themselves out going to clubs and parties. Their relationship was primarily one of identification. They were two party animals, they both liked to take it easy, and although Brooke was more verbal, they both liked to have a good time with friends. Wesley, however, missed the complementary give-and-take that he could find with Dana. She pushed him on things, challenged his opinions (which Brooke rarely did), and teased him in a playful way. Wesley unconsciously responded to this interactive friendship with Dana. If not careful, however, his relationship with Dana could ruin his marriage.

How to *Double* Your Compatibility

What if I were to tell you that there's a way to double your compatibility—would you be interested in making a good relationship *twice* as good? It may sound like a pipe dream, but it isn't. There really *is* a way to get twice the amount of pleasure you're getting from your relationship, and in the process you'll be twice as happy as you are today.

The secret lies in understanding narcissistic attraction. That's the key because it inevitably leads to narcissistic pleasure, which means enjoying things you have in common with your partner. The first thing you want to do is to learn how to sense when you're getting narcissistic pleasure from a relationship—any relationship.

We all get a certain amount of narcissistic pleasure from our relationships. If you're involved with someone who has the same birth order as yourself, your relationship is predominantly based on narcissistic pleasure. You're getting narcissistic pleasure when you stand side by side and look out a window together, when you're together in a car enjoying the scenery passing by, when you're on a train looking in the same direction, when you both do similar tasks like washing the dishes, sweeping the floor, or doing the laundry. Performing chores together and enjoying working side by side is a narcissistic pleasure because you're doing something similar.

Additionally, when you have a conversation with someone and agree on everything, that's a narcissistic moment. You're the same, your minds are one, you're reveling in your agreement. Narcissistic pleasure can also occur when you hug someone who looks a lot like you. Did you ever notice how tickled lovers get when they find that they're wearing similar clothes? For example, if you're both wearing white shirts and blue jeans you're going to look like twins, and if you sit on a couch and begin looking into each other's eyes, you might as well be looking in a mirror.

Kissing someone who kisses like you can also be a narcissistic moment. My research into kissing styles revealed that there are over sixty different kinds of romantic kisses, everything from the French kiss to the vacuum kiss to neck and ear kisses. There's a difference in intensity, duration, and tempo in kissing that can make the experience infinitely variable. But when you get on the same wavelength, when you kiss in short little pecks while your partner does the same thing, when you give long, slow, intimate kisses at the same time your partner does the identical thing to you or when you suck the air out of your partner's mouth while he does the same back to you—all of this is narcissistic pleasure because you're so similar you're like mirror copies of each other.

Once you become aware of how narcissistic pleasure operates, you'll begin to notice yourself slipping into the narcissistic mode all the time. This is a good thing, because the more aware you are of how similar people enjoy similar things, the more enjoyment you'll get out of your relationship.

But enjoying similarities is just *half* the fun.

In addition to enjoying similarities, it's important to enjoy differences. As mentioned earlier, all relationships have the potential for both kinds of pleasure: narcissistic and interactive. When you interact with someone, you're enjoying the differences between you, and that's the important other half of the equation. For example, when you kiss a partner aggressively and she's reticent and less responsive, that's interactive pleasure. When you have a good discussion and your partner expresses a contrary viewpoint, that's interactive pleasure. When you wear long pants and your partner wears shorts, that's interactive mode at work because you're different. Being sensitive to when you slip into an interactive mode can help you enjoy your time with a partner more, because interactive relationship mode is often the most deeply satisfying.

Now comes the fun part. It's possible to become aware of when you make the transition from enjoying narcissistic pleasure to enjoying interactive pleasure. Everyone makes this transition in all their relationships, but very few people are aware of it. The process of transitioning from narcissistic to interactive mode can happen in the blink of an eye, but if you watch for it, you can see it happening.

Jeffrey and Amber have been married for twenty-two years. Jeff is a middle child with older and younger sisters. Amber is a firstborn with a younger brother. They know each other well, enjoy each other's company, and like being together. But there are times when things get a little rocky and difficult. For instance, when they're in the car and Amber is driving, Jeffrey can be a horrible backseat driver, telling her what to do, how fast to go, and criticizing everything she's doing wrong. This is his older-brother persona coming to the fore, controlling, demanding, and guiding. Because Amber is a firstborn, she doesn't like being told what to do, and it leads to conflict.

"We're having a great time in the car, relaxing and listening to the radio, and having a nice conversation, when all of a sudden, out of the blue, his mood will change and he'll start giving orders," says Amber. "It throws me off and gets me in a bad mood."

I told Amber that when Jeffrey got like that he was simply segueing into his big-brother persona. She should watch for this to happen and expect it. Just like hearing a car shifting into a higher gear, if she looked for the change in his personality and demeanor, she'd notice it. I told her that when he was acting like a big brother there was still a way to enjoy being with him. Since she was a big sister and knew how much *she* liked giving orders, she should be less annoyed by his switching into this controlling mode. If she could ride out the storm of his commands and try to perceive his suggestions as helpful advice rather than interfering criticism, she would get a whole new pleasure out of being with him in the car.

A few weeks later she reported that she had tried the suggestion. "I noticed that his personality changed when we came to an intersection or a stop sign," she said. "It was amazing. Just like you predicted. And once I told myself that it was his big brother side, I had to laugh. He sounded just like *me* when I tell people what to do. So I started to get comfortable with it. He noticed it too, and he calmed down and gave me less orders. And before we had gone a mile he had miraculously shifted back to his younger brother role and we were laughing and enjoying a great conversation. I actually noticed him making the shift."

Amber learned to double her compatibility by adopting the simple expedient of observing her husband and being aware when he shifted into his big brother role. Now when she catches him doing this, she can laugh to herself and realize that he's acting just like her. She can get narcissistic pleasure from being with him when he's in that mode. In this way she can ride out what had hitherto been rough patches in their relationship. When Jeffrey finally switches back into his little brother role, she can really enjoy their relationship since that's what she likes best.

You can accomplish the same thing with your relationships. All you need to do is become sensitive to when people shift into their different modes of personality. Everyone has a little bit of the boss in them, just as everyone—even the biggest bully—has a bit of the baby in their personality. These switches are most noticeable with middle children and honorary laterborns. But you can even notice such shifts with firstborns, lastborns, only children, and twins. By going with the flow and meshing your temperament with theirs, you can get both narcissistic and interactive pleasure from any relationship and literally double your compatibility—with even the most difficult of partners.

How to Get the Most from Your Narcissistic Relationships

- Enjoy them. There are many pleasures to be gained from a narcissistic relationship when you do things side by side.

- Make a conscious effort to incorporate more interaction and give-and-take with your partner, especially if you have identical birth orders.

- Set up times to debate issues and take opposite sides. Try not to butt heads and be overly confrontational, but treat differences in opinion in a fun, interactive, playful way.

- Find differences between you that you can enjoy. For example, enjoy when your partner wears clothes that accentuate his male beauty or her female allure. If one is acting particularly solicitous, take comfort and pleasure from being helped. If you wish to be helpful, encourage your partner to receive assistance without objection.

- Play games together, which can heighten interaction.

- Make friends with couples that are from more interactive relationships so you can learn from their method of interacting. This will entail finding out whether you have any firstborn-lastborn friends and then trying to visit more often with them.

- Realize that you may be powerfully tempted to stray outside the relationship because people who offer you a more interactive relationship will exert a magnetic attraction on you. Cultivate them as friends, enjoy their company, but don't keep it a secret from your partner. Indeed, your partner should be able to derive as much pleasure from their company as you do. For example, if you and your wife are both firstborns, you may enjoy an occasional visit from a lastborn friend. That lastborn will likely provide plenty of interactive fun for *both* of you.

Conclusion

We're near the finish line, and I can feel you straining at the bit in your eagerness to rush off and try all the nuggets of birth order information you've learned. But before I let you run away to snare that ideal match, here's a quick summary of birth order and compatibility theory, touching upon the most important points, and concluding with one final new bit of information that I think you'll find helpful.

Birth order isn't something you can see like a hat or a jacket or a sign someone wears around his neck. And yet it does produce measurable effects upon personality that are pervasive, profound, and long-lasting. If you become sensitive to its effects, you'll begin to notice patterns in people that are as manifest and real as if they were wearing a t-shirt saying, "I'm a Firstborn—I demand respect," or "I'm the Baby of the Family—I'm so friendly you'll love me." Once you know what to look for, the effects of birth order are really this clear.

The key points we've already covered are, first and foremost, the fact that any two people can be compatible no matter *what* their birth order—provided they understand one another. We demonstrated that birth order is a good way to understand a potential lover's personality. The correlation between being firstborn and being dominant, conscientious, and controlling, for example, is clear beyond the shadow of a doubt. It's similarly the case with the other portraits of the various birth orders painted earlier. Once you understand how each person is unique, in part because of the effects of birth order, you can begin to understand your romantic partner in new ways, and getting along with lovers, friends, and family will seem like a much easier task. If you're also aware of the effects of loss, of narcissistic attraction, and of the concept of honorary laterborns, your knowledge of the subject will be sufficient for you to begin to be a good matchmaker—especially for yourself.

We also considered the competing theories of homogamy and the duplication theorem. In looking at the research on the subject, we showed that although both approaches have their supporters and although both work to make relationships tick, the duplication theorem is more likely to produce deeply satisfying matches, especially if there is no radical social revolution going on at the time. Keeping this in mind, we also explained how to *double* your compatibility by becoming aware of narcissistic attraction. Knowing this little trick and knowing how middle children are personality switch hitters can give you the ability to recognize patterns of behavior that are invisible to others.

Once you recognize these birth order concepts at work, you'll start to feel like you have compatibility X-ray vision. You'll perceive people in a whole new way, and you're apt to get along with your partner better than ever.

When it comes to romance, another piece of advice will make your life easier—ask potential dates about their birth order. Be aware that many people will be hesitant to reveal their family tree to a total stranger—or sometimes even to a close friend. This hesitancy can work against you, especially if you ask in a prying manner and continually dig for information at the outset of a relationship.

A better way to find out what you want is to volunteer information about *yourself* first. When you voluntarily disclose personal information, others are more likely to reciprocate. If you tell someone, for example, "I'm a firstborn and I have a younger sister and two younger brothers," they'll often reply in kind and tell you at least where they fall in the family tree, namely, first, middle, or last.

Another way to find out what you want is to make an educated guess. I've done this many times, and it usually works in a nonthreatening way to get people to open up and talk about themselves. Let's say you're riding in a car with a woman you've just met, and you notice that she has a tendency to interrupt you when speaking. She's also not the best driver in the world. She acts rather nervous, especially at intersections. Yet she's fashionably dressed. She's also got a to-do list tacked up on the dashboard. You pause a moment, lean back, and then say, "I bet you're a firstborn."

She may immediately admit it, or she may say, "How did you know?" You then say, "Firstborns are usually more organized, and you seem like a very organized person." Naturally you'll want to focus on her strengths and all the good things about being firstborn. In many cases, you'll be right in your assessment, but even if you aren't, she'll usually correct you and say, "No, I'm a middle child." That admission, in and of itself, can lead to a further discussion about siblings, especially if you begin to reveal things about your own family tree.

The rest is up to you, for I've given you all the advice you'll need. You have enough information to do what the gods of love themselves could *never* do—make a reasoned, rational romantic choice. For heaven's sake, you have more knowledge now about who's right and wrong for you than Cupid himself, and you can shoot your *own* invisible little arrows and darts into the heart of your intended. When you meet that firstborn of your dreams, you'll be coming out with quips like, "I really like your work," which will flatter the little egotist, or "you're the most organized person I know," which will ruffle his feathers the right way. And when you meet that lastborn who sets your heart aflutter, you'll give her leeway to amuse you in the manner you know only lastborns can, letting her ramble on, charming you by chatting about one thing after another as if she were lost in a maze. You, however, pupil extraordinaire, you'll find your way through the maze of any romantic encounter. Clad in the armor of knowledge, you can use the tools we've discussed to win your prize, the sweet and wonderful match you were born to love.

Appendix

Research on Mate Selection and Compatibility

In *Birth Order: Its Influence on Personality* (1983), Swiss research-ers Ernst and Angst examined a prodigious amount of clinical data, and as part of their investigation, they looked at four studies[1] on mate selection by birth rank[2] and seven studies[3] on Walter To-man's duplication theorem. They concluded that birth rank has no influence on who people marry, and they also concluded that the duplication theorem is unsupported by the evidence.[4]

Ernst and Angst are generally considered to be careful research-ers. However, when I reexamined the original studies they relied upon, I found substantial support for the premise that birth rank *does* influence marital choice. There is even more substantial sup-port for Toman's duplication theorem.

The first four studies selected by Ernst and Angst examined the issue of whether birth rank influenced mate selection. They con-ceded that the first and second studies did find that birth rank influ-ences mate selection.[5] The second study was also supportive of ho-mogamy since it reported that the persons studied, two hundred faculty members at a large university, tended to marry persons of the same birth rank. This second study went on to state that its re-sults provided "further evidence for the pervasiveness of birth-order effects."[6] In the third study, a researcher stopped two hundred pe-destrians on a large city corner and, upon questioning them, found no correlation between birth order and mate selection.[7] However, this third study failed to inquire as to age gaps between subjects and their siblings, which is an important consideration.[8] Ernst and Angst concluded that the fourth study contradicted the hypothesis that birth rank influences mate selection; however, it actually provided overwhelming *support* for the duplication theorem, finding that birth order complementarity was important for marital satisfaction.[9]

My reanalysis indicates that birth order is more important for mate selection than previously thought. As the following discussion will show, birth order is even more important when it comes to compatibility and marital satisfaction.

The next seven studies selected by Ernst and Angst examined the validity of Toman's duplication theorem. The first study was rated as not supporting Toman, but in fact the study concludes that complementary birth order is *crucial* for marital satisfaction. One of the study's many findings in support of the duplication theorem was that "men with older sisters . . . are happier when . . . the wives have only younger brothers, not both older and younger brothers."[10] The study also confirmed Toman's duplication theorem by finding that, "where the wife is apparently dominant—she has only younger siblings and the husband only older ones—this leads to greater satisfaction for the husband than where the dominance structure seems unstable, as when both husband and wife are oldest."[11] Clearly this study supports Toman.

Ernst and Angst also claim the second study doesn't tally with Toman,[12] but it actually provides strong support for the duplication theorem, stating, for example, that "complementarity of birth rank makes for a better marriage."[13] The second study also found, consonant with the duplication theorem, that when firstborn women were married to lastborn men there was an extraordinary degree of marital satisfaction.[14] Clearly this study also supports Toman.

The third study did not support Toman since it found that birth rank didn't affect power distribution in marriage, but the questionnaire used on domestic problems may not have been the best method for measuring this parameter.[15]

The fourth study attempted to find out whether happy and unhappy couples differed based on how well they were matched according to Toman's theory. The study did not find any significant correlation between complementarity and marital satisfaction,[16] however this fourth study has been criticized for using insufficiently differentiated sample groups, which can lead to a false negative result.[17]

In the fifth study, researchers looked at sixty-four college couples and found that those with sex *and* rank complementary positions (older brother of sister with younger sister of brother, and younger brother of sister with older sister of brother) were happiest. They also found that *rank* complementary pairs were more successful than *sex* complementary pairs. In other words, it's more important to avoid rank conflict than to avoid sex conflict.[18] This study concluded that complementary relationships were happiest. The researchers stated that the "closer [that] heterosexual dyads duplicated the sibling experience of each pair member, the more likely the dyad was successful." They also found that "rank complementary pairs were more successful than sex complementary pairs."[19] Once again they confirmed that it's more important to avoid rank conflict than sex conflict, all of which provides strong support for Toman and is in accord with his duplication theorem.[20]

The sixth study looked at 123 university dating couples and failed to find support for either homogamy or heterogamy; however, this study didn't inquire as to conflict with parents, an important factor, and it also failed to take into account subjects who were middle children, which would be expected to have a significant impact on coding results.[21]

The seventh and final study strongly supported Toman in finding that rank *complementary* pairs were more successful than those with rank *conflict*.[22] In other words, an oldest married to a youngest (rank complementary) is more successful than two firstborns or two lastborns (rank conflict). In looking at these seven studies, my reanalysis clearly shows that the preponderance of evidence supports Toman's theory, with four of seven clinical studies supporting it, and the three studies that did not support it having methodological problems. The evidence thus supports the claim that birth order is a factor in mate selection and that it is an even more important factor in marital satisfaction and compatibility.

Those who, like Ernst and Angst, argue that neither homogamy nor heterogamy play an important role are making the mistake of taking a black and white view; they see some studies supporting homogamy, and some supporting heterogamy, and they conclude that neither theory is correct. What they fail to consider is that these approaches aren't mutually exclusive, that human interactions are overdetermined (that is, they have more than one cause), and that both homogamy *and* heterogamy can simultaneously contribute to attraction and marital satisfaction—*even in the same relationship*. As we have shown throughout this book, both the theory that *opposites attract* and the theory that *like attracts like* have something important to contribute to our understanding of compatibility.

It's clear that numerous factors contribute to making us compatible with others. The idea that *opposites attract* as well as the notion that *like attracts like* are fundamental forces at work in all romantic relationships. Our review of the literature reveals that we have the ability to bond with those who are similar as well as with those who are different, so it certainly should help to understand both approaches. This way, when you do fall in love with someone new, you can use your knowledge of birth order to determine whether Cupid's darts have hit the right mark.

Acknowledgments

A wise man once warned me against saying thank you too much, but I owe a great debt of thanks to many people who helped me with this book. First and foremost, then, thanks must go to Michelle Wolfson at Artists and Artisans Literary Agency for unflagging and insightful help during the initial stages of this work. I'm also grateful to Adam Chromy at Artists and Artisans for enthusiastic assistance. I would like to sincerely thank Brian E. Barreira, Esq., and Judy Youngson for feedback on my early manuscript about younger sisters—the former for scathing criticism, the latter for effusive support. I also remember with gratitude the work of Mitch Douglas at ICM and Carla Glasser at the Betsy Nolan Literary Agency who helped with an earlier version of this work.

Generous and constant help and assistance from Jennifer Walton saw me through many rough spots along the way. Philip Walton offered useful insights and comments about celebrities he's met.

In the professional arena, my debt to Frank Sulloway cannot be overstated. For his helpful advice, for his courage in challenging the status quo, for his discovery of the concept of honorary laterborns, and for his ever-tactful suggestions which opened my eyes to the idea that alternatives to the duplication theorem might be worth considering, I thank him wholeheartedly.

I'm also deeply indebted to the late Walter Toman for generous assistance at an early stage of my research, as well as for my initial introduction to birth order. I am grateful to him for having had the courage to put forward the idea of the duplication theorem in the first place, which, at the time, was a radical notion and which has held up surprisingly well over the years, despite the other approaches to compatibility that are also explored in this book.

Additional psychologists who gave helpful feedback along the way include my father, Philip D. Cristantiello, Wilson Bryan Key, and Ben Pologe.

Many other people offered positive and negative feedback over the thirty-five years that I've been researching this subject. I would like to single out and thank my mother for instilling in me a love of libraries, my sister, Susan, my brothers Philip and John, and the other members of my family who answered questions and let me pry into their lives and the lives of their friends on numerous occasions with my inquiries about birth order.

Special thanks to Katie McHugh, a terrific reader and editor, whose enthusiasm for this manuscript was inspirational. I also appreciate the careful copyediting by Jane Haenel at Wordcraft. For reading and giving feedback on various chapters, I'm deeply indebted to Susan Batkin, Melanie Brown, Rob Glasser, Mina Kavcar, Audrey Kim, Michael Adrienne O'Hagan, Effie Panagopoulos, Paul Scotto, and Joe Whelski.

At Boston College I would like to thank Paul C. Doherty for a writing class I'll never forget. Thanks also to the librarians at the O'Neill and Babst libraries for selecting books that opened my eyes and mind. Although law school can be a rather stultifying place at times, while I was attending Boston College Law School I was fortunate to receive from the late James L. Houghteling and the late Sanford J. Fox some surprisingly good writing advice. Thank you to the many librarians who saved me hours of work by pointing me in the right direction at New York University's Bobst Library, the Boston Public Library, and the New York Public Library.

Thanks to Kevin and Jayne Moore at the Contemporary Issues Agency for arranging speaking engagements at hundreds of colleges and universities. And thanks to James Cunningham, an extraordinary comedian, for his professional feedback on my birth order lecture.

To all the uncredited people who contributed to this manuscript, including thousands who I grilled about their birth order over the years—limousine drivers, waitresses, students, actors, teachers, physicians, and all the rest—I hope I've paid you back for all the prying questions by including what I learned from you in this book. And last but not least, a special note of thanks to my wife, Marilyn, for being the muse behind the man.

Notes

Introduction

1. Sulloway 1996:202. Birth order is approximately ten times more important than gender in shaping personality. Sulloway 2007a.
2. Daniel C. Dennett points out that we all have to make important decisions, and we often rely on external aids to help us decide. These external aids, sometimes known as systems of divination (for example, the *I Ching*, astrology, graphology, and phrenology), may or may not be based on rational evidence, but they nonetheless help in a number of ways, such as by making us *confident* about our decisions and assisting us in thinking about the *factors* that go into our decision-making process. In this way, even invalid systems can serve useful functions (Dennett 2006:132–134). It is, of course, the premise of this book that birth order is much more than a primitive method of divination. I demonstrate throughout that birth order is a *valid* system of making relationship choices, that it is based on rational evidence, and that it is a reliable method of finding a compatible match.
3. A more complete explication of Toman's duplication theorem can be found on page 225.
4. Sulloway 1996:xvii, 434, 519n.79.

An Overview of Our Subject, or What Is Birth Order? And Why Does It Matter?

1. Touhey 1971:618.
2. Ward, Castro, and Wilcox 1974:61.
3. Rank 1929.
4. Adler 1979.
5. Toman's work has influenced clinical researchers as well as popularizers such as Kevin Leman, Ronald and Lois Richardson, and Lucille Forer.
6. McCrae and Costa 1987:81–90.
7. Sulloway 1996:68–70. Sulloway did for birth order what Darwin did for

evolution; his book and the research behind it unequivocally established birth order as an empirically verifiable science.

8. "Perhaps I am biased against Frank Sulloway's theory because I myself am a firstborn with heterodox views" (Harris 1998:44). All humor contains a kernel of truth, and this may, indeed, be part of the reason for some of the objections to the argument that birth order has measurable effects on personality. When I met him in 1992, Walter Toman told me that much antipathy against birth order came from the fact that the bulk of the research was rather negative about laterborns. Ironically, with the publication of *Born to Rebel*, the situation has been reversed, and there's now plenty of anti-firstborn ammunition available, which may be one of the reasons so many researchers with younger siblings, such as Harris and Conley, resist Sulloway's findings.

9. In other words, firstborns may be bossy, dominant, and nurturant within the family with their younger siblings, but they're not going to act that way when outside the family, say, in school, on the job, or in a marriage. Harris 2006:112.

10. Harris 2006:251.

11. One of the most impressive discussions of how genetics can influence us appears in *Fantastic Voyage: Live Long Enough to Live Forever* by Ray Kurzweil and Terry Grossman (2004).

12. For example, Jerome Kagan called Harris's work "total nonsense" and "crazy." When her book came out, he told *Newsweek*, "I am embarrassed for psychology" (quoted in Shea 2004). "She's all wrong," says psychologist Frank Farley of Temple University, adding, "Her thesis is absurd on its face" (quoted in Begley 1998).

13. Conley 2004:245–246n.4, 246n.7.

14. Conley, quoted in ABC News 2004.

15. For example, the work of Sulloway, Toman, and innumerable others, many of whom are discussed in the Appendix.

16. "My own research demonstrates that a categorical dismissal of any and all birth order effects is not only premature but demonstrably erroneous," says Ray Blanchard, professor of psychiatry, Faculty of Medicine, University of Toronto (Blanchard 2000:157). B. G. Rosenberg, from the University of California, Berkeley, agrees: "Despite literature to the contrary, 35 years of research and observation by myself and my colleagues tells me that siblings have a profound and lasting influence on one another's personalities" (Rosenberg 2000:171). This is just a sampling of the many researchers and social scientists who support the proposition that birth order influences personality in clear and measurable ways.

17. Sulloway 1996:42, 47, 72–73.

18. One of the earliest and most astute proponents of this theory was Robert F. Winch of Northwestern University. See, for example, Winch 1958:332–336.

19. "There can be no doubt that persons tend to marry other persons of similar

234

age, residence, race, religion, socio-economic status, and education" (Schellenberg 1960:157). See also Winch 1958:3–5, who argues that although homogamy is a force in mate selection, it's not the *only* psychological force at work; complementarity is also affecting mate selection.

20. The issue of homogamous relationships based on birth order similarity is covered throughout this book and is the subject of Chapter 19 on narcissistic relationships. See also Toman 1993:89–91, who suggests that homogamous relationships are less mature than complementary relationships; and Sulloway 1996:xviii, 434, 519n.79, who suggests that homogamous relationships work better in times of radical social revolution.

21. Hoffman claims that the notion that "opposites attract" is silly, obsolete, and totally wrong; what we need, instead, is a partner who is quite similar, especially in regard to inner personality. Hoffman 2003:13–14.

22. Homogamy was also found to impact mate selection in a study of 146 faculty members at a large state university. Teachers married others with the same birth order. Ward, Castro, and Wilcox 1974:62.

23. Wright 1965:127. See also Winch 1958:4. Winch concluded that homogamy provides a "field of eligibles" and that we then find a mate based on complementary needs *from* this subset of the population. Winch 1958: 331–333.

24. The best and worst match sections of Parts I, II, and III of this book are filled with examples of how heterogamy and homogamy operate in romantic relationships. A few additional examples will illustrate how they can operate simultaneously. A lastborn man marries a firstborn woman: heterogamy at work. She also has a childish playful side (learned from her lastborn mother), which he enjoys: homogamy at work. Another example: a middleborn woman marries a firstborn man. Heterogamy describes their complementary roles when she's in laterborn mode, but homogamy describes their similar roles when she switches to firstborn mode. A third example: Two firstborns marry and are happy together: homogamy at work. But they also enjoy the company of a lastborn friend so much that they joke about making her a permanent part of their family by adopting her: heterogamy at work. Any comprehensive theory of romantic relationships must take into account the contributions of both heterogamy *and* homogamy.

25. Sulloway 1996:xvii, 434, 519n.79.

26. Toman 1993:82–85. See also Richardson and Richardson 1990:16–17.

27. Toman 1993:78.

Chapter 1: Older Brother of Brothers

1. McCrae and John 1992:175–215; Healey and Ellis 2007:58–59.

2. An example of this relationship is Billy Bob Thornton (who grew up with two younger brothers) and Angelina Jolie (who has one older brother), who were married from 2000 to 2003.

3. A study of outstanding jet pilots revealed that most were firstborns with close father-son relationships (Reinhardt 1970:732).

4. Sulloway 1996:356.

5. www.msnbc.msn.com/id/8420203.

Chapter 2: Older Brother of Sisters

1. For example, lastborn men are more agreeable and easy to be with (Saroglou and Fiasse 2003:23).

2. During radical social revolutions, however, you may find that she opposes you if you're too conservative for her liberal tastes (Sulloway 1996:xvii, 434, 519n.79).

3. Fighting usually is most pronounced if siblings are three to five years apart. If they're closer in age or if the age gap is more than five or six years, they fight less.

4. Toman 1993:11.

5. Hall 1965:155.

6. Weller, Natan, and Hazi 1974:797.

7. Levinger and Sonnheim 1965:143. This observation is a nice summary of the pleasures of the narcissistic relationship where two firstborns align themselves and work in harmony. The vast possibilities of human interactions make possible the fact that two firstborns don't always fight over leadership. Sometimes, in the best of scenarios, they work together and admire in one another those traits that are most positive in themselves. These narcissistic elements of a relationship undoubtedly come into play when a middle girl is in firstborn mode and interacts pleasantly with a firstborn boy.

8. King Henry VIII's last wife was the most compatible with him, and she was a firstborn who respected his authority (Sulloway 1996:280–282).

9. Winch 1958:333–334.

10. As Sartre would say, you're not living up to your full potential in such a relationship; you're being inauthentic (Sartre 1943:86–89).

11. Two much younger brothers, Andrew and Edward, who are ten and fourteen years younger, respectively, would have contributed little to his personality, making him effectively an older brother of a sister, with the older brother of brothers characteristics so diminished and attenuated as to be of little practical consequence for his psychological profile.

12. Is it merely a coincidence that Princess Diana married a man with the same first name as her brother? There is a rather convincing theory that similarity of names can lead to narcissistic attraction between people. I was recently at a school and met a cute couple named Kylie and Kyle. I asked Kylie whether she thought that the similarity of names might have led to their attraction for one another, and she smiled and readily agreed that it had. If you look at your friends and family, don't be surprised if you find a number of people who share similar first names and who often joke about it. Those jokes may well contain a degree of accuracy since narcissistic attraction

works on many levels, one of which is your name. I am indebted to my sister for pointing this out to me.

13. The fact that she had two older sisters is largely immaterial to her relationships with the opposite sex. The key point is her opposite-sex sibling, her younger brother.

14. Prince Charles received much criticism for marrying Camilla Parker-Bowles due, in large part, to thinking related to the British royal family. His own parents did not attend the wedding ceremony as it was thought unroyal for them to do so.

15. Charles was always closer to his uncle, Lord Mountbatten, than to his own father. Mountbatten's former secretary has remarked that "Charles and Prince Philip always had a difficult relationship" (Graham 2006:30).

16. When a firstborn encounters substantial parental conflict, it can make him an "honorary laterborn." This means he'll have many characteristics of the lastborn (although also quite a few of the firstborn as well). This "developmental glitch" predominantly affects those from the lower classes (Sulloway 1996:123). So in Charles's case, since he was from royalty, he may have felt only minimal effects on his personality from his conflict with his father. Those conflicts, however, may have been sufficient to make him especially susceptible to the charms of women with younger brothers, such as Princess Diana and Camilla Parker-Bowles.

17. See Sulloway 1996:121–128, for a discussion of "developmental glitches" in which firstborn children with significant parental conflict become "honorary laterborns." The discussion adds a fascinating new insight into what makes firstborns tick.

Chapter 3: Older Sister of Sisters

1. If you're the first girl, we'd expect you to follow a pattern seen with most firstborns, namely, you'd identify with your parents, conform to a cookie-cutter image of what a good child should be, and as a result become conservative and conventional. But Frank Sulloway has pointed out that gender comes into the mix and changes all that. Unlike firstborn males, firstborn females with younger brothers, and firstborn females with a *number* of younger sisters (all of whom tend to conform), firstborn females with only one younger sister are the *least* conforming of all girls. Only younger sisters of brothers tend to be more nonconformist. The reasons for this difference aren't currently well understood, but the older sister in a two-girl family is clearly different on measures of conformity from older sisters in families with three or more sisters (Sulloway 1996:149–151). Lack of conformity can have important implications for finding a mate since girls who don't conform tend to attract men who like this trait, such as lastborn men and older brothers of sisters.

2. Healey and Ellis 2007:58–59.

3. Toman 1993:167–168.

4. Sulloway 1996:150.
5. Sulloway 1996:150; Sulloway 2007b:302. So-called instrumental traits—aggressiveness, dominance, assertiveness, competitiveness, and forcefulness—are thought of as more masculine than feminine, even though women can also possess such traits. Older sisters of sisters possess these traits more than other girls, although older sisters of brothers also score high on these measures.
6. Most firstborns score higher on scores of neuroticism (one of the Big Five personality traits) than middle or lastborn children (Sulloway 1996:73). If you're a firstborn and this bothers you, think of Woody Allen. People will love you for these traits.

Chapter 4: Older Sister of Brothers

1. McGill University researcher Blema S. Steinberg has studied the impact of birth order on leadership, concluding that "first-born women, like first-born men, are overrepresented among political leaders" (Steinberg 2001:89).
2. Sulloway 2000:192.
3. Nelsen 1981:632.
4. Firstborns have been shown to be more religious than middle children (Saroglou and Fiasse 2003:23).
5. This is an especially good match if the boy had a good relationship with his older sister while a child (Birtchnell 1977:26). During times of political upheaval, however, you may find that a lastborn will oppose you if you're too conservative for his liberal tastes (Sulloway 1996:519n.79).
6. Plutarch 2001:497.
7. Research indicates that "firstborns have a greater achievement level and different personality characteristics than other children" (Kardener and Fuller 1972). Their survey showed that 92 out of 160 physicians doing a psychiatric residency were firstborns, approximately 57 percent, which is a statistically significant result.
8. Sometimes comparing people in your mind can help you see their essential traits easier than analyzing them in isolation. When you look at the Clintons side by side like this, many of Hillary's older-sister-of-brothers traits come into high definition: her strength, her dominance, and her fundamental I'm-in-charge-here attitude.
9. Conason and Lyons 2000:85.

Chapter 5: Younger Brother of Brothers

1. Jackie Mason, for example, is on Comedy Central's list of 100 Greatest Stand-Up Comedians, and he's had his own Broadway comedy show. He grew up with three older brothers and says he tried to "overcompensate" by being funny.

2. The more older brothers one has, the more likely one is to experiment with homosexual behavior (Blanchard and Bogaert 1996:27–31).

3. Nietzsche 1887:228.

4. Frank Worsley, one of most fearless members of the expedition, was a last-born with a brother four years older and a sister two years older (Thomson 1999:14). Tom Crean had numerous older brothers, including one who was six years older. Like many younger brothers of brothers, he left home early after a disagreement with his father. Crean was only fifteen years old at the time, and he immediately enlisted in the Royal Navy (Smith 2002:20–21).

5. Finding that they had landed on the wrong side of South Georgia Island, Crean and Worsley hiked across the uncharted mountains with Shackleton and successfully reached the whaling station after three days of harrowing adventures in the freezing snow. There are numerous accounts of the Imperial Trans-Antarctic Expedition of 1914, but the most riveting is Alfred Lansing's *Endurance: Shackleton's Incredible Voyage* (1959). Highly recommended.

6. During radical social revolutions, however, you may find that she opposes you if you're too liberal for her conservative tastes (Sulloway 1996:xvii, 434, 519n.79).

7. Sulloway 1996:xvii, 434, 519n.79.

8. Sulloway 2001b:14060.

9. He actually had both older brothers *and* sisters, but the theory is the same.

10. Leamer 2005:14.

11. Even before he came to the United States, Schwarzenegger used his competitive nature to excel at bodybuilding. "When I was ten years old I got this thing that I wanted to be the best in something, so I started swimming," says Schwarzenegger. "I won championships, but I felt I couldn't be the best. . . . Then I started weight lifting through the other sports and I enjoyed it the most. I won the Austrian championship in 1964 but I found out I was just too tall. So I quit that and went into bodybuilding. Two years later I found out that that's it—that's what I can be the best in" (Gaines 1974:21).

12. His lines for his first movie, *Hercules in New York* (1970), had to be dubbed because producers feared people wouldn't understand him.

13. "I feel very blessed to have four brothers," said Shriver on CBS. "My brothers always say, 'Oh, you know, we prepared you for the world of journalism. We prepared you for Arnold. We prepared you for everything.' And in a way they're right. Because you know, they take no prisoners. They were very tough. They tease a lot. They have no patience for tears. They have no patience for waiting. They have no patience for asking for special treatment. And they're all very bright. They're all very attractive. They're all very funny. They're all very driven. They're all very competitive. They're all very athletic. And yet they're very different." She added, "I talk to all of my

brothers every week. Several of them, I talk to every day. They are my best friends. They're totally involved in my life." Having grown up surrounded by brothers, she clearly understands men, understands their strengths and weaknesses, has compassion for them, likes being with them, and most importantly is used to being with them. Arnold made a great choice.

Chapter 6: Younger Brother of Sisters

1. Marlon Brando, a super younger brother of sisters and a passionate advocate of the American Indian, declined the Academy Award in 1973 on the basis that the American film industry had treated Indians poorly.
2. During times of radical social revolutions, however, you may find that she opposes you if you're too conservative for her liberal tastes (Sulloway 1996:xvii, 434, 519n.79).
3. At one school I visited, one of the participants in the kissing show, Anna, had a twin brother. She was dating Atom, who had an older sister. "Anna was very excited when she learned that I had a sister," Atom told me. "She wanted to meet her and see us together. She asked me all kinds of questions about her. It was kind of weird, her super keen interest in my relationship with my sister. I thought, whoa—what's this girl trying to find out?" All Anna was trying to find out was whether Atom had as close a relationship with his sister as she had with her twin brother. Unconsciously a twin will want to see that kind of closeness, something they're used to from day one. If you can't give it to her, she'll always feel something is missing.
4. Sulloway 1996:433–434.
5. Hamilton 1988:132.
6. Salinger 2000:195.
7. The best biography is *Salinger* (1999) by Paul Alexander, which chronicles all of the writer's many eccentricities.
8. Maynard 1998:71–206.
9. When women dated J. D. Salinger, he would tell them that he was in contact with Holden, the protagonist of *The Catcher in the Rye*. His imagination was so active that he talked about Holden as if he were a real person. He also told his dates that he was in communication with some of his dead buddies from the war and that he could talk with his ex-wife in his dreams. These statements shocked many of the women he was seeing (Alexander 1999:166–167).
10. Maynard 1998:206–227.

Chapter 7: Younger Sister of Sisters

1. *Movers and Shakers* 2003:240.
2. Slater and Slater 2006:147.
3. Koehn 2001:175.
4. Kent 2003:116.

Chapter 8: Younger Sister of Brothers

1. See, for example, Toman 1993:177–181; and Richardson and Richardson 1990:114–120.
2. Toman 1993:77.
3. Toman 1993:179. During times of radical social revolutions, however, you may find that a firstborn opposes you if you're too conservative for his liberal tastes (Sulloway 1996:xvii, 434, 519n.79).
4. An example of this relationship can be seen in the close friendship of Elizabeth Taylor and Montgomery Clift, who had a twin sister.
5. Sulloway 1996:xvii, 434, 519n.79.
6. Toman 1993:179.
7. Sulloway 2001b:14060.

Chapter 9: The Male Only Child

1. Leman 1985:95–112; Leman 1989:85–123.
2. Meditation is an effective tool for stress reduction and has worked for many people, including firstborn director David Lynch (Lynch 2006). Prayer works similarly for some. But whether or not you believe in the religious ideology that goes along with many meditation and prayer systems, the simple act of relaxing and concentrating on something pleasant can have real physiological benefits. Researchers have recently discovered that meditation alters brain structure in a positive way by thickening the prefrontal cortex and right anterior insula, and they concluded that meditation may help offset age-related cortical thinning (Lazar et al. 2005:1893).
3. Sulloway 1996:489n.47.
4. Of the first twenty-three American astronauts, nineteen were firstborns and two were only children (Leman 1998:17). The Mercury astronauts were all first or only sons (Wolfe 1979:354).
5. Jacobs and Stadiem, 2003:57–58.
6. Jacobs and Stadiem 2003:202.
7. Jacobs and Stadiem 2003:202.
8. Kelley 1987:270.

Chapter 10: The Female Only Child

1. Polit, Nuttall, and Nuttall 1980:99. Toman's research, however, comes to a slightly different conclusion and finds that female only children can impress others as being egotistical (Toman 1993:181).
2. Sulloway 1996:489n.47.
3. Sulloway 1996:23.
4. Richardson and Richardson 1990:179.
5. Downs 1971. http://en.wikipedia.org/wiki/Carol_Burnett.
6. Tsui and Rich 2002:74.
7. Toman 1993:182.

8. Richardson and Richardson 1990:178.
9. Toman 1993:181–82.
10. Moughan 1999.
11. Mileti 2004:332.
12. Wood 2006.

Chapter 11: Twins

1. Louis Keith, M.D., obstetrician and cofounder of the Center for the Study of Multiple Birth in Chicago, quoted in Abbe and Gill 1980:147. Louis cofounded the center with his twin brother, Donald Keith. The center has a helpful Web page, multiplebirth.com, and offers information and links for research on twins.
2. "When we quibble, it's about small things, like, why put that bed over here?" says Rocio Aragon, talking about her relationship with twin sister Yarmila. "But inherently, we just get along very, very well. We always have. We have similar tastes" (quoted in Abbe and Gill 1980:77).
3. Segal 1999:101.
4. Segal 1999:101.
5. Lawrence Wright discusses the specialness twins feel simply by virtue of being a twin (Wright 1997:54).
6. "My twin sister and I have finally come to an epiphany in our lives," says one young woman. "We suddenly realized that we love each other too much to split up and move in with different men. The problem is that neither one of us wants to do anything without the other dating wise [sic]. We've fought and cried over this issue and finally just came to the same conclusion: we need to date twin men. We figure that no other person would understand us as well as another twin." Quoted from a Web site devoted exclusively to dating twins: twinsrealm.com/dating_page.htm.
7. Of the three young celebrities that Aaron Carter dated—Lindsay Lohan, Hilary Duff, and Paris Hilton—his best match was Paris Hilton, who has two younger brothers.
8. Quoted in Abbe and Gill 1980:88.
9. "When I was young, I sort of resented being a twin. I wanted individuality," says Aldo Andretti, twin brother of racing legend Mario Andretti (quoted in Abbe and Gill 1980:119).
10. Quoted in Abbe and Gill 1980:122–123.
11. Heyman 2006.

Chapter 12: Middle Children

1. Sulloway 2001b:14060; Toman 1993:32.
2. Sulloway 1996:303.
3. Kevin Federline, who she married in 2004 and divorced two years later, is an older brother of two brothers.

4. Firstborn Nicole Kidman has one sibling, a sister who's three years younger. Cruise and Kidman married in 1990 and divorced eleven years later.

Chapter 13: Firstborn Rank Conflict

1. Contrary to common wisdom, 50 percent of marriages don't end in divorce, only about 30 percent do, but this is still a rather daunting statistic. http://en.wikipedia.org/wiki/Divorce (accessed June 4, 2007).

2. A major premise of Frank Sulloway's *Born to Rebel* is that firstborns and lastborns get into conflict during radical social revolutions. Firstborns follow a conservative line and support the status quo, whereas laterborns think against the grain and support new ideas and contrarian thinking. This is a type of Darwinian rank conflict: firstborns and lastborns replicating in the social arena how they fought for parental investment in the crucible of the family. The implications of Darwinian rank conflict for political and scientific revolutions are profound, tending to make firstborns and laterborns political and scientific enemies (Sulloway 1996:356). But when it comes to *romantic* relationships, this kind of difference in thinking is often the glue that holds couples together and attracts partners to one another, especially when there is no social revolution taking place. According to Toman, in the *romantic* sphere, rank conflict occurs when two *firstborns* get together or when two *lastborns* get together, and it disappears when a firstborn and a lastborn are in a relationship. After Sulloway's research, however, we can never say that Darwinian conflict between opposite birth orders totally disappears. That conflict may manifest itself as teasing romantic banter and may, as we argue in this book, generally support the notion that *opposites attract*, but we cannot forget that during radical social revolutions such conflict may manifest itself in more troublesome ways.

3. Sulloway 1996:100.

4. As Frank Sulloway has convincingly demonstrated, however, during radical social revolutions people from similar birth orders close ranks and bond well together, so you may find that two firstborns are a better match when revolution is in the air (Sulloway 1996:xviii, 434, 519n.79).

5. Having similar names contributes to narcissistic attraction, a form of attraction discussed in Chapter 19.

6. Although Toman and others have found a correlation between birth order and mate selection, the link may not be particularly robust. Others have found that birth order does not impact *mate selection* so much as it affects *marital satisfaction* (Kemper 1966:347–348). The reason the link between birth order and mate selection may be weak, whereas the link between birth order and marital satisfaction is higher, is that at the outset of a relationship couples are entranced by other factors and don't focus as much on compatibility. Which is why it's important to think about compatibility *before* you get married. Take the time to look beyond superficial factors that draw you to someone—physical attractiveness, social similarity, and

propinquity—to consider underlying compatibility, which is crucial for long-term happiness.

7. Sulloway 1996:xvii, 434, 519n.79.

8. Toman suggests that working and living "parallel lives, pursuing their own careers, and recruiting the children of their own sex for themselves" is the best way of handling the marriage of two firstborns, such as an older brother of brothers and an older sister of sisters (Toman 1993:152).

9. The ideal match for the older sister of sisters is a younger brother of sisters. But the ideal match for *him* would be the older sister of *brothers*, because that's what he's used to. Another good match for the older sister of sisters would be a male only child. Toman 1993:169.

10. On the relationship of the older sister of sisters to older men, see Chapter 3. Toman 1993:168; Sulloway 1996:150.

11. Paul Newman is a lastborn with one older brother.

12. Sigmund Freud first described transference in the context of psychoanalysis, but the process works equally in the classroom, as many teachers and students can attest. The term refers to a redirection of feelings for one person (such as a parent) toward someone else (such as a teacher). In the context of a classroom, many students will feel a transference of feelings. If they had problems with their father, for example, they'll rebel against male teachers. If, like most older sister of sisters, they had mostly positive feelings toward their father, they'll feel a pull of unconscious attraction toward male professors.

13. Kemper 1966:347–349.

14. Personal comment by Walter Toman to the author, July 1992. At the time, Toman said that it was clear that many people didn't accept birth order theory because it seemed to favor firstborns.

15. Actually the intellectual difference between firstborns and laterborns is small. "Being firstborn is associated with eminence, although the effect is moderate" (Sulloway 1996:109).

16. Every birth order has its pluses and minuses. For example, "Firstborns are more responsible, achievement oriented, organized, and planful" but less "easygoing, cooperative, and popular" than laterborns (Sulloway 1996:73). The key to making use of birth order information is becoming aware of those pluses and minuses so that you can understand yourself and get along better with others.

Chapter 14: Lastborn Rank Conflict

1. Another reason is that they diversify and try to find things that will get parental attention, and being the funny man gets them attention.

2. This is Toman's duplication theorem (Toman 1993:78).

3. See, for example, Kemper 1966:348; Weller, Natan, and Hazi 1974:796; Mendelsohn et al. 1974:208; Baxter 1965:151; and Toman 1962:48.

4. For more on this last point, see the discussion of Elizabeth Taylor and Rich-

ard Burton and Sarah Jessica Parker and Robert Downey Jr. in this chapter.

5. Heymann 1995:270.

6. Heymann 1995:281.

7. Their lastborn rank conflict was certainly compounded by the fact that Elizabeth Taylor grew up with an older brother, Howard, who was only two years her senior. Precisely because she was so close in age, you would expect her to have very strong lastborn traits. Richard Burton had eleven older siblings and, although he did have one younger sibling, was raised as a lastborn. His mother died when he was only two, after which he was adopted by his sister Celia and raised by her and her husband. Every two or three days they would go back to their father's home and the young Burton would be doted on by his four older sisters.

8. Heymann 1995:323.

9. The ideal match for someone like Sophia Lauren (an older sister of a sister) would be someone like Richard Burton (a younger brother of sisters). See Toman 1993:169.

10. For a discussion of the difference between interactive and narcissistic relationships, see chapter 19 as well as Toman 1993:89–90.

11. Their problems were compounded by the fact that Parker grew up with three older siblings very close in age: a sister two years older, and two brothers three and four years older. This close age gap means she should have very strong lastborn traits. She also has four younger half siblings, but they didn't live with her. Robert Downey Jr. was, in many ways, her female counterpart. His sister, Allison, is only two years older, so the birth order effect should be even more pronounced in his case.

12. Rader 2006.

13. Kiefer Sutherland, *Playboy* magazine interview, February 2004.

14. Toman 1993:179.

15. Sulloway 1996:112.

16. As Frank Sulloway observes, however, people from the same birth order have been known to avoid such clashes when they work together during a radical social revolution to achieve a common political, scientific, or religious goal against common enemies (Sulloway 1996:xvii, 434, 519n.79).

Chapter 15: Sex Conflict

1. Sex conflict is a term coined by Walter Toman to describe the difficulties that children from single-sex sibling constellations experience in trying to understand partners of the opposite sex (Toman 1976:84).

2. Walter Toman has suggested that having same-sex siblings might cause some element of sex conflict even if one *has* opposite-sex siblings (Toman 1976:264). This would mean, for example, that even though a boy had younger sisters, the fact that he also had younger *brothers* would cause some degree of sex conflict with any woman he dates. This is because he

learned to treat younger siblings as boys and would tend to treat women he dated like boys. Toman seemed to suggest, however, that this type of sex conflict was less problematic than that which occurs when a person grows up without *any* opposite-sex siblings. This also follows intuitively since a boy who had both sisters *and* brothers would have a good amount of experience dealing with the opposite sex and should be expected to have minimal difficulty understanding them.

3. Toman 1993:82.
4. Personal communication, October 1992.
5. Scheidt 1976.
6. Sex conflict is also relevant for gay relationships. For example, a boy who grew up with only sisters would have sex conflict with male partners. To analyze gay relationships, look primarily at the individual's same-sex siblings as well as the same-sex siblings of the potential partner. For example, a younger sister of sisters would be compatible with an older sister of sisters. A younger sister of brothers, however, would have sex conflict with a woman but would be most compatible with a partner who had younger sisters.
7. Stoneman, Brody, and MacKinnon 1986:495.
8. Lee 1982:147.
9. Toman 1961:73.
10. The younger brother of brothers, while being very masculine, nevertheless often strikes people as very friendly and personable.
11. Levinger and Sonnheim 1965:144.
12. Levinger and Sonnheim 1965:144.

Chapter 16: Communication Problems

1. Toman 1993:174.
2. Tannen 1990:188–189.
3. Don Imus has a brother, Fred, who is two years younger, making Don a super firstborn with strong characteristics of the older brother of brothers: confidence, bossiness, and sternness.
4. A similar personality is firstborn Rush Limbaugh, whose boasting, know-it-all persona fills the airwaves and mesmerizes listeners. He directs his sarcasm and invective at liberals. Both Imus and Limbaugh are older brothers with a brother two years younger.
5. Men regularly interrupt women in conversation as a sign of dominance (Tannen 1990:188–215).

Chapter 17: Conflicting Values

1. Alexander 1999:233–234.
2. The issues experienced by Shelly and Henry are similar to the scientific, religious, and political conflict described by Frank Sulloway in *Born to Rebel*,

conflict that can pit firstborns against lastborns during radical social revolutions. Sometimes such firstborn-lastborn conflict can hamper couples even when revolution is *not* in the air, which is why it's so important to understand how your partner differs from you. Knowledge leads to better understanding and ultimately the potential for greater harmony and compatibility.

Chapter 18: Loss of a Parent or Sibling

1. Homosexual men are more likely to come from families of divorce, to have an absent father, or to be lastborn. Homosexual women are more likely to have a deceased mother or to be lastborn. Frisch and Hviid 2006:533.
2. Parental loss varies in effect depending on whether a surrogate parent comes into the family or whether the eldest has to take on the parental role. If (as in most lower-class families) the eldest takes on the parent's role, laterborns become very radical. Sulloway 1996:136–146.
3. Permanent loss of a parent or sibling can cause a person to seek out others who have experienced loss, others who will leave him, or others whom he can leave (Toman 1993:43).
4. Chase-Lansdale et al. 1995:1614.
5. Frisch and Hviid 2006:533.
6. Bloch et al. 2007:516.
7. Anderson and Reid 2002:44.
8. Sulloway 1996:123.
9. Sulloway 1996:121–128.
10. During her rock concerts, for example, she was extremely controlling and dominant as the leader of the band. At the same time, she has many lastborn traits, including rebelliousness, creativity, and diverse interests.

Chapter 19: Narcissistic Attraction

1. Levinger and Sonnheim 1965:143.
2. In his seminal monograph *On Narcissism: An Introduction* (1914), Freud stated that there is a "primary narcissism in everyone which may in the long run wind up dominating his object-choice." By primary narcissism he meant normal self-love. When you look in the mirror and like what you see, that's primary narcissism or normal self-love. Freud distinguished this from secondary narcissism, a pathological condition in which a person turns almost all his attention inward toward the self so that very little psychic energy is available to be directed outward toward others. Primary narcissism, according to Freud, might be the basis for a lover's object-choice, meaning that you would use your normal self-love to find a partner who is substantially similar to you.
3. Toman 1993:91.
4. This distinction is drawn largely from the work of Toman and the observation of numerous relationships of firstborns and lastborns. Toman 1993:90.

Appendix

1. The first four in table 40 on page 180 of Ernst and Angst 1983: Altus 1970; Ward, Castro, and Wilcox 1974; Touhey 1971; and Kemper 1966.

2. *Birth rank* means ordinal place in a sibship (first, second, third . . .), *birth order,* sometimes used synonymously, is a more general term encompassing firstborn, lastborn, middleborn.

3. The last seven in the chart on page 180 of Ernst and Angst 1983: Kemper 1966; Weller, Natan, and Hazi 1974; Pinsky 1974; Levinger and Sonnheim 1965; Mendelsohn et al. 1974; Critelli and Baldwin 1979; and Baxter 1965.

4. Ernst and Angst 1983:181.

5. Ernst and Angst 1983:177. The first two studies are Altus 1970 and Ward, Castro, and Wilcox 1974.

6. Ward, Castro, and Wilcox 1974:62.

7. Touhey 1971:618.

8. See infra at page 91.

9. Kemper 1966:348.

10. Kemper 1966:348.

11. Kemper 1966:348.

12. Ernst and Angst 1983:178.

13. Weller, Natan, and Hazi 1974:796.

14. Weller, Natan, and Hazi 1974:796.

15. Pinsky 1974.

16. Levinger and Sonnheim 1965:141–143.

17. Toman 1965:145–146.

18. Mendelsohn et al. 1974:208.

19. Mendelsohn et al. 1974:208.

20. Toman 1993:88.

21. Critelli and Baldwin 1979:468–471.

22. Baxter 1965:151–152.

Bibliography

Abbe, Kathryn McLaughlin, and Frances McLaughlin Gill. 1980. *Twins on Twins.* New York: Clarkson N. Potter.

ABC News. 2004. Does Birth Order Determine Personality? From *2020.* John Stossel (May 21). http://abcnews.go.com/2020/story?id= 124276 (accessed June 1, 2007).

Adler, Alfred. 1979. *Superiority and Social Interest: A Collection of Later Writings.* 3rd ed. New York: Norton.

Alexander, Paul. 1999. *Salinger: A Biography.* Los Angeles: Renaissance Books.

Altus, W. D. 1970. Marriage and Order of Birth. *Proceedings of the 78th Annual Convention of the American Psychological Association* 5:361–362.

Anderson, Ian M., and Ian C. Reid (eds.). 2002. *Fundamentals of Clinical Psychopharmacology.* London: Martin Dunitz.

Bank, Stephen, and Michael Kahn. 2003. *The Sibling Bond.* New York: Basic Books.

Baxter, James C. 1965. Parental Complementarity and Parental Conflict. *Journal of Individual Psychology* 21:149–153.

BBC. 2005. Q&A: Queen's Wedding Decision. http://news.bbc.co.uk/1/hi/ uk/4289417.stm (accessed March 11, 2007).

Begley, Sharon. 1998. The Parent Trap. *Newsweek* (September 7). http:// home.att.net/~xchar/tna/newswk1.htm (accessed June 1, 2007).

Birtchnell, John. 1977. Toman's Theory: Tested for Mate Selection and Friendship Formation. *Journal of Individual Psychology* 33:18–36.

Blanchard, R., and A. F. Bogaert. 1996. Homosexuality in Men and Number of Older Brothers. *American Journal of Psychiatry* 153:27–31.

———. 2000. Fraternal Birth Order, Maternal Immune Reactions, and Homosexuality in Men. *Politics and the Life Sciences* 19:157–179.

Bloch M., I. Peleg, D. Koren, H. Aner, and E. Klein. 2007. Long-Term Effects of Early Parental Loss Due to Divorce on the HPA Axis. *Hormones and Behavior* 51:516–523.

Chase-Lansdale, P. Lindsay, Andrew J. Cherlin, and Kathleen E. Kiernan. 1995. The Long-Term Effects of Parental Divorce on the Mental Health of Young Adults: A Developmental Perspective. *Child Development* 66:1614–1634.

Chodorow, Nancy. 1978. *The Reproduction of Mothering.* Berkeley: University of California Press.

Conason, Joe, and Gene Lyons. 2000. *The Hunting of the President: The Ten-Year Campaign to Destroy Bill and Hillary Clinton.* New York: St. Martin's Press.

Conley, Dalton. 2004. *The Pecking Order: Which Siblings Succeed and Why.* New York: Pantheon.

Critelli, Joseph W., and Amy C. Baldwin. 1979. Birth Order: Complementarity vs. Homogamy as Determinants of Attraction in Dating Relationships. *Perceptual and Motor Skills* 49:467–471.

Dennett, Daniel C. 2006. *Breaking the Spell: Religion as a Natural Phenomenon.* New York: Penguin.

Downs, Joan. 1971. Here's to You, Mrs. Hamilton. *Life* (magazine) (May 14), 93–97.

Ernst, Cécile, and Jules Angst. 1983. *Birth Order: Its Influence on Personality.* New York: Springer-Verlag.

Forer, Lucille K. 1976. *The Birth Order Factor: How Your Personality Is Influenced by Your Place in the Family.* New York: Pocket Books.

Freud, Sigmund. 1914. On Narcissism: An Introduction. In *Essential Papers on Narcissism*, edited by Andrew Morrison, 17–44. New York: New York University Press, 1986.

Friday, Nancy. 1977. *My Mother/My Self: The Daughter's Search for Identity.* New York: Delacorte Press.

Frisch, M., and A. Hviid. 2006. Childhood Family Correlates of Heterosexual and Homosexual Marriages: A National Cohort Study of Two Million Danes. *Archives of Sexual Behavior* 35:533–47.

Gaines, Charles, and George Butler. 1974. *Pumping Iron: The Art and Sport of Bodybuilding.* New York: Simon and Schuster.

Gerometta, Laurel K. 1982. The Prediction of College Roommate Compatibility from Toman's Birth Order Duplication Theorem. Master's thesis, Southern Illinois University, Edwardsville.

Gold, Stephen Bruce. 1985. Birth Order, Marital Quality, and Stability: A Path Analysis of Toman's Theory. PhD diss., Oklahoma State University. http://e-archive.library.okstate.edu/dissertations/AAI8528846/ (accessed June 6, 2007).

Graham, Caroline. 2006. *Camilla Charles: The Love Story.* Rev. ed. London: John Blake Publishing.

Hall, Everette. 1965. Ordinal Position and Success in Engagement and Marriage. *Journal of Individual Psychology* 21:154–158.

Hamilton, Ian. 1988. *In Search of J. D. Salinger*. New York: Random House.

Harris, Judith Rich. 1998. *The Nurture Assumption: Why Children Turn Out the Way They Do: Why Parents Matter Less Than You Think and Peers Matter More*. New York: Simon & Schuster.

———. 2002. Why Do People Believe That Birth Order Has Important Effects on Personality? (January 17). http://xchar.home.att.net/tna/birth–order/believe.htm (accessed June 1, 2007).

———. 2006. *No Two Alike: Human Nature and Human Individuality*. New York: Norton.

Healey, Matthew D., and Bruce J. Ellis. 2007. Birth Order, Conscientiousness, and Openness to Experience: Tests of the Family-niche Model of Personality Using a Within-Family Methodology. *Evolution and Human Behavior* 28:55–59.

Heyman, Marshall. 2006. MK. *W Magazine* (January). www.style.com/w/feat_story/120705/full_page.html (accessed June 4, 2007).

Heymann, C. David. 1995. *Liz: An Intimate Biography of Elizabeth Taylor*. New York: Carol Publishing Group.

Hoffman, Edward, and Marcella Bakur Weiner. 2003. *The Love Compatibility Book: Twelve Personality Traits That Can Lead You to Your Soulmate*. Novato, CA: New World Library.

Jacobs, George, and William Stadiem. 2003. *Mr. S: My Life with Frank Sinatra*. New York: Harper.

James, Oliver. 2006. *They F*** You Up: How to Survive Family Life*. New York: Marlowe & Company.

Kardener, Sheldon H., and Marielle Fuller. 1972. The Firstborn Phenomenon among Psychiatric Residents. *American Journal of Psychiatry* 129:350–352.

Kelley, Kitty. 1987. *His Way: An Unauthorized Biography of Frank Sinatra*. New York: Bantam.

Kemper, Theodore D. 1966. Mate Selection and Marital Satisfaction According to Sibling Type of Husband and Wife. *Journal of Marriage and the Family* 28:346–349.

Kent, Jacqueline C. 2003. *Business Builders in Cosmetics*. Minneapolis, MN: Oliver Press.

Koehn, Nancy F. 2001. *Brand New: How Entrepreneurs Earned Consumers' Trust from Wedgwood to Dell*. Cambridge, MA: Harvard Business School Press.

Kurzweil, Ray, and Terry Grossman. 2004. *Fantastic Voyage: Live Long Enough to Live Forever*. New York: Rodale.

Lansing, Alfred. 1959. *Endurance: Shackleton's Incredible Voyage*. New York: McGraw-Hill.

Lazar, S. W., C. E. Kerr, R. H. Wasserman, J. R. Gray, D. N. Greve, M. T. Treadway, M. McGarvey, B. T. Quinn, J. A. Dusek, H. Benson, S. L. Rauch, C. I. Moore, and B. Fischl. 2005. Meditation Experience Is Associated with Increased Cortical Thickness. *Neuroreport* 16, no. 17: 1893–1897.

Leamer, Laurence. 2005. *Fantastic: The Life of Arnold Schwarzenegger*. New York: St. Martin's Press.

Lee, Aldora G. 1982. Psychological Androgyny and Social Desirability. *Journal of Personality Assessment* 46:147–152.

Leman, Kevin. 1985. *The Birth Order Book: Why You Are the Way You Are*. New York: Dell.

———. 1989. *Growing Up Firstborn: The Pressure and Privilege of Being Number One*. New York: Dell.

———. 1998. *The New Birth Order Book: Why You Are the Way You Are*. 2nd ed. Grand Rapids, MI: Revell.

Lenburg, Jeff. 1983. *Dustin Hoffman, Hollywood's Anti-hero*. New York: St. Martin's Press.

Levinger, George, and Maurice Sonnheim. 1965. Complementarity in Marital Adjustment: Reconsidering Toman's Family Constellation Hypothesis. *Journal of Individual Psychology* 21:137–144.

Lieberg, Carolyn. 1998. *Little Sisters*. Berkeley, CA: Wildcat Canyon Press.

Lynch, David. 2006. *Catching the Big Fish: Meditation, Consciousness, and Creativity*. New York: Tarcher.

MacLaine, Shirley. 2000. *The Camino: A Journey of the Spirit*. New York: Pocket Books.

Maynard, Joyce. 1998. *At Home in the World: A Memoir*. New York: Picador.

McCrae, Robert R., and Paul T. Costa Jr. 1987. Validation of the Five-Factor Model of Personality across Instruments and Observers. *Journal of Personality and Social Psychology* 52:81–90.

McCrae, Robert R., and Oliver P. John. 1992. An Introduction to the Five-Factor Model and Its Applications. *Journal of Personality* 60: 175–215.

Mendelsohn, Mark B., James Linden, Gerald Gruen, and James Curran. 1974. Heterosexual Pairing and Sibling Configuration. *Journal of Individual Psychology* 30:202–210.

Mileti, Nick J. 2004. *Closet Italians: A Dazzling Collection of Illustrious Italians with Non-Italian Names*. Philadelphia: Xlibris.

Milton, Joyce. 2000. *The First Partner: Hillary Rodham Clinton*. New York: HarperCollins.

Moughan, Meg. 1999. "Paint as I See, Not as Others Paint": The Life and Career of Blondelle Malone. *Caroliniana Columns: Newsletter of the University South Caroliniana Society* (Spring). http://www.sc.edu/library/socar/uscs/99spr/blond.html (accessed June 6, 2007).

Movers and Shakers: The 100 Most Influential Figures in Modern Business.
2003. New York: Basic Books.

Nelsen, Hart M. 1981. Religious Conformity in an Age of Disbelief: Contextual Effects of Time, Denomination, and Family Processes upon Church Decline and Apostasy. *American Sociological Review* 46:632–640.

Nietzsche, Friedrich. 1887. *The Gay Science.* Translated by Walter Kaufman. New York: Vintage Books, 1974.

Overbye, Dennis. 2000. *Einstein in Love: A Scientific Romance.* New York: Viking.

Parker, Barry. 2003. *Einstein: The Passions of a Scientist.* Amherst, NY: Prometheus.

Paxton, Michael. 1997. *Ayn Rand—A Sense of Life.* Documentary produced by AG Media Corporation.

Pinsky, Harvey Joel. 1974. The Effect of Sibling Constellation on Mate-Selection. PhD diss., Boston University Graduate School.

Plutarch. 2001. *Plutarch's Lives.* Vol. 2. Translated by John Dryden. New York: Modern Library Classics.

Polit, Denise F., Ronald L. Nuttall, and Ena V. Nuttall. 1980. The Only Child Grows Up: A Look at Some Characteristics of Adult Only Children. *Family Relations* 29:99–106.

Rader, Dotson. 2006. "Sarah Jessica Parker: Why This Star Deserves Her Fame." *Parade Magazine* (January 29).

Rank, Otto. 1929. *The Trauma of Birth.* London: Routledge & Kegan Paul.

Reinhardt, Roger F. 1970. The Outstanding Jet Pilot. *American Journal of Psychiatry* 127:732–736.

Richardson, Ronald W., and Lois A. Richardson. 1990. *Birth Order and You: How Your Sex and Position in the Family Affects Your Personality and Relationships.* North Vancouver, BC: Self-Counsel Press.

Rosenberg, B. G. 2000. Birth Order and Personality: Is Sulloway's Treatment a Radical Rebellion or Is He Preserving the Status Quo? *Politics and the Life Sciences* 19:170–172.

Salinger, Margaret. 2000. *Dream Catcher: A Memoir.* New York: Washington Square Press.

Saroglou, Vassilis, and Laure Fiasse. 2003. Birth Order, Personality, and Religion: A Study among Young Adults from a Three-Sibling Family. *Personality and Individual Differences* 35:19–29. http://www.psp.ucl.ac.be/psyreli/2003.BirthOrder.pdf (accessed June 3, 2007).

Sartre, Jean-Paul. 1943. *Being and Nothingness.* Translated by Hazel E. Barnes. New York: Washington Square Press, 1956.

Scheidt, Rick J. 1976. Same-Sex Dyads and Toman's Theory of Birth-Order Compatibility. Paper presented at the Annual Meeting of the Western Psychological Association, Los Angeles, California, April 8–11.

Schellenberg, James A. 1960. Homogamy in Personal Values and the "Field of Eligibles." *Social Forces* 39:157–162.

Schilling, Renee M. 2001. The Effects of Birth Order on Interpersonal Relationships. *The McKendree College Journal of Undergraduate Research.* Issue 1. http://faculty.mckendree.edu/scholars/2001/schilling.htm (accessed June 5, 2007).

Segal, Nancy L. 1999. *Entwined Lives: Twins and What They Tell Us about Human Behavior.* New York: Dutton.

———. 2005. *Indivisible by Two: Lives of Extraordinary Twins.* Cambridge, MA: Harvard University Press.

Shea, Christopher. 2004. The Temperamentalist. *Boston Globe* (August 29). http://www.boston.com/news/globe/ideas/articles/2004/08/29/the_temperamentalist?pg'full (accessed June 5, 2007).

Slater, Elinor, and Robert Slater. 2006. *Great Jewish Women.* Rev. ed. Middle Village, NY: Jonathan David Publishers.

Smith, Michael. 2002. *Tom Crean: Unsung Hero of the Scott and Shackleton Antarctic Expeditions.* Seattle, WA: The Mountaineers Books.

Steinberg, Blema S. 2001. The Making of Female Presidents and Prime Ministers: The Impact of Birth Order, Sex of Siblings, and Father-Daughter Dynamics. *Political Psychology* 22:89–110. http://www.blackwell-synergy.com/links/doi/10.1111/0162-895X.00227/abs/ (accessed June 5, 2007).

Stoneman, Zolinda, Gene H. Brody, and Carol E. MacKinnon. 1986. Same-Sex and Cross-Sex Siblings: Activity Choices, Roles, Behavior, and Gender Stereotypes. *Sex Roles* 15:495–511.

Sulloway, Frank J. 1996. *Born to Rebel: Birth Order, Family Dynamics, and Creative Lives.* New York: Pantheon Books.

———. 2000. Born to Rebel and Its Critics. *Politics and the Life Sciences* 19:181–202.

———. 2001a. Birth Order, Sibling Competition, and Human Behavior. In *Conceptual Challenges in Evolutionary Psychology: Innovative Research Strategies,* edited by Paul S. Davies and Harmon R. Holcomb, 39–83. Dordrecht and Boston: Kluwer Academic Publishers.

———. 2001b. Sibling-Order Effects. In *International Encyclopedia of Social and Behavioral Sciences,* vol. 21, edited by Neil J. Smelser and Paul B. Baltes, 14058–14063. Oxford: Elsevier Science.

———. 2007a. Birth Order. In *Evolutionary Family Psychology,* edited by Catherine Salmon and Todd Shackelford, 162–182. Oxford and New York: Oxford University Press.

———. 2007b. Birth Order and Sibling Competition. In *Handbook of Evolutionary Psychology,* edited by Robin Dunbar and Louise Barrett, 297–311. Oxford: Oxford University Press.

Tannen, Deborah. 1990. *You Just Don't Understand: Women and Men in Conversation.* New York: Ballantine.

Thomson, John. 1999. *Shackleton's Captain: A Biography of Frank Worsley*. Oakville, ON, and Buffalo, NY: Mosaic Press.

Toman, Walter. 1961. *Family Constellation: Theory and Practice of a Psychological Game*. New York: Springer.

———. 1962. Family Constellations of the Partners in Divorced and Married Couples. *Journal of Individual Psychology* 18:48–51.

———. 1965. Comment. *Journal of Individual Psychology* 21:145–146.

———. 1970. Birth Order Rules All. *Psychology Today* (December), 44–49, 68–69.

———. 1971. The Duplication Theorem of Social Relationships as Tested in the General Population. *Psychological Review* 78:380–390.

———. 1976. *Family Constellation: Its Effects on Personality and Social Behavior*. 3rd ed. New York: Springer.

———. 1993. *Family Constellation: Its Effects on Personality and Social Behavior*. 4th ed. New York: Springer.

Touhey, John C. 1971. Birth Order and Mate Selection. *Psychological Reports* 21:618.

Tsui, Ming, and Lynne Rich. 2002. The Only Child and Educational Opportunity for Girls in Urban China. *Gender & Society* 16:74–92.

Vanderkooy, Cornelia J., and Delbert J. Hayden. 1985. Birth-Order Complementarity and Marital Adjustment. *Journal of Marriage and the Family* 47:723–727.

Ward, Charles D., M. Angela Castro, and Anne H. Wilcox. 1974. Birth-Order Effects in a Survey of Mate Selection and Parenthood. *The Journal of Social Psychology* 94:57–64.

Weller, Leonard, Orah Natan, and Ophrah Hazi. 1974. Birth Order and Marital Bliss in Israel. *Journal of Marriage and the Family* 36:794–797.

Winch, Robert F. 1958. *Mate Selection: A Study of Complementary Needs*. New York: Harper.

———. 1967. Another Look at the Theory of Complementary Needs in Mate-Selection. *Journal of Marriage and the Family* 29:756–762.

———. 1971. *The Modern Family*. 3rd ed. New York: Holt, Rinehart and Winston.

Winch, Robert F., Robert McGinnis, and Herbert R. Barringer (eds.). 1962. *Selected Studies in Marriage and the Family*. Rev. ed. New York: Holt, Rinehart and Winston.

Wolf, Abraham, and Grace Eva Wolf. 1965. First Born and Last Born: A Critique. *Journal of Individual Psychology* 21:159.

Wolfe, Tom. 1979. *The Right Stuff*. New York: Bantam.

Wood, Beci. 2006. Brooke Still Loves Agassi. *The Sun*. www.thesun.co.uk/sol/homepage/showbiz/bizarre/online/article216238.ece (accessed October 19, 2007).

Wright, Lawrence. 1997. *Twins: And What They Tell Us about Who We Are*. New York: John Wiley.

Wright, Paul H. 1965. Personality and Interpersonal Attraction: Basic Assumptions. *Journal of Individual Psychology* 21:127–136.

Zajonc, Robert B. 1993. The Confluence Model: Differential or Difference Equation. *European Journal of Social Psychology* 23:211–215.

Zajonc, Robert B., Hazel Markus, and George B. Markus. 1979. The Birth Order Puzzle. *Journal of Personality and Social Psychology* 37: 1325–1341.

Zajonc, Robert B., and Frank J. Sulloway. 2007. The Confluence Model: Birth Order as a Within-Family or Between-Family Dynamic? *Personality and Social Psychology Bulletin* 33:1187–1194.

Index

Adler, Alfred, 2
Affleck, Ben, 20
Age gaps, 91, 133–134
Agreeableness, 2–3

Bacall, Lauren, 107–108
Bardot, Brigitte, 172
Beatty, Warren, 149–150
Beauvoir, Simone de, 103, 199
Best match. *See specific birth order,*
    best matches for
Birth order. *See also specific birth order*
    asking your date about, 222–223
    benefits of knowing, 197, 201
    definition of, 1
    marital satisfaction affected by, 153
    mate selection and, 225–228, 243
    personality affected by, 2–4, 21–222
    predicting of, 196–197
    research of, 1–2
    romantic compatibility and, 4–5
Boy-boy twins, 124
Boy-girl twins, 123–124
Brando, Marlon, 240
Breaking up
    with female only child, 116
    with male only child, 105
    with middle child, 140
    with older brother of brothers, 17
    with older brother of sisters, 26–27
    with older sister of brothers, 49
    with older sister of sisters, 39

with twins, 127
with younger brother of brothers,
    61
with younger brother of sisters,
    71–72
with younger sister of brothers, 92
with younger sister of sisters, 81–82
Brothers. *See specific birth order*
Bullock, Sandra, 155–156
Burnett, Carol, 111
Burton, Richard, 163–164, 245
Bush, Barbara, 123
Bush, Jenna, 123
Business leadership, 12–13

Career
    female only child, 117
    middle child, 141–142
    older brother of brothers, 19
    older brother of sisters, 28–29
    older sister of brothers, 50–51
    older sister of sisters, 40–41
    twins, 128–129
    younger brother of brothers, 62–63
    younger brother of sisters, 72–73
    younger sister of brothers, 93–94
    younger sister of sisters, 82–83
Carter, Aaron, 123, 125, 242
Charm
    of older brother of sisters, 21–22
    of younger brother of sisters, 21–22
    of younger sister of sisters, 76–77

China, 112
Cleopatra, 47
Clinton, Bill, 15, 52, 104–105
Clinton, Hillary, 15, 51–52, 104–105
Cobain, Kurt, 209–210
Communication
    firstborn style of, 180–181,
        185–186
    gender-based differences in, 177
    lastborn style of, 178–179, 182–183
    middleborn style of, 181–182,
        187–188
    only child style of, 179–180,
        183–184
    twins style of, 188–189
Compatibility
    doubling of, 216–219
    romantic, 4–5
Compromising, 135–136
Conformity, 237
Connery, Sean, 172
Conscientiousness
    description of, 2–3
    by firstborns, 155
    by older brother of brothers, 12
    by older sister of sisters, 31
Crean, Tom, 239
Creativity, 76–77, 165
Cruise, Tom, 167

Darwinian rank conflict, 243
Dating
    female only child, 115
    male only child, 104–105
    middle child, 139–140
    older brother of brothers, 16–17
    older brother of sisters, 25–26
    older sister of brothers, 48–49
    older sister of sisters, 38–39
    twins, 126–127, 188, 200–201
    younger brother of brothers, 60–61
    younger sister of brothers, 89–91
    younger sister of sisters, 80–81
Decision making, 233
Diaz, Cameron, 79
Divorce, 203–208, 243
Dominance
    by older sister of brothers, 43, 180

    by older sister of sisters, 34–35,
        180
Doubling of compatibility, 216–219
Downey, Robert Jr., 73, 165, 245
Duff, Hilary, 123, 242
Duplication theorem, 4, 7, 222, 226

Emotional connections, 157–159
Empathy, 86–87
External aids, 233
Extraversion, 2–3

Federline, Kevin, 242
Female only child
    authority and, 109–110, 115, 117
    best matches for, 113–114
    breaking up with, 116
    career of, 117
    celebrity case study of, 118–119
    communication style of, 179–180,
        183–184
    dating, 115
    firstborn males and, 111
    friendships, 116–117
    imitation by, 110–111
    male only child and, 104, 114–116
    mercurial nature of, 110
    mother of, 110
    older brother of brothers and, 14,
        114
    older brother of sisters and, 24,
        113–114
    overreliance by, 112–113
    romance by, 111, 199–200
    strengths of, 109–110
    weakness of, 112–113
    worst match for, 104, 114–115,
        125
    younger brother of brothers and,
        58, 114
    younger brother of sisters and, 69,
        114
Firstborn(s)
    academic success of, 152
    achievement levels of, 238
    communication style of, 180–181,
        185–186
    conscientiousness by, 155

entitlement feelings by, 146
as honorary laterborn, 208–209, 237
lastborns and, 150, 154–156, 164, 166, 208–209, 212, 243
marriage of, 244
older brother of brothers. *See* Older brother of brothers
older brother of sisters. *See* Older brother of sisters
older sister of brothers. *See* Older sister of brothers
older sister of sisters. *See* Older sister of sisters
parental conflict, 208–209
perfectionism by, 31, 101, 195
romantic values of, 195
traits of, 43, 131, 244
Firstborn rank conflict
avoidance of, 155–156
celebrity case study of, 148–149
coping with, 156
description of, 146–147
difficulties in detecting, 147, 50–151
lack of perception of, 153
lastborn rank conflict vs., 160
outward happiness, 150–151
professional, 147–148
temptations, 149–150
understanding of, 156
Five-year age gaps, 91
Four-year age gaps, 91
Fraternal twins, 122
Freud, Sigmund, 28, 212, 244, 247
Friendships
female only child, 116–117
male only child, 105–106
middle child, 140–141
older brother of brothers, 17–19
older brother of sisters, 27–28
older sister of brothers, 49–50
older sister of sisters, 39–40
sex conflict and, 171
twins, 127–128
younger brother of brothers, 61–62
younger brother of sisters, 72
younger sister of brothers, 92–93
younger sister of sisters, 82

Gardner, Ava, 107–108
Garner, Jennifer, 20
Gay relationships, 246
Girl-girl twins, 124–125

Hefner, Hugh, 13
Helpfulness, 45–46
Heterogamy, 5, 235
Hilton, Paris, 43, 79, 123, 129, 242
Hoffman, Edward, 5
Homogamy, 5, 212, 222, 235
Homosexuality, 206, 247
Honorary laterborn, 208–209, 237
Hypothalamic-pituitary-adrenal axis, 206

Identical twins, 122
Imus, Don, 11, 180, 246
Instrumental traits, 238
Interactive pleasure, 218
Interactive relationships, 7

Jackson, Janet, 88
James, Jesse, 155
Jolie, Angelina, 235
Jung, Carl, 12, 18, 28, 180

Kidman, Nicole, 167, 243
King, Martin Luther Jr., 135–136
Kissing, 150–151, 217, 240

Lachey, Nick, 148–149, 170
Lastborn(s)
attention seeking by, 160–161
celebrity case study of, 163–164
communication style of, 178–179, 182–183
creativity of, 165
firstborns and, 150, 154–156, 164, 166, 208–209, 212, 243
focus on, 160–161
risk taking by, 56–57
romantic values of, 195, 198
traits of, 131, 159
traveling by, 56–57
younger brother of brothers. *See* Younger brother of brothers

Lastborn(s) *(continued)*
  younger brother of sisters. *See*
    Younger brother of sisters
  younger sister of brothers. *See*
    Younger sister of brothers
  younger sister of sisters. *See*
    Younger sister of sisters
Lastborn rank conflict
  attention seeking, 160–161, 163
  avoidance of, 161–162, 166
  description of, 146–147, 157
  firstborn rank conflict vs., 160
  result of, 160
  signs of, 165
  temptation, 164
Lauder, Estée, 83–84
Leadership, 11–13, 19
Leto, Jared, 79
Like attracts like theory, 2–3
Limbaugh, Rush, 246
Lohan, Lindsay, 123, 242
Loren, Sophia, 33, 164, 245
Loss of parent or siblings
  dealing with, 206–208, 210
  example of, 203–205
  homosexuality and, 206, 247
  impact of, 205–208
  knowledge of, 203
  through divorce, 203–206
Love, Courtney, 209–210

Male friendships
  older brother of sisters, 28
  older sister of brothers, 49–50
  older sister of sisters, 39–40
  younger sister of brothers, 92–93
Male only child
  best matches for, 101–104
  breaking up with, 105
  career of, 103–104, 106–107
  celebrity case study of, 107–108
  communication style of, 179,
    183–184
  dating, 104–105
  female only child and, 104,
    114–116
  firstborn personality of, 102–103
  friendships, 105–106

lastborn personality of, 102–103
mother of, 105
older sister of brothers and, 47–48,
  102
older sister of sisters and, 36, 102
privileged position of, 99
romantic values of, 199
traits of, 99
worst matches for, 79, 89, 104, 125
younger sister of brothers and, 89
younger sister of sisters and, 79
Marital satisfaction, 153
Marriage, 243–244
Mason, Jackie, 238
Mate selection, 225–228, 243
Maternal instinct, 44–46
Meditation, 241
Middle child
  age gaps, 133–134
  best match for, 137–138
  breaking up with, 140
  career choices for, 141–142
  communication style of, 181–182,
    187–188
  compromising skills of, 135–136
  confusion experienced by, 131,
    136–137
  dating, 139–140
  description of, 131–132
  friendships, 140–141
  negotiating skills of, 135–136
  older brother of brothers and, 14
  older brother of sisters and, 23
  opposite-sex siblings of, 199
  personality switching by, 132–133
  romantic potential of, 136–137, 139
  romantic values of, 198–199
  siblings, 133–135, 138
  worst match for, 138
  younger sister of brothers and, 88
Monroe, Marilyn, 95

Narcissistic attraction
  definition of, 6
  example of, 211–212
  sex conflict and, 170
  understanding of, 216
Narcissistic pleasure, 216–218

Narcissistic relationships
  differences, 217–218, 220
  difficulties in, 215–216
  feelings in, 214–215
  firtborns, 236
  Freudian principles, 212–213, 247
  temptation risks, 220
  tips for enjoying, 220
Negotiation skills, 135–136
Neuroticism, 2–3

Obedience, 11
Object relationships, 213–215
Older brother of brothers
  best match for, 13–14, 77, 88, 114
  breaking up with, 17
  business leadership skills of, 12–13
  career choices for, 19
  celebrity case study of, 20
  communication style of, 180
  conscientiousness of, 12
  dating, 16–17
  early childhood dynamics of, 11
  female only child and, 14, 114
  friendships, 17–19
  leadership traits of, 11–13, 19
  middle girl and, 14
  older sister of brothers and, 15
  older sister of sisters and, 15, 37–38
  risk taking by, 12
  saving face by, 17
  seriousness of purpose, 12
  twin and, 14
  worst match for, 15, 37–38, 48
  younger sister of brothers and, 14,
    19, 88
  younger sister of sisters and, 14, 19
Older brother of sisters
  best matches for, 22–24, 36–37, 77,
    88, 113–114
  breaking up with, 26–27
  career choices for, 28–29
  caring traits of, 26
  celebrity case study of, 29–30
  communication style of, 180
  creativity of, 26
  dating, 25–26
  female friendships, 27–28

  female only child and, 24, 113–114
  friendships, 27–28
  male friendships, 28
  middle girl and, 23
  older sister of brothers and, 25,
    46–47
  older sister of sisters and, 36–37
  romantic charm of, 21–22
  twin and, 24
  worst match for, 24–25
  younger brother of brothers and,
    62
  younger sister of brothers and,
    22–23, 88
  younger sister of sisters and, 23, 77
Older sister of brothers
  best matches for, 46–48, 57–58,
    102
  breaking up with, 49
  career choices, 50–51
  celebrity case study of, 51–52
  communication style of, 180–181
  dating, 48–49
  description of, 43–44
  dominance traits of, 43, 180
  friendships, 49–50
  helpfulness by, 45–46
  male friendships, 49–50
  male only child and, 47–48, 102
  maternal instinct of, 44–46
  older brother of brothers and, 15
  older brother of sisters and, 25,
    46–47
  psychological mirror for, 45
  recognition by, 46
  religiosity of, 43–44
  worst match for, 48
  younger brother of brothers and,
    57–58
  younger brother of sisters and,
    67–68
Older sister of sisters
  best matches for, 35–37, 68, 102
  breaking up with, 39
  career choices for, 40–41
  celebrity case study of, 41–42
  communication style of, 181
  conscientiousness by, 31

Older sister of sisters *(continued)*
control by, 33–34
dating, 38–39
dominance, 34–35, 181
friendships, 39–40
male friendships, 39–40
male only child and, 36, 102
older brother of brothers and, 15, 37–38
older brother of sisters and, 36–37
older men and, 32–33
perfectionism by, 31
submission, 34–35
traits of, 31–34, 237
twin and, 36
worst match for, 37–38
younger brother of brothers and, 35–36, 46, 58
younger brother of sisters and, 35, 46
younger sister of sisters and, 81, 171
Olsen, Ashley, 128–130
Olsen, Mary-Kate, 128–130
Onassis, Jacqueline Kennedy, 41–42
One-year age gaps, 91
Only child. *See* Female only child; Male only child
Openness to experience, 2–3
Opposites attract theory, 2, 156
Opposite-sex siblings, 174, 199

Parent(s)
firstborn's conflict with, 208–209
loss of. *See* Loss of parent or siblings
Parker, Sarah Jessica, 165–166, 245
Partial sex conflict, 167–169
Perfectionism, 31, 101, 195
Personality
birth order effects on, 2–4, 221–222
shifts in, 218–219
Personality traits, 2–3
Piper, Myfanwy, 117
Population growth, 112
Prayer, 241
Prince Charles, 29–30, 236–237
Princess Diana, 29, 135, 236
Professional rank conflict, 147–148

Radical social revolutions, 243
Rand, Ayn, 33, 35
Rank conflict
Darwinian, 243
difficulties in detecting, 147
explanation of, 6, 145–146
firstborn. *See* Firstborn rank conflict
lastborn. *See* Lastborn rank conflict
older brother of brothers and older sister of brothers, 48
older brother of brothers and older sister of sisters, 15
older brother of sisters, 24
professional, 147–148
younger sister of sisters and younger brother of brothers, 79
Rebelliousness, 66–67
Relationships
emotional connections in, 157–159
of identification, 6
narcissistic. *See Narcissistic relationships*
object, 213–215
sex conflict effects on, 168–169
Religiosity, 43–44
Rilke, Rainer Maria, 93
Risk taking
by older brother of brothers, 12
by young brother of brothers, 56–57
Romance
by boy-girl twins, 123–124
by female only child, 111
by middle child, 136–137, 139
by twins, 122
by younger brother of brothers, 60
by younger sister of brothers, 90
Romantic compatibility, 4–5
Romantic values
of female only child, 199–200
of firstborns, 195
of lastborns, 195, 198
of male only child, 199
of middle child, 198–199
of only child, 199–200
of twins, 200–201

Salinger, J. D., 70, 191–192, 240
Salome, Lou Andreas, 93
Same-sex siblings, 245
Same-sex twins, 123–125
Sartre, Jean-Paul, 36, 103, 199, 236
Schwarzenegger, Arnold, 63–64, 239
Sex conflict
    avoidance of, 176
    dealing with, 175–176
    definition of, 6, 167, 245
    dynamics of, 171–175
    examples of, 168–169
    femininity and, 172, 175
    friendship and, 171
    gay relationships, 246
    masculinity and, 172, 175
    mitigation of, 169–170
    narcissistic attraction and, 170
    for older brother of brothers
        and older sister of brothers,
        48
    for older brother of brothers
        and older sister of sisters, 15
    opposite-sex siblings and, 174
    overcoming of, 78, 169–170
    partial, 167–169
    partners with, 171–173
    partners without, 174
    preferring of relationships with,
        171–172
    total, 167–169
Shackleton, Ernest, 134
Shields, Brooke, 118–119
Shriver, Maria, 64, 239
Sibling order, 2
Siblings
    loss of. See Loss of parent or
        siblings
    of middle children, 133–135, 138
    opposite-sex, 174, 199
    research regarding, 2–4
    same-sex, 245
Simpson, Jessica, 148–150, 170
Sinatra, Frank, 107–108
Sisters. See specific birth order
Spears, Britney, 137–138
Stern, Howard, 66
Stress reduction, 241

Sulloway, Frank, 2–3, 5–6, 32, 43, 89,
    110, 148, 155, 208
Sutherland, Kiefer, 165

Tannen, Deborah, 177
Taylor, Elizabeth, 163–164, 245
Teachers, 152
Temperament, 194
Temptations
    firstborn rank conflict, 149–150
    lastborn rank conflict, 164
    narcissistic relationships, 220
Theory of complementary relationships,
    4
Thornton, Billy Bob, 235
Three-year age gaps, 91
Toman, Walter, 2, 4–5, 32, 116,
    167–168, 213
Total sex conflict, 167–169
Transference, 244
Twins
    best matches for, 124–125
    boy-boy, 124
    boy-girl, 123–124
    breaking up with, 127
    career of, 128–129
    celebrity case study of, 129–130
    closeness between, 121–122, 128
    communication style of, 188–189
    dating, 126–127, 188, 200–201
    disappointment concerns, 188
    fraternal, 122
    friendships, 127–128
    girl-girl, 124–125
    identical, 122
    mutual assistance traits, 122
    older brother of brothers and, 14
    older brother of sisters and, 24
    older sister of sisters and, 36
    personal space for, 126
    romance by, 122, 200–201
    same-sex, 123–125
    with siblings, 125–126
    worst match for, 125–126
    younger brother of brothers and, 58
    younger brother of sisters and, 8–69
    younger sister of brothers and, 89
Two-year age gaps, 91

Values
    conflicts in, 192–193
    description of, 191–192
    romantic. *See Romantic values*
    understanding of, 193–195

Wayne, John, 12, 16
Wolfe, Tom, 100
Worsley, Frank, 239
Worst match. *See specific birth order,
    worst match for*

Younger brother of brothers
    best matches for, 35–36, 57–58, 114
    breaking up with, 61
    career choices for, 62–63
    celebrity case study of, 63–64
    communication style of, 178
    dating, 60–61
    description of, 55–56
    female friendships, 62
    female only child and, 58, 114
    friendships, 61–62
    older brother of sisters and, 62
    older sister of brothers and, 46,
        57–58
    older sister of sisters and, 35–36, 58
    only child and, 58
    risk taking by, 56–57
    romance by, 60
    twin and, 58
    worst match for, 58–59, 89
    younger sister of brothers and,
        58–59, 89
    younger sister of sisters and, 59, 79
Younger brother of sisters
    best matches for, 35, 67–69, 78, 88,
        114
    breaking up with, 71–72
    career choices for, 72–73
    celebrity case study of, 73
    communication style of, 178
    dating, 70–71
    description of, 65–66
    female only child and, 114
    friendships, 72
    older sister of brothers and, 35–36,
        46, 67–68

    older sister of sisters and, 35, 68
    only child and, 69
    rebelliousness of, 66–67
    romantic charm of, 21–22
    twin and, 68–69
    worst matches for, 69–70
    younger sister of brothers and, 69,
        88
    younger sister of sisters and, 7,
        69–70
Younger sister of brothers
    best matches for, 22–23, 87–89
    big brothers, 86–87
    breaking up with, 92
    career choices for, 93–94
    celebrity case study of, 95
    communication style of, 179
    critical nature of, 90
    dating, 89–91
    description of, 85–86
    emotional traits of, 90
    empathy by, 86–87
    friendships, 92–93
    male attractions to, 94–95
    male friendships, 92–93
    male only child and, 89
    middle boy and, 88
    older brother of brothers and, 14,
        19, 88
    older brother of sisters and, 22–23,
        88
    rivalries, 86
    romancing of, 90
    studying of, 94–95
    twin and, 89
    worst match for, 58–59
    worst matches for, 89
    younger brother of brothers and,
        58–59, 89
    younger brother of sisters and, 69,
        88
Younger sister of sisters
    best matches for, 23, 77–78
    breaking up with, 81–82
    career choices for, 82–83
    celebrity case study of, 83–84
    charm and creativity, 76–77
    communication style of, 178–179

dating, 80–81
description of, 75–76
distractions, 77
friendships, 82
listening to, 80, 82
male only child and, 79
middle boy and, 78
older brother of brothers and, 14,
    19, 77
older brother of sisters and, 23, 77
older sister of sisters vs., 81
twin with twin sister and, 78
worst match for, 59, 79
younger brother of brothers and, 59
younger brother of sisters and,
    69–70, 78

CPSIA information can be obtained
at www.ICGtesting.com
Printed in the USA
FSHW011749041219
64624FS

9 781600 940415